Race Relations
in the United States

D1601231

Race Relations in the United States

A Chronology, 1896–2005

PAUL D. BUCHANAN

McFarland & Company, Inc., Publishers

Jefferson, North Carolina, and London

LIBRARY OF CONGRESS CATALOGUING-IN-PUBLICATION DATA

Buchanan, Paul D., 1958–
    Race relations in the United States : a chronology,
1896–2005 / Paul D. Buchanan.
        p.   cm.
    Includes bibliographical references and index.

    ISBN 0-7864-1387-5 (softcover : 50# alkaline paper)

    1. United States — Race relations — History — Chronology.
2. United States — Race relations — History — 20th Century —
Chronology.   I. Title.
E184.A1B8325 2005
305.8'0097309'034 — dc22
                                        2005010593

British Library cataloguing data are available

Cover photograph ©2005 Image State

Manufactured in the United States of America

McFarland & Company, Inc., Publishers
  Box 611, Jefferson, North Carolina 28640
  www.mcfarlandpub.com

To Penni Thorpe,
who helps me to appreciate
the colors of life

Contents

Preface 1

The Chronology 3

Bibliography 185
Index 195

Preface

The great irony in writing this book is that, despite the almost innumerable volumes of work published on the subject of race and race relations, to the anthropologist or biologist race is a superficial matter. For the natural scientist, comparing an African American with a European American or an Asian American is much like comparing a yellow-billed magpie with a black-billed magpie: they look a little different, they originated in different places, they sometimes behave a little differently; but they are essentially the same bird.

Alan R. Templeton, Ph.D., professor of biology at Washington University, says, "Race is a real cultural, political, and economic concept in society, but it is not a biological concept." Templeton's study of DNA from global human populations revealed that, while human beings have used the idea of race to define and divide peoples for centuries, there are no substantial genetic differences between the traditional cultures and ethnicities. A human is a human, with important differences occurring more on an individual basis than a collective one.

Socially, the importance of differentiating among races becomes less important with increased familiarity with the individual cultures and individual people. The stereotypes traditionally associated with, for example, persons of Asian ancestry dissipate as one becomes more familiar with Japanese, Philippine, Korean, or Chinese culture. The stereotypes associated with these particular cultures further evaporate when the individual — with his or her own characteristics and behaviors — is further understood. With the appreciation of individual differences, the cloak of race discrimination can be more easily removed.

The information gathered for this project makes it apparent that America is becoming not only a society of multiple ethnicities and cultures, but a society of multiethnic, multicultural persons. The documentation indicates that intercultural marriages and progeny are not only becoming more accepted, they are becoming more prevalent. The lines are blurring, the boundaries are being crossed, the pot is truly melting. Gradually, differences are being rendered irrelevant, because such distinctions — once so feverishly guarded, particularly by the dominant culture — no longer are so clearly perceived.

This chronology focuses primarily on decisions and events in the period from 1896 to 2005 that have had national impact. Some important personalities and incidents have no doubt been missed; in the course of history, after all, every idea and every action is significant to someone, depending on the point of view.

It has been said that it is unfair to judge a past event by today's standards. But in terms of racial injustice, it is imperative to do just that, to study the historical events in terms of what has been learned, to make certain the evils of the past are not repeated.

The Chronology

May 18, 1896

In a decision that would upset the progress of the Reconstruction and severely impede the path toward racial equality for the next 58 years, the United States Supreme Court validates the concept of "separate but equal" in *Plessy v. Ferguson*.

Homer Plessy, of African and European descent, had challenged the constitutionality of a Louisiana statute that required railroads to provide separate but equal accommodations for the two races. Plessy tried to sit in a railroad coach reserved for whites. He was arrested, in accordance with the 1890 law separating railroad cars by race. Plessy appealed the Louisiana Supreme Court ruling, bringing the case before the United States Supreme Court.

Homer Plessy belonged to a New Orleans organization of blacks and Creoles called the Citizens' Committee to Test the Constitutionality of the Separate Car Law. Plessy reportedly appeared to be white, but had been classified as colored because he was one-eighth black. Plessy encroached upon the whites-only coach specifically to create a test case against the "separate but equal" policies of Louisiana.

At the time, the task of interpreting the Constitution had fallen to the archconservative, business-minded Supreme Court, perfectly in step with the contemporary Manifest Destiny, pro-white, imperialistic and paternalistic outlook of the nation.

In an eight to one decision, the Court declared the Fourteenth Amendment guaranteed equality before the law, but not social equality. Justice Henry Brown, writing the majority opinion for the court, determined, "We consider the underlying fallacy of the plaintiff's argument to consist in the assumption that enforced separation of the two races stamps the colored race with the badge of inferiority. If this be so, it is not by reason of anything found in fact, but solely because the colored race chooses to put that construction upon it." Brown's assertion essentially framed the oppression of nonwhite individuals simply as an attitude problem of those being oppressed.

The lone dissenting judge, Justice Marshall Harlan, wrote, "The arbitrary separation of citizens, on the basis of race, while they are on a public highway, is a badge of servitude wholly inconsistent with the civil freedom and equality before the law established by the Constitution. It cannot be justified upon any legal grounds.... We boast freedom enjoyed by our people above all other peoples. But it is difficult to reconcile that boast with the state of the law which, practically, puts the brand of servitude and degradation upon a large class of our fellow citizens, our equals before the law."

In essence, the *Plessy v. Ferguson* decision upheld the so-called Jim Crow laws, designed to deny the civil rights African Americans had attained during Reconstruction. The origin of the Jim Crow image may have been a song and dance tune from the 1830s, the image of the "comic, jumping, rag doll of a man," or perhaps the idiom "black as a crow." Jim Crow personified the separation of the races in services, public forums, public facilities, and jobs. The need for this separation came from the basis of all racial segregation: political, economic, and sexual fears.

The political and economic fears stemmed from a longstanding concern about competition in the work place. Long before the Civil War, free white workers had feared the freeing of black slaves, since this would release more laborers into the marketplace. At the same time, big business had feared the populist coalition forming in the 1890s, which integrated the labor and economic needs of the poor — both black and white — against rich.

The sexual fear was the fear of black males gaining the opportunity to make contact with, and then become sexually active among, white females. The fear not only aroused issues of sexual inadequacy within the white male, but also challenged the image of the passive female and the aggressive male, since the white woman was in a position of social superiority to the black male. The very idea of sexual intimacy between a white woman and a black man completely undermined the white male preoccupation with superiority. (On the other hand, the issue of white males becoming sexually active with black females had not been a fear; rather, it had been a common practice between white masters and their slaves since the dawn of the slave trade. Indeed, the rape of a black woman had been a rape without risk, since there had been no laws to prosecute crimes against slaves.)

Of course, there had been many instances of sexual liaisons between white women and black men. But at the turn of the twentieth century, they had almost always been framed to make the black man the aggressor and the white woman the innocent — no matter who had been the initiator. Lynching turned out to be the recourse against any black male caught — or even just accused — in such a situation.

Finally, the white society feared if African Americans ever attained equal status — after so many decades of submission and suffering under the white man's foot — the retribution wrought by black against white would be terrible indeed.

April 24, 1898

Spain declares war on the United States, beginning the Spanish-American War, fueled by American expansionist ideology and the belief of European American superiority.

By the 1890s, a fervent belief in the superiority of white Americans gripped the country. The Pulitzer and Hearst newspapers pushed for liberation of Cuba from Spain. Massachusetts senator Henry Cabot Lodge advocated for American control of the Pacific Ocean, Latin America, and the Panama Canal. Secretary of state John Hay called it the "splendid little war," which cost relatively little in American lives and forces but ultimately gave the United States control of Puerto Rico, the Philippines, Cuba, Wake Island, and Guam.

Heading the pro-imperialist factions at the time were President McKinley and Vice President Theodore Roosevelt, plus the forces of big business and American colonialism. In the anti-imperialist camp — known as "The Aunties" — stood political orator William Jennings Bryan, suffragist Susan B. Anthony, African American advocate W.E.B. Du Bois, and Mark Twain, who served as vice president of the Anti-Imperialist League from 1900 until his death in 1910.

After only four months of war, the Treaty of Paris was signed on December 10, 1898, giving the United States control of Spanish territory including the Philippines for $20 million.

Depicted as little more than a minor insurgence, in truth the Philippine-American War cost four times more deaths than the Spanish-American War. American troops numbering 126,000 were brought to the Philippines. Although President Roosevelt announced the war's end in 1902, fighting continued in the Philippines for the next dozen years. On June 15, 1913, the last large engagement ended on the island of Mindanao. When the bloodshed finally ended in 1915, the insurgence had cost 4,200 American deaths and 2,800 American injuries. In contrast, an estimated 250,000 to 600,000 Filipinos — mostly civilian — died at the hands of American troops, many after egregious torture.

Throughout the campaigns, pro-imperialist businesses and news media depicted Filipinos, Hawaiians, Puerto Ricans, and Cubans in an inferior light, while white European Americans were presented as fatherly caretakers of the colored, lower forms of humanity. These forces distinguished little between the cultures of the various dark-skinned peoples, but saw them as ignorant savages destined to be trained and indoctrinated in European American Christian civilization. More important, these new colonies were seen as foreign markets for big business. Senator Albert Beveridge expressed the sentiments well, saying, "The Philippines are ours forever ... and just beyond the Philippines are China's unlimited markets.... Our largest trader, henceforth, must be Asia.... The Pacific is our ocean.... The Philippines gives us the door to all the East" (www.isop.ucla.edu).

The magazine *Judge* published a political cartoon called "White Man's Burden." It showed the English representative figure of John Bull and the American cartoon of Uncle Sam carrying the childlike indigenous peoples of the Philippines, Puerto Rico, Hawaii, and Cuba on their backs up to the golden mountain of civilization. This attitude carried over into American attitudes toward Asian immigrants, beginning in the first decade of the twentieth century.

In response to the Filipinos' plight, more than two dozen soldiers from the 24th Colored Infantry defected from the United States Army, joining the Filipino cause in sympathy for their racial plight.

In the end, the pro-imperialists won out. The racist attitudes developed during American expansionism held fast for most of the following century.

July 7, 1898

The Hawaii Treaty of 1898 proves to be the culmination of conspiracy by American settlers to overthrow the Hawaiian monarchy, which had ruled the islands for countless years.

Since the day Captain James Cook set foot on the Sandwich Islands in 1778, the Hawaiian people had suffered an invasion of *haoles* to the otherwise pristine islands. Imported livestock and feral animals ravaged much of the native flora and fauna, while foreign diseases — such as smallpox, leprosy, and alcoholism — decimated the native population, wiping out nearly 80 percent. Faced with the new infirmities, natives turned for cure and comfort toward Christianity, which quickly replaced the traditional *kapu* system and island culture. Finally, American capitalism infiltrated, confiscated, and controlled native resources and labor, while a figurehead constitution replaced the royal family, leaving American business firmly in control of island politics.

The American settlers — mostly businessmen, sugar growers who had come to the islands — had installed a provisional government to negotiate a treaty of annexation. Queen Lili'uokalani, the last in the long line of Hawaiian monarchs, tried to revive the old customs and practices to save her people from complete assimilation. In 1893 she was arrested for treason and confined to quarters within the royal palace.

United States president Grover Cleveland actually opposed the annexation treaty, citing the overthrow as illegitimate and without popular support. While the treaty stalled in the Senate, however, the Spanish-American war broke out. To secure Hawaii as a harbor during the war, Congress passed the treaty through a joint resolution. Thus began the annexation of Hawaii, the suppression of native customs and traditions in the islands.

In the end, American imperialism and racism decimated the island culture. More than a century later, the natives are still looking for ways to revive the ancient island ways.

January 27, 1900

Political cartoons hint at United States prejudices.

On this day, the *Chicago Chronicle* published a political cartoon entitled "Forbidden Book." It depicted the form of President William McKinley standing on a thick bound book titled *True History of the War in the Philippines*. The figure of Uncle Sam stood to the side, attempting to take a peek at the book's contents, under the watchful restraint of McKinley.

In another cartoon highlighting much of the sentiment of the times, *Puck* magazine showed an American Indian sending by wire a message to an equally stereotypical caricature of a Philippine native. The message, which served as the caption for the cartoon, simply read, "Be good, or you will be dead."

April 12, 1900

Congress passes the Foraker Act, which establishes a civil government in Puerto Rico.

The island to the southeast of Florida had become the first incorporated United States territory acquired at the end of the Spanish-American War. The government included the office of governor — Charles H. Allen — plus the governor's cabinet, composed of five Puerto Rican and six American members, and a supreme court. All components of the new regime were to be appointed by the president of the United States.

The cabinet included a Department of Education, which provided classes taught in English, with Spanish as a special subject — a means of incorporating the Puerto Ricans into the "American Way." The Foraker Act, authored by Senator Joseph B. Foraker of Ohio, benefited the United States by incorporating Puerto Rico into the tariff system, establishing a 15 percent tariff on goods flowing from Puerto Rico to the mainland.

"The organization of an appointed, foreign body," says Wagenheim, "to make the laws of the people — a body whose members were at the same time executive heads of departments — was naturally a great disappointment to the Puerto Ricans." Puerto Ricans disliked the measure, since their only representation was the 35-member House of Delegates. Moreover, the island would now operate even less autonomously than under the monarchy of Spain.

The Foraker Act exemplified the expansionist, imperialist United States policy at the turn of the century. Patronizing in its action and racist in its views, the United States would repeatedly underestimate a native people's ability to govern themselves. More pragmatically, particularly in view of the territory, the needs of American business evidently counted much more than the wishes and needs of the people.

June 12, 1901

Cuba ratifies the Platt Amendment, adding its provisions to the newly written Cuban Constitution.

After Spain withdrew from the island, General John R. Brooke had installed a military government. Although the United States had been credited with the victory over Spain, it had been Cuba's rebel forces who had helped exhaust Spain's resources, then finally pinned the Spanish forces on the island.

After the war, the United States provisional government of Cuba helped restore the social infrastructure and worked to eradicate diseases such as malaria and yellow fever, which had plagued the island. The Platt Amendment then restricted Cuban self-determination. It allowed the Cubans to elect officials on a local municipal level, but reserved for the United States ultimate control in national and international affairs through the military government.

Although welcoming the help in normalizing their island, most Cubans felt humiliated at the intrusion the United States placed upon their home.

August 4, 1901

Louis Armstrong is born in a poor section of New Orleans called the Battlefield.

His father was a day laborer who abandoned the family, while his mother was a part-time prostitute. At age five Armstrong was befriended by a Russian Jewish family named Karnofsky, who took him under the family wing, giving him a job and making sure he had food to eat. From the Karnof-sky's, Armstrong borrowed the money to purchase his first coronet.

After his arrest at the age of 13, "Little Louie" became the first coronet player and leader of the marching band at the Home for Colored Waifs orphanage. By the age of fourteen, he was on his own, playing wherever he could: parades, dance halls, and bars throughout New Orleans. Eventually, he joined King Joe Oliver's Creole Jazz Band, falling under the mentorship of King Oliver himself. When Oliver finally left New Orleans for Chicago in 1918, Armstrong stayed behind, taking over the band.

In four years, however, he made the trip north. He rejoined King Oliver in Chicago, setting the stage for the transformation of American music.

October 16, 1901

In a gesture that would startle the nation, President Theodore Roosevelt plays host to Tuskegee University president Booker Taliaferro Washington at a dinner at the White House.

The progressive president, who regarded the African American educator — an advocate of industrial instruction over equal rights, industriousness over rebellion — as a close advisor, considered the invitation as "natural and proper."

Expectedly, Roosevelt's gesture outraged Southern whites. "Roosevelt dines with a Nigger," one headline read. *The Richmond Times*, echoing the covert sexual fears of the separate but equal doctrine, complained, "It means the President is willing that Negroes shall mingle freely with whites in the social circle — that white women may receive attentions from Negro men." Roosevelt seemed to succumb to the tirades of the south, never asking Washington back (Harlan, p. 314).

Not all, however, shared in the offense suffered by the South. The *San Francisco Chronicle* wrote, "The act of President Roosevelt in inviting Mr. Washington to dine with him deserves no more notice than his invitations to other people. He doubtless wished to see him, and asked him to dinner as he would ask anybody else. And the quicker the public comes to take the same view the better it will be for all concerned. A man's social position is properly concerned with his social qualities. His color does not properly enter into the question" ("Roosevelt Stirs Up a Sensation").

Despite the gesture, Harlan writes that there was "no evidence ... Roosevelt intended to inaugurate a new policy of racial liberties." Nevertheless, in a single movement — whether calculated or inadvertent — President Roosevelt raised Booker T. Washington to the position of spokesman for a people. Many African Americans resented this distinction accorded Washington, feeling his perspective to be too complacent and subservient to campaign adequately for their long-awaited rights and liberties. For others, however, the Washington-Roosevelt summit offered a flicker of hope toward future possibilities, a mere 40 years after the onset of the Civil War.

April 29, 1902

The United States Congress passes the Chinese Exclusion Act of 1902, legislation which suspends Chinese immigration indefinitely. The culmination of 20 years of systematic discrimination, the act of 1902 was actually the last of three exclusion measures. The Chinese Exclusion Act of 1882 had passed in response to the great migration of Chinese during the California gold rush. Chinese had come to California in search of financial opportunities not available in the collapsing empire of their home land. By 1867, 50,000 Chinese had immigrated to the United States, many of whom worked to send money to their families back home. Originally intended to be a ten-year policy, the act had been extended in 1892, then was finally made permanent law in by the Exclusion Act of 1902.

The exclusion acts found favor with miners and organized labor alike. The white miners' animosity stemmed from a combination of a fear of competition for employment and financial success — the Chinese generally seemed to be quite industrious — and the fear of a stranger based on appearance; that is, pure racism. White immigrants, such as the Irish or the Russians, used this animosity to strengthen their own positions on hiring line. Chinese already settled in the United States attempted to challenge the measures, but the laws remained.

The exclusion acts met their purposes, as the Chinese population in the United Stated declined rapidly afterwards. The act of 1902 strengthened previous exclusion acts by extending the restrictions on immigration to Hawaii and the Philippines — both American possessions.

January 5, 1903

In deciding the case *Lone Wolf v. Hitchcock*, the United States Supreme Court gives near absolute plenary authority to the United States Congress over Indian affairs, including the sale of Indian land.

In 1901, Congress had used that authority to sell 2 million acres of Kiowa land for non-Indian settlement. Members of the Kiowa tribe had sued, saying the step was a breach of the 1867 Treaty of Medicine Lodge Creek. The plaintiffs had asserted that the treaty required the agreement of three-fourths of the adult male tribal members for the sale of land.

In a 9–0 unanimous decision led by Justice Edward D. White, the Lone Wolf case gave the United States permission to appropriate tribal land and resources under the guise of fulfilling federal trust responsibility. In 1979, a federal judge reportedly called *Lone Wolf v. Hitchcock* "the Indian's Dred Scott" (Hall, p. 511).

February 1, 1903

Souls of Black Folk, a collection of essays reviewing the state of the Negro in America, is published by William Edward Burghardt Du Bois.

In publishing the book, Du Bois (1868–1963) became the John the Baptist of the campaign for racial justice. Reminiscent of Frederick Douglass in his capacity to agitate, Du Bois was critical of Booker T. Washington, saying, "So far as Mr. Washington preaches thrift, patience, and industrial training for the masses, we must hold up his hands and strive with him, rejoicing.... But so far as Mr. Washington apologizes for injustices, North or South, does not rightly value the privileges and duty of voting, belittles the emasculating effects and of caste distinctions, and opposes the higher training and ambition of our brighter minds — so far as he, the South, or the nation does this — we must unceasingly and firmly oppose them" (Davis, p. 233).

Born in Massachusetts, Du Bois had been the first African American to receive a Ph.D. at Harvard, in 1895. At the time of the release of *Souls*, he was teaching as a professor at Atlanta University.

In *Souls*, Du Bois writes of the "two-ness" of the American Negro, the paradox of a systematically oppressed being living in the land of the free: "this sense of always looking at one's self through the eyes of others, of measuring one's soul by the tape of a world that looks on in amused contempt and pity ... an American, a Negro; two souls, two thoughts, two unreconciled strivings, two warring ideals in one dark body, whose dogged strength alone keeps it from being torn asunder."

Du Bois also introduced the concept of the Talented Tenth, the percentage of the African American community — as in all other communities — with the intelligence, talent, and inspiration to lead the community to its fullness, without reliance upon the patronage of the white man. Finally, he advocated for the three things that the community needs to attain its wholeness: the right to vote, civic equality, and the education of youth according to ability. This education, he believed, would equip the Talented Tenth with the tools they needed to guide the people to wholeness.

April 30, 1904

An anthropological exhibition by W.J. McGee depicting the concept of "cephalization" is featured at the 1904 World's Fair in St. Louis, Missouri.

Cephalization, as the term was then used, supposedly depicted the increase of size of human cranium according to race features, supposedly to explain human progress in terms of some kind of racial evolution.

In his bizarre menagerie, McGee displayed different aboriginal tribes from Africa, Japan, Patagonia, the Philippines, and North America. Finally, the exposition offered the Caucasian, as representative of "the perfected man."

Later sociological, anthropological and biological studies showed that there is no difference in cranial capacity among the races and, in fact, that the whole concept of race as a means of categorizing humans is one that is superficial at best. Yet, the exposition at the World's Fair posed another example of an era in which white America upheld itself as the superior race, the savior of the world's peoples, and the holder of Manifest Destiny.

July 15, 1904

The mutilated body of Kitt Bookard is found floating in the Santee River, Berkeley County, South Carolina. Bookard's hands, bound behind him, indicate he has been the victim of a lynch mob.

Bookard had reportedly been jailed for arguing with a white man, but an angry mob had broken into the jail house, carrying Bookard away, ultimately to his horrifying doom.

Lynching is the illegal killing of an individual by a mob. In the early part of the twentieth century, 80 percent of all lynchings victimized African Americans. According to Dr. Arthur Raper, 3,724 people were lynched in the US between 1889 and 1930. Four-fifths of the victims were Negroes; those not black might have spoken up sympathetically for the black man's plight. Between 1919 and 1922, 239 blacks were lynched, ten of them returning World War I soldiers in uniform. All totaled, between 1865 and 1965, more than 2,400 African Americans were lynched. Of the tens of thousands of lynchers and onlookers, only 49 ever faced indictment; only four were ever sentenced.

Ida Bell Wells-Barnett, the great African American journalist and reformer, waged a tireless campaign against lynching throughout her career. Born a slave in Holly Springs, Mississippi, in 1862, she reportedly began investigating lynchings in 1892, after three of her friends were hanged in Memphis. She conducted an investigative study of 505 lynchings between 1896 and 1900, gleaning information from the *Chicago Tribune* which, on the first day of each year, published statistics concerning the previous year. In the midst of her study, she wrote to President William McKinley, asking him to take a stand on the despicable acts: "Nowhere in the civilized world save the United States of America do men, possessing all civil and political power, go out in bands of 50 to 5000 to hunt down, shoot, hang, or burn to death a single individual, unarmed and absolutely powerless. Statistics show that nearly 10,000 American citizens have been lynched in past 20 years. To our appeals for justice the stereotyped reply has been the government could not interfere in a state matter."

Southern whites justified lynching as the only way to keep down the crime of rape, as perpetuated by a black man against a white woman. (Little was ever said of the reverse, as white men have been raping black women since the days of slavery.) They perpetuated the myth that Southern white women could not bear to testify against a black man in court, so a lynching — complete without trial — could be the only remedy. In truth, statistics reveal that less than one sixth of lynchings had been for the crime of rape.

Jane Addams, the famed Chicago social reformer, replied to the justification for lynching in a letter to *Independent Magazine*. She wrote, "To those who say that most of these hideous and terrorizing acts have been committed in the name of chivalry, in order to make the lives and honor of women safe, perhaps it is women themselves who can best reply that bloodshed and arson and ungoverned anger have never yet controlled lust.... Perhaps it is women who can best testify that the honor of women is only secure in those nations and localities where law and order prevail."

George Henry White was the last former slave to serve in Congress, and the only African-American of his era to serve in the House of Representatives. White proposed a bill in January 1901 making the lynching of an American citizen a federal crime. He demonstrated that 87 of the 109 victims of lynching in 1899 had been African Americans. White felt anyone actively participating or acting as an accessory in a lynching should be convicted of treason.

Despite the congressman's passionate plea, his bill was easily defeated.

May 5, 1905

Robert Sengstacke Abbott publishes the first edition of the *Chicago Defender*, after an initial investment of 25 cents.

He ran 300 copies of the four-page weekly out of his landlord's apartment. Within ten years, it became the greatest, most influential black newspaper in the United States.

Abbott was born in Georgia in 1870 to former slaves. He studied printing at Hampton Institute from 1892 to 1896, receiving a degree in law from Kent College of Law in Chicago. Barred from practicing law in several states because of his race, Abbott became a self-made millionaire as a publisher. When Abbot died of Bright's disease in 1940, his nephew, John Sengstacke, assumed editorial control of the newspaper.

The *Chicago Defender* became famous for its editorials, in which Abbott launched sensational attacks on issues such as white oppression, military segregation, and lynching. Read extensively throughout the south, the *Defender* became instrumental in encouraging African Americans to leave the rural South for the industrial North, fostering the Great Migration. Celebrated writers such as Langston Hughes, Ida Wells-Barnett, and Gwendolyn Brooks all had their prose featured in the *Defender*.

By 1929, the *Chicago Defender* sold 250,000 copies a week, two-thirds of which sold beyond the city limits of Chicago. Becoming the *Chicago Daily Defender* in 1956, it was the largest black-owned daily newspaper in the world.

July 11, 1905

W.E.B. Du Bois and others form the Niagara movement.

Professor W.E.B. Du Bois of Atlanta University headed a small band of educated, bold, and unhappy Negro professionals who met in the city of Niagara Falls, Ontario, Canada. Together, they formed the "Niagara movement," issuing a blazing manifesto to white America.

In what became known as the Niagara Platform, these African Americans vowed to stand and fight for the Negroes' "manhood rights," to denounce and defeat oppressive laws, and to demand voting rights and school integration. Of the struggle for equal treatment, Du Bois wrote, "The prouder he is, or has a right to be, of the blood of his black fathers, the more doggedly he resists the attempt to load men of that blood with ignominy and chains. It is race pride that fights for freedom; it is the man ashamed of his blood who weakly submits and smiles" (Weinberg, p. 306).

Although the Niagara Movement eventually developed branches in 30 cities, the campaign survived as such for only five years. However, it proved an important development in the struggle for civil rights, as many of its ideals and precepts became the blueprint for the National Association for the Advancement of Colored People (NAACP), which emerged four years later.

May 8, 1906

The United States Congress enacts the Burke Act, which seeks to modify the Dawes Severalty Act of 1887, ostensibly passed to protect Indian land holdings from whites.

The Burke Act upheld the earlier measure, which granted to Indians who renounced their tribal allegiance full title to between 80 and 160 acres of reservation land after a probationary period of 25 years. However, unlike the Dawes Act, it granted citizenship only after the probationary period was over. The act also forbade the sale of alcohol to Indians who were not citizens. Many Indians resented the patronizing flavor of the act, and campaigned for full citizenship to all Indians; this was finally granted in 1924. Many saw the Burke Act, and similarly the Dawes Act, as attempt by the white man to break up the traditional tribes and to further indoctrinate Indians into white society.

Wary of deception and firmly protective of their lands and traditions, few Indians agreed to leave their tribal lands.

February 24, 1907

First affirmed on this date in a Japanese diplomatic note, the Gentleman's Agreement of 1907 is a secret executive agreement between the United States and Japan, limiting Japanese immigration to the United States.

Between 1867 and 1925, approximately 275,000 Japanese emigrated from their homeland. This amounted to about one-tenth of one percent of the total United States population, a mere pittance compared to the 30 million European immigrants who arrived between 1856 and 1924. The racially-based outcry against Japanese immigration was totally out of proportion with census realities. Yet the concern, fueled by reports of Japanese invasions in the Russo-Japanese War, received the attention of the administration, which seemed to share the discriminatory outlook.

Racial hostility toward Japanese arrivals had grown in California. The school district in San Francisco, California, had called for segregation of Japanese children from white children. To avoid this segregation, President Theodore Roosevelt convinced the Japanese government to withhold passports for laborers wishing to come to the United States.

The Gentleman's Agreement took place in the midst of emerging California state legislation to limit Japanese immigration into the state. In 1900, California had declared Japanese aliens ineligible to be citizens, something reserved only for free white persons. In 1913, the Heney-Webb Alien Land Law would prohibit ownership of land by people ineligible for citizenship. Finally the 1920 Alien Land Law would close loopholes in the 1913 law, further preventing Japanese acquisition of land.

Like the Chinese Exclusion Act of 1902, the Gentleman's Agreement and subsequent alien acts were racially-motivated attempts to restrict immigration from Asia to the United States — the same United States that had welcomed millions of European Americans.

July 2, 1908

Thurgood Marshall is born in West Baltimore, Maryland.

His mother was Norma Ariza Marshall, a school teacher in a segregated Baltimore elementary school. His father, William Caufield Marshall, was a dining car waiter on the Baltimore and Ohio Railroad; he would eventually become chief steward at the prestigious Gibson Island Club.

Young Thurgood was outspoken and boisterous in school, a characteristic which often landed him in trouble. For his punishment, he was regularly exiled to the school basement with a copy of the United States Constitution. Before long, he thoroughly memorized the document.

His parents raised him in a secure, affectionate home. They encouraged him to stand up against prejudice, to stand for his dignity and rights in the face of racial oppression.

Marshall received his undergraduate degree from Lincoln University, Pennsylvania, studying law at Howard University in Washington, D.C.

February 12, 1909

The National Association for the Advancement of Colored People (NAACP) is founded.

The originators purposely chose the symbolism of the birthday of Abraham Lincoln, the Great Emancipator. A multiracial group of more than 60 citizens, including W.E.B. Du Bois and Ida Bell Wells-Barnett, joined in the historic formation at Harpers Ferry, West Virginia, site of the legendary raid by fanatical abolitionist John Brown.

Du Bois went on to create the journal of the NAACP, which he called *The Crisis: The Record of the Dark Races.* Du Bois edited and published this periodical, which featured success stories of blacks in the fields of art, business, and philosophy. The journal also worked toward the enforcement of anti-lynching laws.

The need for a watchdog organization such as the NAACP had become exemplified in the Springfield Race Riot of 1908. When on July 4, a white woman falsely accused a black man of raping her, hostilities flared until a white mob invaded and destroyed the city's black district. Eight African Americans were murdered, with more than 2,000 fleeing Springfield. The Springfield Race Riot had been fueled by flickering hostilities among growing white, European immigrant, and African American communities. The race riot illustrated the great need to monitor those hostilities.

Over the next 90 years, the NAACP — through its legislative advocacy and legal defense — would be a leading force in the attainment of racial equality and justice.

February 17, 1909

The Apache leader Geronimo dies and is buried at Fort Sill, Oklahoma.

Following the death of Cochise in 1874, Geronimo led the last campaign of the Chiricahua Apache against the white man, after 4,000 Apaches were removed from their tribal homeland of southeastern Arizona to San Carlos, New Mexico. His campaign solidified the image of the Apache as a fierce warlike tribe, carrying on in the tradition of the great Cochise.

Geronimo waged war for ten more years, until induced to surrender by Brigadier General Nelson A. Miles in 1886. Miles promised Geronimo he and his tribe would be allowed to return to their Arizona homeland. The promise — like so many white promises in the past — was never kept.

After keeping him at hard labor for two years, the government moved Geronimo to Fort Sill, Oklahoma. He ostensibly attempted to adopt European American ways, making meager attempts to farm and even joining the Dutch Reform Church. After more than 20 years of this existence, he petitioned President Theodore Roosevelt to allow him to return to his homeland. Citing the animosity the white people of Arizona still held for the Apache, Roosevelt denied his request.

At the age of 85, Geronimo fell off his horse while riding one day and lay in a ditch overnight until discovered. He caught pneumonia, dying a few days later.

The last great chief of the Apaches never returned to his native lands.

January 22, 1910

San Francisco opens Angel Island in the northern corner of San Francisco Bay.

The island had originally been intended as the Ellis Island of the West, an entryway for immigrants from Europe. Instead, most of the persons passing through Angel Island came from Asia, particularly China. Of the 250,000 individuals who passed through Angel Island, 175,000 — or 70 percent — were Chinese. In response to West Coast animosity to Asian immigrants, Angel Island became a prison-like detention center, a place where immigrants might be detained for days, weeks, or months before their final destination was determined.

Chinese immigrants had found a loophole in the Exclusion Act of 1902: anyone who could prove citizenship through paternal lineage would be granted entry into the United States. Those without true fathers in the United States often purchased falsified documents identifying them as offspring of American citizens, making them "paper sons" or "paper daughters." With no official records available, even extensive interrogations could be futile.

The United States government closed the immigration station on Angel Island on November 5, 1940.

July 4, 1910

John Arthur "Jack" Johnson successfully defends his title as undisputed world champion heavyweight boxer by defeating former champion James Jeffries before 20,000 people in Reno, Nevada.

The match had become more of a war between the races than a simple pugilistic campaign. Johnson had already defeated a white fighter named Tommy Burns in Sydney, Australia. Now Jeffries, 35, was called upon to redeem the white man from the indignities he had suffered. Before the contest, one white journalist wrote, "if Johnson wins, the Negroes in the Southern states may be encouraged to acts which formerly they would not dare to commit" (Jennings, p. 41).

Although the fight lasted 15 rounds, the flamboyant Johnson — in the peak of physical condition — seemed to toy with his opponent, delaying the knockout punch until the final moments. Jeffries, a California native who had come out of retirement as the "Great White Hope," seemed totally outmatched in the contest.

In response to Johnson's victory, riots broke out around the country, leaving 11 dead and hundreds wounded. One black intellectual wrote, "It was a good deal better for Johnson to win and as few Negroes to have been killed in body, than for Johnson to have lost and the Negroes to have been killed in spirit" (Jennings, p. 42).

White Americans had to grapple with the reality that a black man could best a white man in anything. After the fight, law enforcement pursued Johnson, locking him in jail on trumped-up morals charges. Although Johnson's career quickly faded into obscurity, he would forever be regarded as the man who, on center stage in Reno, defeated the Great White Hope.

September 29, 1910

The Committee on Urban Conditions Among Negroes, the predecessor of the National Urban League, is formed at an inaugural meeting in New York City.

A response to the great migration of African Americans to northern urban America, the committee was created under the direction of two initial leaders of the movement: Mrs. Ruth Standish Baldwin was a member of one of America's oldest families, the widow of a railroad magnate, and a fearless champion of poor and disadvantaged; Dr. George Edmund Haynes was a social worker and educator, a graduate of both Fisk and Yale universities. Haynes was the first African American to earn a doctorate degree from Columbia University. He was named the first executive director of the committee in 1911.

Within a year, the Committee on Urban Conditions Among Negroes merged with the Committee for the Improvement of Industrial Conditions Among Negroes in New York, and the National League for the Protection of Colored Women, to form the National League on Urban Conditions Among Negroes. The organization became the National Urban League in 1920.

In all its forms, the mission of the Urban League was to help African Americans who had migrated from the rural South to escape the oppression of the Jim Crow laws achieve social and economic equality. Focusing on the northern cities, the Urban League worked with newly arrived blacks, who had escaped the brutal economic, social, and political oppression of the white South only to find a new set of oppressions plaguing them in the North. Often these people could find only menial jobs, with poor housing and education opportunities, and terrible social and economic conditions.

The National Urban League worked to end racial discrimination by campaigning to increase the political and economic power of blacks and other minorities. They became famous for their boycotts of businesses that would not hire African American workers. The League counseled black migrants from the South, providing employment training and developing black social workers to continue the training. These social workers focused on issues such as employment opportunities, recreation, housing, health and sanitation, and education.

Eventually the National Urban League included 114 affiliates in 34 states and the District of Columbia. Dr. Haynes went on to serve as special assistant to the secretary of labor from 1918 to 1921.

May 25, 1911

The presidency of Portfirio Diaz falls to revolutionary Francisco Madero, Jr.

Diaz is exiled to Paris, France, from Mexico, ushering in the Mexican Revolution and the northward migration of Mexican laborers.

Economic and social injustices flourished under the 35-year reign of

Diaz — particularly toward the end. Influenced by the thinking of American business in Mexico, the Diaz administration regularly practiced discrimination against dark-skinned Mexicans and Mexican Indians. The low standards of living for poor Mexicans sank even lower, as jobs in mining and railroads disappeared in northern Mexico. The depressed economy encouraged a wave of Mexicans to move to United States, with as many as one million Mexicans emigrating to the U.S. between 1910 and 1920. The migration would lead to future bitter clashes of culture among Mexican immigrants, Mexican Americans, and European Americans.

July 4, 1911

The Cincinnati Reds sign two Cuban ball players deemed to be talented enough — and light skinned enough — to play in the Major Leagues.

Armando Marsans stood 5'10", weighed 164, and batted and threw right handed. He would accumulate a .269 lifetime average playing for the Reds, the St. Louis Browns, and New York Yankees, as well as the St. Louis Terriers in the Federal League. Rafael Almeida, at 5'9" and 164 lbs., played three seasons with Cincinnati. He stood 5'9", weighed 164, and batted and threw right handed. At their signing, Marsans and Almeida become the first Hispanic players in the Major Leagues.

In 1914, the Boston Braves signed Cuban pitcher Dolf Luque, destined to be the first Latin-American star of the Major Leagues. Luque would play 21 years in the majors, including stints with the Cincinnati Reds, the Brooklyn Dodgers, and the New York Yankees. His finest season would be 1923, when he posted a record of 27–8, with a 1.93 earned run average. He would be known as the "Pride of Havana," 12 years after Cuba gained independence from the United States following the Spanish-American War.

The litmus test for Latin or Hispanic players entering the major leagues seemed solely to depend on the color of the skin. Because the skin of Marsans, Almeida, and Luque appeared light enough, they could be allowed into the league. Other fine ball players, such as Jose Mendez, had to sign in the Negro Leagues. The distinction was purely by color, having nothing to do with culture, nationality, sportsmanship, or skill level.

August 29, 1911

Ishi, last of the Yahi people, is discovered.

On this day, a man in his fifties, thought to be the last remnant of a wild (not yet confined to a reservation) tribe of Indians, was captured outside a slaughterhouse near Oroville, California.

He was found in the vicinity of Mill Creek and Deer Creek, naked except for a thin covered-wagon canvas used as a poncho. Sheriff J. B. Webber took the Indian into custody, as much for the Indian's safety as any other reason. Quickly, word spreads of the wild Indian, who became the object of great curiosity and fear.

The Indian's presence in the jail came to the attention of two professors of anthropology at University of California, Berkeley: T.T. Waterman and Alfred L. Kroeber. They determined him to be the member of a tribe called the Yahi, the southernmost branch of the Yaha linguistic family of tribes — long thought to be extinct. Kroeber gave the survivor the name "Ishi," meaning "man" in the Yahi language. Yet, the Indian spoke a dialect completely indigenous to himself and whatever remained of his tribe. However, it resembled the language of the Northern and Central Yana enough that Waterman found he could communicate with him.

Meanwhile, the discovery of Ishi sent imaginations and fears soaring throughout the country. The 1900 census had indicated that the American Indian population had reached its lowest point in history at fewer than 240,000, less than ten percent of the pre–Columbus estimate of 2 to 18 million. Still, great trepidations rose among white Americans about other "unknown" wild tribes that might be wandering about uncontrolled and uncivilized in the wilderness.

As the controversy grew in Oroville around Ishi, the anthropologists decided to move him to San Francisco, to the Museum of Anthropology. They set up an apartment for him. Ishi soon became the subject of study for scientists, a curiosity for the public, and fun for the children.

Unfortunately, Ishi's fate followed that of countless Native Americans before him, unable to develop immunities to foreign diseases. Shortly after arriving in San Francisco, Ishi contracted a cold, which turned into a respiratory infection by 1914. By the spring of 1915, he developed tuberculosis. He died on March 25, 1916.

The reputed last wild Indian, who had lived healthily for 50 years in the northeast California wilderness, died within five years of entering the twentieth century civilization of European Americans.

July 6, 1912

A Native American competes in the Olympic Games.

On this day, King Gustav of Sweden opened the fifth Olympiad of the modern era in Stockholm. The 1912 games prominently featured the prowess of arguably the finest athlete of the twentieth century, Jim Thorpe. A Sac and Fox Indian born in a one-room cabin in Oklahoma, Thorpe captured gold medals for both the pentathlon and the decathlon in the 1912 Stock-holm Olympics. His performance inspired King Gustav V of Sweden to call him "the greatest athlete in the world." His Indian name, "Wa-Tho-Huk," is translated as "Bright Path."

Thorpe built one of the greatest careers in the history of American athletics. An All-American in 1910 and 1912, he had played football for Carlisle Indian Industrial School in Oklahoma. Tiny Carlisle won the national championship in 1911, at one point beating Harvard 18–15, with Thorpe scoring a touchdown and four field goals. Thorpe went on to play outfield for the New York Giants, the Boston Braves, and the Cincinnati Reds. He also performed as running back for the New York (football) Giants. In 1950, a survey of the national press selected Thorpe as the most outstanding athlete of the first half of the twentieth century.

However, by 1913, the International Olympic Committee stripped Thorpe of his gold medals. It was discovered that between 1909 and 1910, Thorpe had played semi-professional baseball in Oklahoma, at $25 a week. This meager stipend violated the IOC's rule on amateur status. Not until 70 years later, after a vigorous campaign by his daughter Grace, were Thorpe's Olympic achievements reinstated and appropriately recognized.

February 4, 1913

Rosa Louise McCauley is born in Tuskegee, Alabama, home of Tuskegee University, founded by post–Civil War reformer Booker T. Washington.

Her father was a brick layer and a carpenter, her mother a teacher. Her father left her family when she was five, and she moved to live with her grandparents in Pine Level, Alabama. She picked cotton for a time as a seven-year-old, and attended Alabama State Normal School in Montgomery, then called Montgomery Industrial School.

She married Raymond Parks, a longtime activist for the National Association for the Advancement of Colored People. She joined the NAACP herself, eventually becoming the secretary of the Montgomery chapter, while she learned to be a seamstress at a Montgomery department store. One day in December 1955, she went for a bus ride that would change a nation.

March 10, 1913

Harriet Tubman, called the "Moses of the Civil War," dies in her home at Auburn, New York.

Tubman had been the best known and most successful conductor of the Underground Railroad, the passage to freedom for slaves before the War Between the States.

Born Harriet Ross into slavery in Maryland in 1819 or 1820, Tubman won her freedom in 1851. Once free, she returned to the South 19 times, primarily to her home state of Maryland, to personally lead 300 to 800 slaves to freedom. Enraged Southern plantation owners at one point offered $40,000 for her capture.

Marrying Nelson Tubman after the Civil War, she settled in Auburn, New York, where she died. She was buried at Fort Hill Cemetery in Auburn with full military honors. On June 14, 1914, a large bronze plaque was placed in the Cayuga County Courthouse, with a civic holiday declared in her honor.

May 19, 1913

Governor Hiram Johnson signs California's Heney-Webb Alien Land Act.

Building on the Gentleman's Agreement of 1907, the Alien Land Act prohibited the owning and leasing of land by aliens not eligible to become naturalized citizens. At the time, federal law prohibited all nonwhite, non–African immigrants from becoming naturalized citizens.

The act clearly targeted Asian immigrants, particularly the Japanese, based on anti–Japanese sympathies rooted in the nineteenth century.

The first demonstration of anti–Japanese sentiments came in 1906, when San Francisco tried to segregate Japanese school children. President Roosevelt's administration quashed the segregation idea, instead devising the Gentleman's Agreement. California legislators had considered several versions of the Alien Land Act between 1907 and 1913, until the passage of this measure.

The Californians' fear of the Japanese was based on several erroneous assumptions, mostly racial. Many Californians saw the Japanese as competition not only as laborers, but as land owners, possibly more skilled and ambitious than themselves. Many feared the immigration of "picture brides" coming to California instead of male laborers, banned by the Gentlemen's Agreement of 1907. They feared the women would presage a new population of native-born Japanese, who would be American citizens.

At the signing of the Heney-Webb law, many Japanese land owners circumvented the law by entrusting their land to their American-born children, or to white friends for safekeeping.

August 15, 1914

The fabulous Panama Canal, the American engineering marvel that placed the country's stamp on the modern age, opens to passage of vessels along the Isthmus of Panama, between the Atlantic and Pacific Oceans.

The American press had regularly depicted the phenomenon as the handiwork of contented white American laborers blissfully working in the sun. In truth, the canal was built on the backs of laborers of color, mostly blacks, mostly from islands in the Caribbean Sea. Of the thousands of laborers who toiled on the project between 1904 and 1914, 80 percent were non–American people of color.

The black laborers were fed and housed separately, often in highly deplorable conditions. They were paid in silver instead of gold, with strict color lines maintained. Black men rarely reached supervisory levels, and were never in a position over a white man. The death rate due to disease and accident for blacks numbered five times that for whites. In the last year of construction alone, of the 414 deaths on the canal, 384 involved people of color.

David McCullough later wrote in *The Path Between the Seas*: "Official visitors ... could not help but be amazed, even astounded, at the degree to which the entire system, and not simply the construction, depended on black labor."

February 8, 1915

Under the title of *The Clansman*, *The Birth of a Nation* premieres in Los Angeles at Clune's Auditorium.

It premiered under its more familiar name on March 3 in New York. The film, by D.W. Griffith, was immediately denounced by the National Association for the Advancement of Colored People as "the meanest vilification of the Negro race" (www.filmsite.org). The NAACP launched a nationwide protest against the film, as well as its racist portrayal of blacks, which ignited riots in several cities.

The film portrays the Ku Klux Klan as heroes, while Southern blacks are depicted as villains. While it explores skewed themes of black empowerment and interracial sex, most of the important black roles are portrayed by white actors in black face. Despite its obvious shortcomings, the film introduced numerous technical innovations to filmmaking. It proved to be an extraordinarily successful film, grossing more than 18 million dollars by the late 1920s.

It is difficult to ignore the timing between the release of the film and the rebirth of the Ku Klux Klan later the same year.

June 21, 1915

Guinn v. United States, a test case brought by the NAACP, is decided by the United States Supreme Court.

The Court ruled that the so-called "grandfather clause," which exempted from certain financial and educational requirements persons whose fathers, or grandfathers, had voted before 1867, was unconstitutional. Essentially, this clause would have disenfranchised all blacks, since no black gained the right to vote before 1867. The state of Oklahoma had attempted to include such a clause in its constitution.

The Court ruled the clause to be a clear violation of the Fifteenth Amendment, which assured equal voting rights to all men regardless of race, color, or previous condition of servitude.

September 10, 1915

Henry Roe Cloud, a full-blooded Winnebago Indian and a graduate from Yale, establishes the American Indian Institute in Wichita, Kansas.

It was the first college preparatory institution created by a Native American for Native Americans. It provided a non-industrial education for Native American boys for the next 13 years.

November 14, 1915

Booker T. Washington dies at Alabama's Tuskegee Institute, where he had served as president since 1881.

Born as a slave in 1856, he went on to help found Tuskegee Normal and Industrial School, turning it into one of the world's leading centers for education for African Americans. With his Atlanta Compromise speech before the Cotton States and International Exposition in 1895, he became the de facto leader of African Americans.

Because of his placating viewpoint, Washington often found himself in the position of default spokesperson for his race — despite the fact that many African Americans did not agree with his philosophy. Nevertheless, Washington proved to be one of the most influential and recognized men in the country. His rags-to-riches dream for Southern blacks may have been the appropriate political and social road for his time, a road upon which future loftier sojourns could be planned. He preached the virtues of hard work and economic survival through education and advancement into professions, believing character value to be of more importance than political agitation. "The wisest among my race," he said in 1895, "understand that the agitation of social equality is the extremest of folly" (Harlan, p. 219).

Known throughout his life for the quiet endurance with which he sought to raise his people, Washington made an unusual invitation to the

Institute just a month before his death, to a man who would soon become known for his flamboyance and his aggressive nature.

Marcus Garvey never made it to Tuskegee.

November 24, 1915

William J. Simmons, a Spanish-American War veteran turned self-proclaimed preacher, rides with 15 other men on a bus from Atlanta to Stone Mountain, Georgia, to inaugurate the twentieth century version of the Ku Klux Klan.

Simmons was apparently inspired by the release of the film *Birth of a Nation* earlier in the year. Before a flaming pine cross on Thanksgiving eve, Simmons revived the nineteenth century organization, which had been more or less terminated in the 1860s.

The Ku Klux Klan was originally organized at the end of the Civil War, by white Civil War veterans in Tennessee. What had started out, according to some historians, as something of a farce quickly turned into a serious means of intimidating minority groups in the Southern states. The name Ku Klux Klan is thought to be a derivative of the Greek "kuklos" meaning "circle" or "cycle." The most revered of the early leaders was former Confederate general Nathan Bedford Forrest. The Klan named Forrest the first imperial wizard, who in 1867 and 1868 traveled around the South on a mission to establish additional chapters and memberships. The Klan members donned white cloaks and hoods — soon developing a culture of secrecy, violence and intimidation of poor unionizing whites and blacks — in an effort to restore the aristocratic wealthy white prewar seat of power.

Several elements combined to support the rebirth of the KKK. More than 23 million immigrants from Europe stoked the fear of foreigners overwhelming the American workplace. The war in Europe brought hundreds of minorities from the United States, exposing them to cultures in which they could be honored and valued despite their skin color. Finally, there was the advent of the populist movement, in which the poor white and the black voter joined forces against the interests of the rich. Into this mix the Ku Klux Klan reemerged, terrorizing not only Negroes, Catholics and Jews, but also immigrants, Asians, and unionists.

Over the next decades, the targets of the Klan's intimidations expanded to include all those determined to be immoral, or traitors to the white race.

March 9, 1916

At approximately 4:15 A.M., the New Mexico border town of Columbus is raided by a force of 485, led by Mexican revolutionary general Francisco "Pancho" Villa.

Surprising the 13th United States Cavalry stationed at Columbus, population 400, Villa's attack cost at least 17 American casualties. Villa also confiscated 80 horses, 30 mules, and a substantial collection of American military equipment. In turn, 90 of Villa's men were killed in the skirmish.

Historical opinions differ on the purpose of the Villa's strike. Some contend he simply sought a source of loot by which to replenish his campaign against Mexican president Venustiano Carranza. Others, however, see the attack as a statement aimed at both Carranza and United States president Woodrow Wilson. Villa believed Carranza and Wilson had come to an agreement to make Mexico a United States protectorate.

Whatever the reason for the attack, Wilson decided that Villa's strike merited retaliation. Within a week, Wilson sent a 10,000-man punitive force, led by Spanish-American War hero General John Pershing, deep into the Mexican state of Chihuahua. Among those selected to pursue Villa were the 10th Cavalry, known as the "Buffalo Soldiers," composed of African Americans commanded by white Americans. Despite the American show of force, Pancho Villa managed to elude the punitive expedition, solidifying in his countrymen's eyes the mythic image of the revolutionary who defied the might of the northern neighbor.

Villa's attack on Columbus, along with Pershing's raid into Mexico, raised already existing tensions between Mexico and United States. Furthermore, the Pancho Villa image — of the dust-covered Mexican bandito in sombrero, on horseback, with bandoliers crossing his chest — was impressed upon the imaginations of Americans. Mexican Americans and immigrants would find the stereotype an impediment for decades to come.

March 24, 1916

Jamaican-born Marcus Mosiah Garvey arrives in New York City penniless, staying with a Jamaican family in Harlem.

Within a year he organized the Universal Negro Improvement Association (UNIA), publishing the first issue of its newspaper *The Negro World* in 1918. Garvey preached that African Americans can never receive justice in a land populated mostly by whites, suggesting blacks consider returning to the homeland to settle and live. He believed that Northern Africa had been the wellspring of civilization.

Garvey's philosophy actually echoed a creed previously espoused by African Methodist Episcopal bishop Henry MacNeal Turner, who, in the late nineteenth century, touted Liberia as the true "American Dream" for blacks. Turner had actually traveled to Liberia on a goodwill tour, but returned from the country with his dream somewhat dampened.

Outspoken and flamboyant, Garvey frequently wore a braided uniform with a plumed military hat, preaching racial pride. In the wake of the Great Migration northward, Garvey encouraged the black community to purge itself of its self-hatred. He said, "The time has come for the Negro to forget and cast behind him his hero worship and adoration of other races, and to start out immediately, to create and emulate heroes of his own. Sojourner Truth ... Crispus Attucks and George William Gordon ... Toussaint L'Ouverture ... Africa has produced countless numbers of men and women, in war and in peace, whose luster and bravery outshine that of any other people. Then why not see good and perfection in ourselves?" (Marcus Garvey and UNIA). This philosophy ushered in the period in New York City known as the Harlem Renaissance.

Through the UNIA and *The Negro World*, Garvey would eventually reach between 2 million and 4 million people with his "Back to Africa" message. Supporters sent thousands of dollars, which he used to set up black businesses. His ultimate goal was to initiate the Black Star Line of ships, with a dream to bring disillusioned African Americans from the land of their birth to their homeland.

February 5, 1917

Congress passes the Immigration Act of 1917, imposing a literacy requirement on all immigrants.

The act excluded all "aliens over sixteen years of age, physically capable of reading, who cannot read the English language or dialect, including Hebrew or Yiddish." The act also expanded the list of aliens excluded for mental health and other reasons, including "all idiots, imbeciles, feeble-minded persons, epileptics, insane persons ... persons with chronic alcoholism; paupers, professional beggars; vagrants, persons afflicted with tuberculosis of any form or with a loathsome or dangerous disease."

The Immigration Act also further restricted Asian immigrants, creating a "barred zone" for persons from what would be known as the Asia-Pacific triangle. The legislation also greatly broadened the deportable classes of aliens from the United States, introducing the requirement of deportation without statute of limitations for serious cases. Additionally, the act increased the entry head-tax to $8 per person.

Massachusetts Senator Henry Cabot Lodge argued for the literacy test, while Presidents Woodrow Wilson, William Howard Taft, and Grover Cleveland all argued against it. Aimed at curbing the influx from southern and eastern Europe, the literacy requirement of the Immigration Act of 1917 ultimately inhibited immigration from Mexico.

March 2, 1917

The Jones Act is passed, extending United States citizenship to all Puerto Ricans.

The act also created two Puerto Rican houses of legislature, whose representatives would be elected by the people, and decreed English to be the official language of Puerto Rico

The Jones Act, named for Congressman William H. Jones of Virginia, provided a resident commissioner who supposedly was to represent the people in Congress. However, the Puerto Rican people had no means of directing the commission, since they had no vote on measures the commissioner would consider.

In addition, the power to appoint the territorial governor, the resident commissioner, the attorney general, and the Puerto Rican Supreme Court remained firmly in the hands of the president of the United States. Furthermore, Congress kept veto power over all acts of the Puerto Rican legislature.

Although American legislators no doubt viewed the act as magnanimous, many Puerto Ricans saw the measure as a "colonizing" gesture, imposing American citizenship whether the islanders wanted it or not. The Puerto Ricans became United States citizens without vote, in a republic without true representation.

July 28, 1917

Ten thousand protesters march down New York City's Fifth Avenue in a protest organized by W.E.B. Du Bois and the National Association for the Advancement of Colored People.

Called the "Why We March," Du Bois used the movement to protest continued lynching, discrimination, and segregation in the federal government.

Due to protests such as these, the NAACP finally pressured President Woodrow Wilson to make — in August of 1917 — a public statement against the scourge of lynching. Realizing the need for Negro support for the war in Europe, Wilson spoke out against lynching and mob violence, saying it played into the hands of German propagandists. Wilson wanted to repair ties to the Negro community, now that the United States had declared war on Germany in April of 1917. He knew the armed forces and industries would be in need of African American workers and soldiers to support the war in Europe. However, he reportedly never mentioned the plight of Negroes, nor advocate for any kind of federal legislation banning lynching.

The NAACP had been striving for a law against lynching since its inception in 1909. At the same time, Wilson's record on racial justice seemed abysmal. Jim Crow had essentially become the hiring policy for United States government. Federal offices remained segregated, and few African American held any federal positions.

November 5, 1917

The Supreme Court deals a blow to housing segregation.

In the decision of *Buchanan v. Warley*, the United States Supreme Court took a step down the road away from *Plessy v. Ferguson*, conceding that states can not restrict or officially segregate African Americans into residential districts and declaring unconstitutional a 1914 Louisville, Kentucky, ordinance that required residential segregation by race.

This case involved the sale of property by a white seller named Buchanan to a black purchaser named Warley. Buchanan had sold a residence in a Louisville neighborhood to Warley, as well as several other African American customers. According to the Louisiana ordinance, a black person could not live on a block on which more white individuals than black resided. Buchanan challenged the ruling, calling it a violation of the Fourteenth Amendment, which protects the life, liberty, and property of an American citizen from removal without due process of law. Buchanan sued to challenge the ordinance and allow the sale of the property to Warley to remain valid.

In a unanimous decision, the Supreme Court declared the Louisiana law unconstitutional. Justice William R. Day, in writing the opinion, stated the solution to racial hostility "cannot be promoted by depriving citizens of their constitutional rights and privileges."

The fact that the case involved the rights of both a black man and a white man had no doubt prompted the unanimous decision. *Buchanan v. Warley* became a precedent on which later housing discrimination cases — particularly *Shelley v. Kraemer* in 1948 — were based.

November 11, 1917

Queen Lili'uokalani, the last monarch of Hawaii, dies at the age of 79, following a stroke.

Raised in the Protestant mission, Lili'uokalani nevertheless remained proud of her native culture, language, and people, striving to revive and restore the ancient ways in the face of the invasion of American *haoles,* the outsiders.

A skillful musician, Lili'uokalani wrote many songs, including the famous "Aloha Oe,'" meaning "Farewell to Thee." It is said she tearfully wrote this song of two lovers parting as she sat under house arrest in the Iolani Palace, watching the Stars and Stripes being raised on the flagpole of her beloved home, while the United States officially annexed the Hawaiian Islands. Following annexation in 1898, Lili'uokalani lived privately for 19 years.

Following the death of Hawaii's last queen, Hawaiian natives struggled to retain the customs and traditions Lili'uokalani held so dear.

January 1, 1918

The first African American officer sets foot in France.

When the 15th Infantry Regimental Band of New York arrived in Paris, it was led by a musician from Alabama named James Reese Europe. The French gave the 15th Infantry — later to be designated as the 369th Infantry — a rousing welcome. Europe and his band traveled all over the continent, infiltrating some of the fiercest battlegrounds of the European theater. Lieutenant Europe became the first African American officer on the combat lines in World War I. Meanwhile, his regimental band thrilled European audiences with its unique, syncopated, early version of American jazz. In turn, the band was treated with the respect and dignity so difficult to find in its own oppressive and bigoted homeland. The black troops were welcomed as heroes all over Europe.

Arriving back home after World War I, African Americans found the same brutality and racism they left. In the first year after the end of World War I, at least 70 blacks were found lynched. Ten of them were soldiers, several of them still in uniform.

On February 12, 1919, a parade up Fifth Avenue in Harlem welcomed home the 369th Infantry. James Reese Europe and his band immediately began a tour around the country, gathering fans and followers wherever they went.

Tragically, on May 9, 1919, at a concert tour in Boston, Europe was fatally stabbed in the neck with a penknife by a member of his own band. Europe was given an official New York funeral, the first ever for an African American.

January 31, 1919

Jack Roosevelt Robinson is born in Cairo, Georgia, the son of an sharecropper.

Abandoned by her husband, his mother, Mallie McGriff Robinson, raised Jackie and his siblings in an all-white neighborhood in Pasadena, California. Jackie Robinson excelled in all sports at both Pasadena Junior College and the University of California at Los Angeles. All the while, he endured taunts from his nonblack classmates. It was an experience he shouldered well into adulthood, when he once again — but on a much greater scale — would be a lone African American thrust into an all-white world.

February 18, 1919

The Second Pan-African Congress, arranged by American scholar W.E.B. Du Bois, draws up the Pan-African Congress Resolutions, demanding the League of Nations develop a special bureau to oversee the treatment of black Africans in their homeland.

Meeting in Paris, the Congress hoped to see black Africans become landowners, be free from outside financial exploitation and slavery, be educated to read and write in their own languages, and participate in the governments of their countries. Independence for African colonies would not be demanded until the Fifth Congress, which met in Manchester, England, in 1945. By highlighting the plight of black Africans, Du Bois and the Pan-African Congress brought attention to the hardships faced by African Americans.

July 27, 1919

The death of Eugene Williams, a black youth who drowned at the 29th Street Beach in Chicago, Illinois, triggers five days of rioting in what would be known as Red Summer.

By the first of August, 38 people had died, and more than 290 were wounded or maimed.

Williams reportedly had been trying to float ashore on a railroad tie, between 26th Street and the 29th Street beach, when he was struck on the head by a rock thrown at him by a white male. Despite aid offered by a friend, Williams reportedly panicked and drowned in the Lake Michigan waters. The white male reportedly ran off as rioting began on the beach. A police officer refused to arrest the white male, but reportedly arrested a black male for trying to use a designated "white beach." The rioting continued and escalated, fueled by innuendo and rumor concerning the drowning death of Williams.

The Chicago coroner's office reportedly spent 70 days on an inquest into the death of Williams. The resulting report featured recommendations for dealing with the festering economic and social conditions in Chicago.

Red Summer exemplified the growing tensions created in Chicago and other northern cities. The combination of the African American migration and the European immigration was causing the melting pot to boil over with racial and cultural fears.

January 12, 1920

The American Civil Liberties Union (ACLU) is formed in New York City by social workers Crystal Eastman and Roger Baldwin and attorney Albert DeSilver.

In October 1917, Eastman and Baldwin had organized the National Civil Liberties Bureau (NCLB). When the NCLB folded, they came back to New York to form the ACLU.

The first public interest law firm of its kind, the ACLU worked to defend the Bill of Rights against government oppression and the tyranny of the majority. The ACLU adopted the policy of impartially defending civil liberties, including the freedom of speech, in all circumstances. The ACLU did not discern among the contents of free speech, but consistently defended the freedoms provided by the first ten amendments of the Constitution.

At first, much of the work of the ACLU focused on the rights of the individual laborer. Transformed from the NCLB, it was "reorganized and enlarged to cope more adequately with the invasion of civil liberties incident to the industrial struggle, which had followed the war" (Walker, p. 46).

The ACLU quickly procured the reputation of defending civil liberties for everyone — no matter the race, religion, national origin, or lifestyle. The ACLU stood alone to condemn the interment of Japanese Americans during World War II. The organization defended those denied education and public services due to race long before other organizations. The ACLU confronted threats to civil liberties on any and all fronts.

January 13, 1920

As if in response to Marcus Garvey urging, "No more fears, no more cringing ... no more begging and pleading," New York's Andrew "Rube" Foster begins the Negro National League.

Foster, a former big league pitcher who had organized the Chicago American Giants baseball team in 1911, became black baseball's first impresario.

The league — actually called the National Association of Colored Professional Baseball Clubs — started out with eight teams: the Kansas City Monarchs, the Indianapolis ABCs, the Dayton Marcos, the Chicago Giants,

Chicago American Giants, the Detroit Stars, the St. Louis Giants, and the Cuban Giants. Its first game was played on May 2, 1920, with the Indianapolis ABCs beating the Chicago American Giants 4–2. The Negro Leagues featured three big stars: Pitcher Smokey Joe Williams, flame thrower Joe Rogan, and fleet-footed Oscar Charleston.

By 1923, Foster's league was a great success, drawing more than 400,000 black fans in that single year. Seeing the profits the Negro Leagues was earning, white businessmen started up rival leagues, such as the Eastern Colored League. The rival leagues lured Foster's players away. By 1926, Rube Foster was a financial and physical wreck, institutionalized. He died in 1930, but the idea of the Negro Leagues continued for 30 more years, producing some of the finest players baseball — any baseball — would ever see.

August 1, 1920

A delegation of the Universal Negro Improvement Association, founded by Marcus Garvey in 1914, draws up the *Declaration of Rights of Negro Peoples of the World* in New York City.

The document railed against the injustices, discriminations, and "inhuman, unchristian, and uncivilized treatment" suffered by descendants of Africa throughout the world. (This document would one day become the model for the United Nations' *Universal Declaration of Human Rights*.) The declaration stated that all blacks are "free citizens of Africa, the motherland of all Negroes," and they have the right "to reclaim the treasures and possessions of the vast continent of their forefathers." At the same time, Garvey adopted a "nation" flag with the colors of red, green, and black, declaring himself "Provisional President of Africa."

Meanwhile, the Bureau of Investigation of the Department of Justice placed Garvey under surveillance, as the predecessor of the FBI looked for a way to indict and deport Garvey — still a Jamaican citizen — out of the United States. By this time, Garvey had purchased the first vessel of the Black Star Line — which he envisioned as the medium for his "Back to Africa" movement. The ship, called the S.S. *Yarmouth*, set sail on January 17, 1920, from New York for Havana, Cuba, carrying a cargo of whiskey during the initial days of Prohibition. By February 3, the vessel was sinking outside New York harbor, with the U.S. government seizing the cargo.

November 1, 1920

Renaissance man Paul Robeson stars in his first stage production, *The Emperor Jones*, at the Provinceton Playhouse in New York at the age of 22.

Robeson graduated Phi Beta Kappa as valedictorian from Rutgers University, after which he earned a law degree at Columbia University. Robeson then commenced on a career on the stage that would be legendary. He starred in Shakespeare's *Othello*, playing the lead character with an indomitable stage presence. In *Show Boat*, he displayed his rich, warm voice in the rendition of "Ol' Man River." His performances commanded rave reviews, as he became one of the most charismatic figures in American theater history.

Through out his life, Robeson showed himself a man of multiple talents and causes. He learned to speak 20 languages, enabling him to enjoy success on the stage throughout the world. He railed against fascism and, while entertaining troops overseas, advocate for the civil rights of soldiers during World War II. His travels brought him into contact with leftist organizations, African nationalist groups, and finally the Soviet Union. He became a great sympathizer and spokesperson for the Communist movement. In 1950, the State Department revoked his passport, for which he endured blacklisting, which severely curtailed his career as a performer. He eventually became depressed, lost his health, and drifted into obscurity. He died following a stroke in 1976.

May 15, 1921

Downhome Blues, sung by blues goddess Ethel Waters, is the first hit record released by Black Swan Records, the first recording company owned and operated entirely by African Americans.

Entrepreneur Harry Herbert Pace of Covington, Georgia, had founded Black Swan Records in March of 1921. The company was named for a blues singer from the late nineteenth century named Elizabeth Taylor Greenfield, also known as the Black Swan.

The company's logo featured an elegant black swan against a gold field. By then other labels — Okeh, Columbia, Paramount, Vocalion — had their catalogs of "race records" marketed specifically for African Americans. Black Swan's motto, however, would become "only genuine colored records — others are only passing for colored," indicating the authenticity of its ownership and operation. Black Swan artists included Fletcher Henderson, band leader at the Roseland Ball Room, as well as Bessie Smith and Ethel Waters, who virtually kept Black Swan afloat.

June 3, 1921

The Negro Speaks of Rivers is published in *The Crisis*, the newspaper of the National Association for the Advancement of Colored People.

The verse was by a 19-year-old essayist and poet named Langston Hughes. The poem, the first Hughes verse ever published, had been written two years earlier, while Langston and his family crossed the Mississippi River. Known as "Harlem's Poet," Hughes wrote of Harlem during its Renaissance period for decades to come.

Hughes's father, James Hughes, had left for Mexico shortly after the poet's birth in Joplin, Mississippi, in 1902. Hughes was raised first by his grandmother, then by an aunt. His favorite book as youngster was *The Souls of Black Folk* by W.E.B. Du Bois. Hughes and his father did not see eye to eye on many things, but after seeing a copy of Langston's poem in *The Crisis*, the elder Hughes agreed to pay for his son's college education at Columbia University. Before settling in New York, Hughes traveled to Africa and Europe on a sailing ship. He published his first book of poetry — called *The Weary Blues* — in 1926.

In "Theme for English B," Hughes touches on the sights and sounds of Harlem, the theme of much of his work. He writes:

> *It's not easy to know what is true for you or me*
> *At twenty-two, my age. But I guess I'm what*
> *I feel and see and hear, Harlem. I hear you:*
> *hear you, hear me — we two — you, me, talk on this page.*
> *(I hear New York, too) Me — who?*
> *"Well, I like to eat, sleep, drink, and be in love*
> *I like to work, read, learn, and understand life*
> *I like a pipe for a Christmas present*
> *Or records — Bessie, bop, or Bach*
> *I guess being colored doesn't make me not like*
> *the same things other folks like who are other races.*
> *So will my page be colored that I write?*

As a result of the great black migration, Harlem — which came to be known as the Negro Metropolis — grew six times over between 1920 and 1929, with more African Americans than any other northern city. By 1925, an entirely black literary and entertainment mecca was established, attracting whites as well as blacks. Poets included Alain Locke, Countee Cullen and James Weldon Johnson. Among the scholars was historian Arthur Schomburg, who became known for dispelling the myth of black passiveness during the antislavery campaigns of the nineteenth century. Schomburg helped assemble the storied collection of books and papers on black history, culture, and thought at 135th branch of the New York Public Library. Musicians and dancers included Ethel Waters, Bill "Bojangles" Robinson, Duke Ellington at the Cotton Club, and Louis Armstrong at Roseland. Harlem became a social and cultural hub, transformed in a decade by the Depression.

June 15, 1921

Bessie Coleman earns the Fédération Aéronautique International (FIA), becoming the first African American woman to earn an international pilots license.

In 1920, Coleman went to France's Ecole d'Aviation des Freres Caudron at Le Crotoy in Somme. She had been inspired by her brothers' stories of World War I, but when she tried to attend flight school in the United States, discrimination against both race and gender barred her way. She was advised by *Chicago Defender* editor and publisher Robert S. Abbott to go to Europe, where she would find no such prejudice to keep her from her dream. She studied French to proficiency at night school in Chicago, eventually traveling to France in 1920.

Coleman was born in Atlanta, Texas, in 1892, soon moving to Waxahachie, Texas. She lived in poverty, picking cotton with her mother and her siblings to earn a living. An avaricious reader, she attended Colored Agricultural and Normal University in Langston, Oklahoma, in 1910, then moved to Chicago, where her two brothers lived, in 1915. She enrolled in Burnham School of Beauty Culture, winning a contest for manicurists in 1916. The stories of flight told by her brothers inspired her to learn to fly.

Returning from France in 1921 to begin her career as an aviator and a speaker, Bessie Coleman became the darling of the white press, as well as a beacon of inspiration to African American women and anyone else with a dream.

Bessie Coleman died tragically in an airplane accident in 1926, thrown from the cockpit after the plane's controls jammed.

January 12, 1922

Marcus Garvey is arrested by federal law enforcement for using mail to defraud investors in the Black Star Line.

Thirteen days later, Garvey met with Grand Wizard Edward Young Clarke of the Ku Klux Klan, whom Garvey said he appreciated more than his hypocritical white so-called supporters. Soon he incurred the wrath of black leaders, as well as that of the overall American public. W.E.B. Du Bois called Garvey a lunatic or traitor, calling his "Back to Africa" efforts "filled with spiritual bankruptcy and futility" (Marcus Garvey and UNIA). Garvey and Du Bois had been at odds for some time, as some of Garvey's writings seemed to favor dark-skinned blacks over light-skinned blacks — like Du Bois. Labor advocate A. Philip Randolf — an integrationist rather than a separatist — portrayed Garvey's philosophy as unreasonable and unrealistic.

Garvey published retorts to critics in his newspaper *The Negro World*, calling his critics race-defenders, traitors, turncoats, and sinners.

August 8, 1922

Having headed north during the Great Migration, Louis Armstrong arrives in Chicago, after answering a telegram from his old mentor, King Joe Oliver.

Armstrong joined Oliver and his Creole Jazz Band, playing at the Lincoln Gardens on Chicago's south side. Armstrong played amazing duets with Oliver, developing the thunderous, intricate, syncopated style which soon made him known as one of the world's greatest jazz coronet and trumpet players. Armstrong was among the first to employ scat singing in his performances. Soon he would be recording some of the most important classic jazz recordings in history.

The emergence of jazz is owed in part to the Great Migration and in part to Prohibition which, of course, never curtailed consumption of alcohol, but simply made it more exciting and glamorous. With the closing of legal bars and public houses, speakeasies opened all over the country. The new establishments needed musicians willing to work in illegal arrangements; this gave black musicians who had moved north in the migration, opportunities to perform for financial gain.

Louis Armstrong played the Lincoln Garden for two years before moving to the Roseland Ballroom in New York. He would return to Chicago two years later.

February 19, 1923

The United States Supreme Court decision in *U.S. v. Bhagat Singh Thind* declares Asian Indians ineligible for naturalized citizenship.

This decision reversed *U.S. v. Balsara* in 1910, at which time Asian Indians had been considered Caucasian, and therefore eligible for citizenship.

The case involved one Bhagat Singh Thind, a United States World War I veteran living in Oregon. Thind had been granted a certificate of citizenship by the district court in Oregon, over the objections of the United States' naturalization examiner. A bill of equity was filed to cancel the certificate of citizenship, saying Thind was not a white person and therefore was not entitled to naturalization. The district court dismissed the bill, sending the case through appeals until it eventually arrived in the Supreme Court.

The statutes in question fell under Section 2169 of the Revised Statutes, which stated that the provisions of the Naturalization Act "shall apply to aliens being free white persons and to aliens of African nativity and to persons of African descent."

In drafting the opinion of the Court, Justice George Sutherland presented a somewhat precipitous distinction between "white" and "Caucasian," saying "What we now hold is that the words 'free white persons' are words of common speech, to be interpreted in accordance with the understanding of the common man, synonymous with the word 'Caucasian' only as that word is popularly understood. As so understood and used, whatever may be the speculations of the ethnologist, it does not include the body of people to whom the appellee belongs." Suddenly, according to Sutherland's view, white was no longer synonymous with Caucasian, and therefore Asian Indians were no longer eligible for naturalization.

Between 1870 and 1965, it is estimated only 16,013 Asian Indians immigrated to the United States. However, between 1923 and 1926, the Immigration and Naturalization Service tried to revoke the naturalization certificates of 70 Indians. The case appeared to be a part of an overall wave of oppression toward Asian immigrants, characteristic of the early years of the twentieth century.

April 5, 1923

Louis Armstrong appears on a recording for the first time.

The record, called "Chimes Blues," features King Oliver and the Creole Jazz Band and was produced by Gennet Records of Richmond, Indiana. Armstrong had only a supporting role in the piece, but his omnipresent trumpet can be heard above the band.

Three years later, while playing to nightly standing-room-only performances at the Vendome Movie Theater in Chicago, Armstrong released "Heebie Jeebies," through Okeh Race Records. He introduced scat singing on "Heebie Jeebies" and took Chicago by storm.

June 13, 1923

Fighting under the name of Pancho Villa, Filipino American Francisco Guilledo captures the title of World Flyweight Champion, the first Asian American to hold the title.

In 1922, he had defeated Johnny Buff for the American Flyweight title. But at the 1923 World Flyweight bout at the Polo Grounds, the underdog Guilledo knocked out Jimmy Wilde in the seventh round.

Guellido continued to fight for two years, until his career ended tragically on July 4, 1925, in Oakland, California. Guilledo entered his bout with

Jimmy McLarin while suffering complications from a wisdom tooth extraction. He died ten days later from a tooth infection.

May 26, 1924

The Oriental Exclusion Act — also known as the Johnson-Reed Act, the Permanent National Origins Act, and the Immigrant Quota Act — is passed by the United States Congress.

Particularly targeting immigrants from Asia (as well as eastern Europe), the act virtually eliminated entry of Asians to the United States, supporting racial prejudice and exclusion of Asian immigrants on a national level.

The Immigrant Quota Act of 1924 was sponsored by Senator James A. Reed of Missouri and Senator Hiram W. Johnson of California. As California governor in 1913, Johnson had signed into law the first of the state's alien land laws. The 1924 federal measure reduced the immigration quotas set by the U.S. Emergency Quota Act of 1921 by 50 percent. The regulations set quotas from individual nations; unsurprisingly, the majority of allowed immigration slots came from Ireland, England, and Germany. With the passage of the act, the quota for the number of immigrants stood at 164,447, and the annual immigration for any group was limited to 2 percent of that group's U.S. population, according to the 1890 census. The limit was changed to 150,000 in 1927, in response to the 1920 census.

The Johnson-Reed Act was the latest in a series of acts aimed squarely at the Asian immigrant. In addition to California's alien land acts passed in 1913 and 1920, other states — including Arizona and Oregon — had passed alien land acts, limiting immigration, commerce, and land ownership by Asian immigrants.

The ignoble Cable Act, passed in 1922, dictated that any American female who married "an alien ineligible for citizenship shall cease to become an American citizen." This act — whose proponents warned "marry an alien, lose your citizenship" — remained in force until 1936. Though many of the acts passed for fear of economic competition from Asians, a primary motivation was the simple racism felt by many white American citizens. The same year, the United States Supreme Court decided in *Takao Ozawa v. United States* that the Japanese were not eligible for naturalized citizenship.

June 2, 1924

Largely as a show of gratitude for their service in World War I, Native Americans are granted full citizenship as Congress passes the Indian Citizenship Act.

The 1924 measure — sometimes known as the Snyder Act — was an extension of the 1919 Indian Citizenship Act, which granted citizenship to Native Americans who had served in World War I. During the Great War, any number from 8,000 to 17,000 Native Americans served, at least 6,000 of whom volunteered.

In essence, Native Americans now had dual citizenship: as a member of a particular Indian tribe, considered a sovereign state, with which the United States had a government-to-government relationship; and as a citizen of the United States. Prior to this act, some members of specific tribes had been granted citizenship, but not all.

Some states prevented Native Americans from voting until as late as 1953. In 1948, the Arizona Supreme Court finally declared unconstitutional the disenfranchising interpretation of the state constitution. Utah still had a law in 1953 declaring that a person on a reservation was not a resident of the state and could not vote. In 1954, certain tribes in Maine, not yet recognized by the federal government, at last gained suffrage. Finally, in 1962 New Mexico extended the right to vote to all.

Many felt that citizenship had been conferred upon the Native American not so much as a response to a demand by them, but as a further effort to absorb them into the mainstream where "they would do better." After being granted citizenship, many Native Americans chose to remain on their reservations, the lands they had reserved for themselves during the creation of treaties with the United States government. Even though the community resources of the reservations — which the United States government had promised to provide in exchange for the land — suffered, many chose to remain there. On their own lands, at least, they maintained some hope of preserving the native culture which they held dear.

Chief Clinton Rickard of the Tuscarora tribe said, "United States citizenship was just another way of absorbing us and destroying our customs and our government.... The Citizenship Act did pass in 1924 despite our strong opposition. By its provisions all Indians were automatically made United States citizens whether they wanted to be so or not. This was a violation of our sovereignty. Our citizenship was in our nations. We had a great attachment to our style of government. We wished to remain treaty Indians and preserve our ancient rights" (Camurat, p. 7).

However, citizenship failed to bring Native Americans into the mainstream of American life. Native Americans had lived for at least 10,000 years in relative dignity and health before the arrival of Europeans. Under the Manifest Destiny mode of thought, Americans of European descent believed the advent of their civilization would assist the Native Americans in raising themselves up from pagan savagery. It also justified — or at least rationalized — the massive genocidal period that followed European settlement of the continent.

The greatest crime of the United States against Native Americans was coercing them to deny their cultural identity. In the early part of the twentieth century Native Americans remained under constant pressure to give up their traditional dress, customs, and ceremonies. Inherent racism — the belief the Indian needed intervention from a superior people — brought this oppressive treatment upon them. The big difference: while other races and cultures left their homes for America, the Native Americans had their homes taken right from under them.

May 19, 1925

Malcolm Little is born in Omaha, Nebraska.

His father Earl Little, a disciple of Marcus Garvey, was killed by a streetcar in 1931, although young Malcolm grew up believing he had been the victim of white racists. Malcolm's mother, Louise Norton Little, was committed to a mental hospital when Malcolm had turned just 12. The boy spent the remainder of his childhood in foster homes.

Little moved to Boston in 1941, quickly becoming active in Boston's criminal element, and was finally incarcerated in 1946 for burglary. While in prison, Little joined the Nation of Islam, which cultivated his personal dignity and pride, and stoked his anger toward white people. In 1952 he renounced his slave name, becoming known to the world from that point forward as Malcolm X. Soon, he emerged as the greatest preacher the Nation of Islam ever knew.

August 25, 1925

The Brotherhood of Sleeping Car Porters is founded at Elks Hall in Harlem, under the direction of African American labor organizer A. Philip Randolph.

A group of railroad porters, knowing of Randolph's efforts to organize blacks in Harlem, came to him to help organize a railroad porters' union to bargain for better wages and improvements in work conditions. Since Randolph did not work as a porter, the organizers estimated he would be immune to Pullman Company influence.

To work as a railroad porter had been among the best means by which an individual African American could gain financial security. For the next 12 years, the Brotherhood worked to achieve collective bargaining for porters, under Randolph's undaunted message: "Black men are able to measure up" (www.apri.org).

Asa Philip Randolph had been born in Crescent City, Florida, in 1889. He moved to Harlem as young man in 1911, attending City College. A socialist during World War I, he strongly opposed W.E.B. Du Bois' recommendation to participate in the war, believing that the American idea of "making world safe for democracy was outright falsity," since blacks were being lynched and oppressed throughout America. He did not believe in the "talented tenth" of Du Bois, choosing a much more pragmatic outlook: he believed once his children were fed, a man could be in a better position to fight for dignity and pride

A. Philip Randolph regularly spoke for all disenfranchised. "The history of the labor movement in America," he said, "proves that the employing classes recognize no race lines. They will exploit a White man as readily as a Black man ... they will exploit any race or class in order to make profits."

In 1935, the Brotherhood of Sleeping Car Porters won a charter with American Federation of Labor. Two years later, the Brotherhood negotiated a contract with the Pullman Company, the first contract between a business and a black union in America. Soon, A. Philip Randolph would be regarded by some as the most dangerous black man in America.

August 26, 1925

As her award for winning the Lewisohn Stadium Concert Award over 300 competing singers, Marian Anderson performs with the New York Philharmonic Orchestra, the first African American woman ever to do so.

Anderson was born on February 17, 1902, in Philadelphia. Her father died when she was young, forcing her mother to work as both a cleaning woman and a laundress to support her family. Marian Anderson first sang at Union Baptist Church Choir at age six, going on to study at the age of 19 with Giuseppe Boghetti, who would be her lifelong teacher. Her magnificent voice was classified as a contralto.

At the age of 23, Anderson received a Rosenwald Foundation Fellowship, allowing her to study and perform in England and Germany. Her concerts throughout Europe were met with rave reviews.

Before long, Anderson would be considered world's greatest contralto. In less than 15 years, she would give a concert in Washington, D.C., which would astonish and amaze the country.

February 7, 1926

Educator and writer Carter Godwin Woodson organizes the first Black History Week.

He chose the second week of February, which commemorates the birthdays of both Abraham Lincoln (February 12) and Frederick Douglas (February 14).

Born in New Canton, Virginia, in 1875, Woodson attended Berea College in Kentucky, obtaining his Bachelor of Arts degree at the University of Chicago in 1907. He continued his studies at Sorbonne University in Paris, eventually gaining his Ph.D. in history from Harvard University in 1912. He became only the second African American to earn such a degree, after W.E.B. Du Bois.

Woodson held educational administrative posts in the Philippines, at Howard University, and at West Virginia State College. A member of the Niagara movement in 1909, Woodson became a regular columnist for Marcus Garvey's *Negro World*. He founded the Association for the Study of Negro Life and History in 1915. He also founded *Journal of Negro History* in 1922.

An energetic advocate for African American pride and identity, Woodson believed that by acknowledging and understanding their history, African Americans — as well as any other people — could develop pride among themselves, as well as greater respect among the larger community. Out of that yearning for pride and perspective, Woodson conceived the idea of Black History Week, which eventually became Black History Month in 1976.

In 1933, Woodson wrote *The Mis-education of the Negro*. Considered a classic of Negro literature, it discusses the difference between education and mind control, which had been imposed on African Americans.

January 7, 1927

The Savoy Big Five — the predecessors of the Harlem Globetrotters — play their first game in Hinckley, Illinois.

Abe Saperstein had organized the team at the Savoy Ballroom in Chicago, the previous year. The team featured the nucleus of the future Globetrotters in the persons of Inman Jackson, Lester Johnson, and Walter Wright. The team became the Saperstein Globetrotters in 1927, transforming into the Harlem, New York, Globetrotters — to emphasize the all-black squad — in 1930.

The Harlem Globetrotters became the most famous and beloved basketball team of all. Starting out as a serious barnstorming team, the Globetrotters eventually developed the crowd-delighting show for which they became famous.

Accompanied by their renowned whistled theme song "Sweet Georgia Brown," the Harlem Globetrotters featured stars over the years such as original clown Reese "Goose" Tatem, sharp-dribbling Marques Haynes, and

Meadowlark Lemon, well known for his wiseacre antics. In all, the Harlem
Globetrotters eventually performed in 90 countries. This included the largest
crowd ever assembled for a basketball game, 75,000 at Berlin's Olympic Stadium in August of 1951.

March 31, 1927

Cesar Estrada Chavez is born in an adobe home near Yuma, Arizona.
He and his family moved to California in 1938. Young Chavez worked
in agricultural fields throughout California, in places such as Oxnard, Atascadero, Gonzales, King City, Salinas, McFarland, Delano, Wasco, Selma,
Kingsburg, and Mendota.

Speaking only Spanish in his home, Chavez faced language and discriminatory barriers at school. Often the only Spanish speaker in his class, he
frequently faced punishment for speaking his native language. He attended
37 schools in all, completing eighth grade but never advancing to high
school. However, he became a lifelong student, studying philosophy and
economic cooperatives. Chavez was particularly inspired by St. Francis of
Assisi and Mohandas Gandhi, the modern author of nonviolent civil protest

Chavez became a migrant worker, learning well the poor pay, terrible
conditions, and bigotry that oppressed the workers. He met and married his
wife Helen Fabela in 1948.

June 14, 1927

George Washington Carver receives his third patent, on the invention
of a process to produce paint and stain from soybeans.

It was the latest in a series of innovations that the brilliant botanist and
chemist would produce in his lifetime at Tuskegee University.

Born into slavery at Diamond Grove, Missouri, c.1865, the world
famous botanist did not complete college until middle age, due to the racial
barriers that barred him from finishing his education. He started his career
as an educator at Iowa Agricultural College.

Lured to Tuskegee University by Booker T. Washington in 1896, Carver
went on to revolutionize agriculture in the South. He traveled about Alabama
in a wagon that became a moveable school, carrying with him seeds, tools,
and plants. He urged sharecroppers to replace "King" cotton with more soil-nurturing crops, such as tomatoes and sweet potatoes. He also educated
sharecroppers about methods of cross fertilization and crop rotation.

Meanwhile, Carver conducted research to develop industrial applications for agricultural products. In his lifetime, he developed more than 1,000 industrial applications for crops such as peanuts, sweet potatoes, pecans, and soybeans.

George Washington Carver died of anemia on January 5, 1943, at Tuskegee University. He was buried on campus beside the grave of Booker T. Washington. On July 14, 1943, President Franklin D. Roosevelt honored Carver by dedicating federal funds toward a national monument near Diamond Grove, to be completed in 1953. It was the first such monument ever dedicated to an African American.

December 2, 1927

Marcus Garvey is deported to Jamaica, after serving four years and five months of his five-year sentence in Tombs Prison, New York, for mail fraud.

Some said the excessive sentence had been a means for the federal government to control the powerful influence Garvey had exerted. His sentence was commuted by President Calvin Coolidge.

After spending three months in Jamaica, Garvey traveled to London on April 29, to start a new branch of the Universal Negro Improvement Association. On March 30, 1929, Garvey returned to Jamaica, to begin a new newspaper called *The Blackman*.

December 4, 1927

Duke Ellington and His Orchestra open at the Cotton Club in Harlem.

Edward Kennedy Ellington was born on April 9, 1899, on the northwest side of Washington, D.C. His father, James Edward, was a waiter and caterer, establishing a comfortable middle class existence for his family. Daisy, his mother, made sure her son received piano lessons as a child, and learned to dress and comport himself with elegance. This elegance earned him the nickname "Duke" while playing piano for clubs in Washington, D.C. His early influences included alto saxophonist Sidney Bechet.

Ellington and his orchestra worked in the Kentucky Club in New York before signing on with the Cotton Club. His exotic, mysterious, and sensual style became known around New York as "Jungle Music." The group served as the Cotton Club's house band until 1932. Ellington, often called America's greatest composer, embarked on an unprecedented period of creativity during which he produced his finest compositions, including "Mood Indigo," "Creole Rhapsody," and "In a Sentimental Mood."

As jazz became more popular in the clubs of Harlem, Manhattan, Chicago, and beyond, young white musicians came to the clubs to learn the craft from the masters. Bix Beiderbecke, Artie Shaw, Benny Goodman, and more spread the impact of jazz, in its many forms, to all corners of American society. Before long, jazz was influencing a whole generation of musicians.

January 15, 1929

Martin Luther King, Jr., is born in Atlanta, Georgia, to Martin and Alberta Williams.

His father served as a minister at Ebenezer Baptist Church, while his mother was a school teacher. King, Jr., attended Booker T. Washington High School in Atlanta, and Morehouse College. He entered Crozer Theological Seminary in Chester, Pennsylvania, in 1948, where he would study the works and philosophy of Henry David Thoreau and, in particular, of Mohandas Gandhi.

A year after King's birth, Mohandas Gandhi began his Great Salt March in southern India. This would have a profound effect on the future civil rights leader. The salt march, which became the epitome of *satyagraha*, or passive resistance, protested Britain's salt tax on India. The tax unfairly impacted the poor, because those engaged in the hardest work needed the most salt.

The 241-mile march began at the Sabarmati ashram and ended at Dandi. Starting with 78 volunteers, thousands of Indians eventually joined in the march, which captured the attention of India and the world for 24 days. The salt march broke the salt tax by urging marchers to go to the sea in Dandi, to pick up their own free salt washed up to the seashore. It was something even the poor could do, something the government could not easily dissuade.

Although 12,000 miles and many years away from King's awareness, Gandhi's actions and technique would have a significant impact on the future civil rights leader and the causes he would champion.

August 29, 1930

The Japanese American Citizens League (JACL) is formed through the efforts of Clarence Arai of Seattle, Saburo Kido of San Francisco, and Thomas Yatabe of Fresno, at a conference in Seattle, Washington.

Establishing initial branches in Washington, Oregon, and California, the JACL included 21 local chapters by 1934. The JACL was destined to become the oldest and largest Asian American civil rights organization in the country.

The original purpose of the JACL was to work to preserve the rights of the *Issei*, or first generation of Japanese immigrants, ostracized by the many land laws passed in California and other states. As World War II approached, the Japanese American Citizens League worked to publicize the loyalty of Japanese residents. Once the Second World War began, the work of the Japanese American Citizens League took a wholly different turn, to provide comfort and advocacy to those unjustly imprisoned in internment camps because of their ethnicity.

March 25, 1931

Nine African American males from Chattanooga, Tennessee, are arrested on a train stopping at Scottsboro, Alabama.

Roy Wright, Eugene Williams, Andy Wright, Haywood Patterson, Olin Montgomery, Willie Roberson, Ozzie Powell, Charles Weems, and Clarence Norrise — ranging in age from 13 to 21— were charged with the rapes of two white women, Ruby Bates and Victoria Price. The young men came to be known as the Scottsboro Nine.

In a clear miscarriage of justice, a white judge and 12 white male jurors convicted eight of the nine of rape, sentencing them to the electric chair in less than a month. The convictions spurred furious protests, particularly in Harlem and overseas in Europe. Appeal petitions were filed, and for the next nine years, the Scottsboro trial garnered much national attention. One of the alleged victims, Ruby Bates, admitted there had been no rape. The worldwide attention shone a glaring light on the inequities of Southern courts and juries.

In the end, charges against five of the nine were dropped. Of the four tried and convicted, three were paroled and the other escaped. But the years in jail took personal tolls on the nine young men, highlighting the dubious scales of justice present in much of the country.

March 4, 1933

President Franklin Roosevelt appoints John Collier as Commissioner of Indian Affairs.

Collier, a cultural anthropologist long critical of the government's failed management of Native Americans and reservations, set out to create a "New Deal for the Indians" amidst Roosevelt's New Deal for America. Collier actually recruited Native Americans to staff the Bureau of Indian Affairs. He proposed ideas for tribal self-government, cultural preservation, and religious freedom. His policies also provided for the return of unsold allotted lands to tribes, and the development of on-site reservation day-schools to replace off-site boarding schools.

Despite his many innovations, Collier met resistance among some Native Americans, who feared losing private property attained during the allotment era. Others criticized Collier's policies, leading to many imposed tribal governments that became puppets for the Bureau of Indian Affairs. While Collier's new approach appeared more humane and just, critics contended that his methods merely provided a different means toward the centuries-old end: the assimilation of the Native Americans into the dominant European-American society.

December 22, 1933

The film *Flying Down to Rio* permieres at Radio City Music Hall in New York City, starring Dolores Del Rio with Fred Astaire and Ginger Rogers.

At the height of her career, Del Rio was among the most successful of the Hispanic performers, who seemed to enjoy widespread acceptance with middle America. In this particular film, Del Rio is presented as a great beauty, while Brazilians are portrayed as sophisticated and charming.

In the 1920s Rudolph Valentino, an Italian, had provided the image of the quintessential Latin Lover in films such as *Four Horsemen of the Apocalypse* and *Blood and Sand*. Stars such as Antonio Moreno, Ramon Novarro, Ricardo Cortez, and Anthony Quinn later followed in his celluloid footsteps.

Besides Del Rio, famous Hispanic movie goddesses included Lupe Velez and Rita Hayworth, who filled the movie screen with images exuding passion, sensuality, and beauty. Showcased as exotic and desirable, the Latin actresses became big stars who could play characters of many different cultures. Furthermore, they could be made to appear light-skinned enough to avoid offending those who felt averse to viewing dark skin in substantial roles on the screen.

February 26, 1934

Elijah Muhammad becomes leader of the Nation of Islam.

Paul Robert Poole, born in 1897, migrated with his family from Georgia to Detroit. He took the name Elijah Muhammad, meaning "Messenger of Allah." At the same time, Wallie Farrad, alias W.D. Farrad, alias Wallace Fard Mohammad, alias Farrad Mohammad, alias "the Prophet," disappeared. In 1930, Farrad had begun to visit the African American homes of Detroit, denouncing the Bible, introducing the Q'uran, and advocating African American power and energy. He had presented his message as a call to power and freedom for black Americans. The sect would later be known as the

Nation of Islam, the foundation of what the media would call the Black Muslim movement.

At a public meeting hall in the Paradise Valley section of Detroit, Farrad had opened the Lost/Found Nation of Islam in the Wilderness of North America, in what was referred to as the Temple of Islam, Number One. Within three years, membership grew to 8,000. Elijah Muhammad opened the Temple of Islam, Number Two, in Chicago, with a list of followers that eventually included Muhammad Ali and Malcolm X.

The Nation of Islam originally accepted only blacks as members. Preaching in a vein like that of Marcus Garvey, Elijah Muhammad encouraged the development of a sense of dignity, equality, and even superiority to whites. Unlike Garvey, Muhammad had no intention of moving back to anywhere else.

Nation of Islam members participated vigorously in the rigors of the religion. The Nation encouraged prayer, discipline, abstinence from vices, and frugality leading to a higher standard of living. The movement preached distrust of whites and, above all, the belief in the beauty and divinity of being black. In the Nation of Islam, African Americans did not need whites in order to achieve full potential and prosperity.

June 18, 1934

Federal legislation restores some Native American lands to tribal ownership and authorizes federal funds to stimulate Indian businesses.

The Wheeler-Howard Act, also called the United States Indian Reorganization Act, is sponsored by Senator Burton K. Wheeler of Montana and Representative Edgar Howard of Nebraska. The act allowed Native American tribes on reservations to adopt their own constitutions for self-government, or to petition the secretary of state for a charter of incorporation. The Bureau of Indian Affairs, though, retained the right to veto tribal decisions. The act restored tribal ownership of surplus land once for sale to homesteaders. It also authorized funds to enlarge tribal land holdings, to support Indian education, and to encourage economic development through federal loans.

Part of the impetus behind the Indian Reorganization Act had come from the findings of the 1928 Miriam Report. Congress had assigned more than 1,000 Native Americans and prominent citizens to investigate widespread allegations of corruption and abuse of the Dawes Act of 1887, which had supposedly been passed to protect Indian property rights. The 800-page report had revealed massive fraud and misappropriations of land associated with the very government agencies charged with administering the act. As a result of these activities, more than two-thirds of the lands owned by Native Americans in 1887 had already been lost by 1928.

November 15, 1935

The Philippines become a self-governing commonwealth following the passage of the Tydings-McDuffie Act.

Authored by Maryland senator Millard Tydings and Alabama congressman John McDuffie, the act started the Philippines on a ten-year transition period from United States territory to independent nation.

Some surmised the act had been passed so that Filipinos could be excluded as immigrants. Prior to 1935, because the Philippines had been a territory, Filipinos could move back and forth from the United States freely. With the passage of the Tydings-McDuffie Act, they were inhibited by the Immigrant Restriction Act and other legislation meant to limit immigration from Asia. The immigration quotas now allowed only 50 Filipinos a year into the United States, while movement from United States to the Philippines remained unrestricted.

The results of the act also restricted trade between the Philippines and the United States. American goods were allowed to enter the islands duty free for the next ten years, while products bound for the United States incurred an increasingly steep tariff after five years.

Manuel Quezon was elected president of the new nation, called the Republic of Philippines, after its liberation from Japan by General Douglas MacArthur on October 20, 1944.

The Philippines became an independent nation on July 4, 1946.

August 3, 1936

Jesse Owens wins the first of four track and field gold medals at the Olympics in Berlin, during the Nazi regime of Adolph Hitler.

Owens grabbed the gold for the 100-meter run, and would win the 200-meter race, the broad jump, and the 400-meter relay as well. Owens shattered the aims of the German dictator, who had hoped the Berlin Olympics would be a global showplace for the superiority of his Aryan race.

James Cleveland Owens was born in Oakville, Alabama, the son of a sharecropper who moved his family to Cleveland when Jesse was seven. Owens became a track star at Ohio State University, setting three world records and tying a fourth. He set seven world records during his startling track and field career.

August 8, 1936

Mourning Dove, also know as Christine Quintasket, dies at the age of 51.

Coyote Stories was published in 1933 by this Salish-speaking Colville tribeswoman of Washington State. It was one of the first collections of native stories gathered and transcribed by a Native American; the first by a woman.

Coyote Stories chronicles the life ways of the Salish and Okanagon peoples, preserving great stores of knowledge that could otherwise have been lost. Many of the stories had been told to Mourning Dove as a child by tribal storytellers. As a child, she thought of the stories as fun and play, never aware she had actually been given a very ancient and effective form of education.

Mourning Dove was born on Colville Reservation, living for a time in Montana and in Portland, Oregon, before attending business college in Calgary, Alberta, Canada. She returned to Colville in 1919, helping to found the Colville Indian Association and soon becoming the first woman ever elected to the Colville Tribal Council. Her first novel, *Cogewea, the Half-Blood*, was published in 1927. It explored the difficulties of being biracial, while examining Native American perspectives on religion.

June 22, 1938

Before a packed house at Yankee Stadium, Joe Louis defeats Max Schmeling with a knockout two minutes and four seconds into the first round, to retain his World Heavyweight Championship boxing title.

Although Louis had won the title a year previous from Jim Braddock, he had particularly anticipated the bout with Schmeling, as the German had knocked him out in the twelfth round of their 1936 bout.

Against the backdrop of the Second World War and Hitler's Thousand Year Reich, Louis and Schmeling — reluctantly — had been drawn into a struggle touted as a duel between the Aryan Race and the Sharecropper's Son. In the 1936 bout, Schmeling outboxed the "Brown Bomber" for 12 rounds before scoring a knockout. Schmeling came home to Germany a hero, the irresolute symbol of Aryan supremacy.

The defeat seemed to cause Louis to intensify his focus as the American people, perhaps for the first time, had rallied behind an African American hero. On June 22, Louis quickly dispatched Schmeling with a combination of punches, landing one massive blow that fractured two vertebrae in the challenger's back.

Reportedly the German broadcast fell silent before its audience could hear the final knockout.

December 12, 1938

The United States Supreme Court issues a 6–2 decision in *Missouri ex rel. Gaines v. Canada*, declaring a violation of the equal protection guarantee under the Fourteenth Amendment of the Constitution.

Lloyd Gaines, an African American, had been refused entry into the law school at the University of Missouri because of the color of his skin. He had completed his required undergraduate work at the all-black Lincoln University. Missouri statutes, however, kept whites and blacks segregated through all levels of school. No law school had yet been established at Lincoln University. Therefore, in order for Gaines to attend law school, the state would have to pay his tuition to an out-of-state school. The National Association for the Advancement of Colored People used the situation as a test case for the Supreme Court.

In its decision, the Court ruled that Lincoln College, by the fact that it had no law school, had violated the equal protection clause of the Fourteenth Amendment, since it denied to Gaines an advantage all Missouri white students enjoyed. Chief Justice Charles Evans Hughes, in writing the majority opinion, stated, "The basic consideration is not as to what sort of opportunities other states provide, or whether they are as good as those in Missouri, but as to what opportunities Missouri itself furnishes to white students and denies to Negroes solely on the ground of color."

January 8, 1939

Wahpeton Sioux physician and writer Charles Alexander Eastman dies.

In 1911 at Columbus, Ohio, he was the co-founder of the Society of American Indians (SAI), which became the first national organization founded and organized by Native Americans. Galvanizing Native American writers, artists, physicians, and philosophers, the SAI encouraged Native Americans to maintain ties to their own culture, firmly withstanding the pressures of the larger mainstream American society.

A hallmark of the SAI was that its members possessed both strong tribal loyalty and connections with the white world. Because of this, factions developed over issues of assimilation into white culture, and the future role of the Bureau of Indian Affairs. The SAI dissolved within four years but set a precedent for Native American thinkers to organize on a national level.

Unique among Native American writers, Eastman was raised as a traditional woodland Sioux. He was educated at Dartmouth, obtaining his medical degree from Boston University. He was the only physician to attend the victims of the Wounded Knee massacre in 1890. Among his better known literary works are *Old Indian Days* (1907) and *The Soul of the Indian* (1911).

January 9, 1939

Poor sharecroppers protest abuses of laws intended to help them.

More than 1,000 sharecroppers — mostly African American — huddled along highways 60 and 61 in southeastern Missouri. Organized by the Reverend Owen Whitfield, a member of the Southern Tenant Farmers' Union (STFU), these small farmers gathered to protest the fallout from Roosevelt's New Deal program, through the Agricultural Adjustment Act.

Money designed to help the small tenant farmer had been siphoned by the larger plantations. These wealthy land owners had found a loophole in the law that let them keep the government money intended for the sharecroppers — provided they fired the current tenants, then hire new ones. They did. Thousands of already poor sharecroppers had been not only deprived of federal aid, but evicted from the lands on which they had worked.

The STFU was formed in 1934 by seven black and 11 white sharecroppers in Arkansas, with the goal of fighting exploitation by the large plantation owners. The STFU became a model for many unions to follow, including Caesar Chavez's United Farm Workers.

Those sharecroppers protesting on the highways of southern Missouri later formed a small community called Cropperville, on 93 acres near Poplar Bluff, Missouri. The town provided a short-lived respite for several hundred tenant farmers looking for land to till and live on. Eventually, though, the migrant farmers — mostly black — were driven from the South by paltry wages, oppressive and discriminatory conditions, and advancing agricultural technology.

Lured by industries burgeoning from the Second World War, thousands of African Americans headed north, creating the second wave of the Great Migration. In 1910, 80 percent of African Americans lived in the South. By 1970, less than half lived in the South, with only one-quarter remaining in the rural South.

April 9, 1939

Internationally renowned contralto Marian Anderson performs in front of 75,000 at the Lincoln Memorial, after the Daughters of American Revolution (DAR) refuse to let her sing at the Constitution Hall in Washington, D.C.

Eleanor Roosevelt, reportedly enraged by the prejudice shown by the

DAR, resigned from the organization, then helped arrange for Anderson to perform outdoors at the Lincoln Memorial on Easter Sunday morning. Anderson's performance became one of the most famous concerts in United States history.

Anderson, in her autobiography *My Lord, What a Morning*, says, "There seemed to be people as far as the eye could see. The crowd stretched in a great semicircle from the Lincoln Memorial to the reflecting pool, onto the shaft of the Washington Monument. I had a feeling that a great wave of good will poured out from the people, almost engulfing me" (Anderson, p. 192).

Numerous Washington dignitaries attend the event. In 1941, Anderson received the Bok Award from city of Philadelphia, given to the citizen of which it is most proud. In 1943, the Department of Interior commissioned a mural commemorating the Easter concert.

April 20, 1939

One of America's most controversial songs is recorded by one of America's most controversial artists: Commodore Records releases "Strange Fruit," sung by blues legend Billie Holiday.

Its startling lyrics graphically describe the horrifying image of a lynching. Written by communist poet and teacher Abel Meeropol, "Strange Fruit" had first been performed by Holiday at the Cafe Society in Greenwich Village a year before. The song stung audiences and listeners alike, as the mainstream press criticized it as too brutal. *Time Magazine* called it a "prime piece of musical propaganda for the NAACP." Despite the scandal surrounding it, the song climbed to number 16 on the charts. It was heralded as "the first significant protest in words and music, the first unmuted cry against racism." Billie Holiday was hailed as a hero of the black and leftist communities.

In a 1930 investigation into lynching, Dr. Arthur Raper reported that as many as 3,700 individuals — four-fifths African Americans — had been lynched in the United States between 1889 and 1930. In addition to hanging, the victims suffered torture, mutilation, castration, and burning. Only one-sixth of the victims were ever accused of rape, the offense initially considered to warrant such a heinous punishment. Of the many thousands of lynchers and accessories — most of whom were white — only 49 ever faced indictment, and only four were ever sentenced.

June 17, 1939

An editorial appears in the *Amsterdam News,* as popular opinion seems to be mounting to bring African Americans into the Major Leagues baseball.

> During this century of Diamond Doings, however, Negro base-
> ballers, in spite of their undoubted ability to bat, run, pitch, snare
> gargantuan flies, cavort around shortstop and the keystone sack and
> think baseball, haven't reached first base insofar as getting into the
> big leagues is concerned. Maybe the first hundred years are the
> hardest after all. For this reason, the progeny of present-day Negro
> baseball players may look forward, but with some degree of appre-
> hension, to playing in the big leagues by the year 2039 [Ward,
> p. 249].

Meanwhile, as the Eastern Colored League folded, Negro teams relied more on barnstorming. Over the years, black teams reportedly played white teams 438 times, with white teams winning 129 and black teams winning 309.

The biggest hitting star of the Negro Leagues was Josh Gibson. He hit 70 home runs in league and nonleague games in 1931, and some believe his lifetime total of round trippers could have exceeded 1,000. Never allowed into the major leagues, Gibson died a pauper.

The greatest pitcher of the Negro Leagues was Satchel Paige. A natural crowd pleaser, Paige offered a host of pitches with which to overcome the bewildered batter. Unlike Gibson, Paige eventually made it to the major leagues, but only after another Negro League star paved the way — much sooner than the *Amsterdam News* predicted.

February 29, 1940

Hattie McDaniel wins the Academy Award for Best Supporting Actress for her role as "Mammy" in *Gone with the Wind.*

McDaniel, a veteran of more than 30 films, was the first black performer to win an Academy Award.

The youngest child of an ex-slave turned Baptist minister, she was born on June 10, 1895, beginning her career in show business as part of a minstrel show in 1910. She made her film debut in 1932 in *Judge Priest.* At the time, the National Association for the Advancement of Colored People chided actors who portrayed maids, buffoons, or butlers. But McDaniel did not consider the roles she played to be demeaning. "I'd rather play a maid and make $700 a week," she said, "than be one and make $7."

On the set for *Gone with the Wind,* McDaniel forced the movie studio to take the word "nigger" from the script. Despite what many considered a negative, stereotypical role, McDaniel managed to make Mammy a complex, emotional character.

Hattie McDaniel became a civil rights activist in the 1940s, purchasing

a 15-room mansion in Los Angeles called Sugartop in 1942. She battled housing covenants in Los Angeles in 1945, taking her case all the way to the United
States Supreme Court. She starred in *The Beulah Show* for $2,000 a year from
1947 to 1950. McDaniel died on October 26, 1952, of breast cancer.

June 10, 1940

Marcus Garvey, the former leader of the Universal Negro Improvement
Association and the back-to-Africa movement, dies in London.

Garvey had suffered a cerebral hemorrhage on January 20, leaving him
aphasic and paralyzed on his right side.

Although his dreams of leading a migration back to Africa had essentially dissolved by 1930, Marcus Garvey left an indelible imprint on American society. He incited the first mass movement of the African American
community. His influence would instill a sense of black nationalism and
racial pride in future generations who would know nothing about him. He
also managed to raise more money than any prior African American leader;
ironically, he died penniless.

Although Garvey died in London, Jamaica, his homeland, brought his
body back in 1964, declaring him the nation's first national hero.

November 27, 1940

A Chinese American legend is born.

On this date, Lee Jun Fan was born at Jackson Street Hospital in San
Francisco's Chinatown. His father, Lee Hoi Chuen, was a performer in the
Cantonese Opera Company, and moved his family back to Hong Kong in
1941. Lee Jun Fan appeared in several movies as a child, then attended La
Salle College in Hong Kong. In 1953, following a severe beating by a Hong
Kong street gang, he began studying martial arts under Sifu Yip Man, mas-
ter of the Wing Chun system of Kung Fu. This discipline would define him
for the rest of his life.

Lee Jun Fan returned to San Francisco in 1959, then moved to Seattle,
where in October of 1963 he opened his Jun Fan Kung-Fu Institute. Within
a year, he began the television and film career that would make him the most
recognizable Asian American star of all time, under the name of Bruce Lee.

March 22, 1941

Congressional legislation creates the all-black 99th Fighter Squadron.
The squadron would train at Tuskegee Army Air Field at Tuskegee

Institute in Alabama, the same institute developed by Booker T. Washington in the nineteenth century. The necessary legislation passed over the objections of both the Army Air Corps and the War Department. Many of the Air Corps white elite felt African Americans would never learn to fly, becoming an inept liability in the air. The squadron, which eventually encompassed the 332nd Fighter Ground and the 447th Bombardiers, became known worldwide as the Tuskegee Airmen. Nearly 1,000 black military pilots emerged from Tuskegee University for World War II.

The overwhelming majority of black troops in World War II served as uniformed laborers, ascribed to tasks such as ditch digging or kitchen patrol. Some, however, such as the 92nd Infantry Division, numbered among the most decorated combat units in the war.

July 1, 1941

A. Philip Randolph, president of the Brotherhood of Sleeping Car Porters, chooses this date for his "March on Washington for Jobs and Equal Protection in Nation Defense."

In a statement on January 14, 1941, Randolph said, "On the contrary, we seek the right to play our part in advancing the cause of national defense and national unity. But certainly there can be no national unity where one tenth of the population is denied their basic rights as American citizens" (www.spartacus.schoolnet.co.uk).

Randolph warned if jobs in the defense industries did not immediately open to African Americans, he would lead a demonstration of 50,000 in Washington. By June, the estimated number of marchers had reached 100,000. President Franklin D. Roosevelt apparently heeded the warning, issuing Executive Order 8802, which made racial discrimination in federal hiring and defense plant jobs illegal.

Randolph canceled the march, much to the displeasure of the younger contingent of organizers such as Bayard Rustin. In 22 years, however, Randolph would see his March on Washington materialize, during very different times and circumstances.

December 7, 1941

At 7:55 A.M., 183 Japanese planes attack Pearl Harbor, Hawaii.

The attack damaged 18 ships and eight battleships, sinking both the *Arizona* and the *Oklahoma*. More than 2,400 American lives were lost, while the Japanese lost 29 aircraft and 100 lives.

Many conjectured that the United States knew an attack had been imminent. Both the Americans and the Dutch had broken the Japanese code, passing warnings of a coming invasive action. But whether due to human frailty, overconfidence, or racism, many Americans — including President Franklin D. Roosevelt — seemed to dismiss the Japanese as a serious threat. Some actually doubted the skill of Japanese fighters, believing them to be nearsighted.

December 8, 1941

President Roosevelt addresses the nation.

On December 8, President Franklin D. Roosevelt delivered his now famous War Message to Congress: "Yesterday, December 7, 1941 — a date which will live in infamy — the United States was suddenly and deliberately attacked by naval and air forces of the Empire of Japan." Within an hour, Japan officially became the enemy as Congress complied with a 388–1 vote for a declaration of war. Pacifist Jeannette Rankin was the lone dissenter.

It was a day of infamy within the United States as well as without. The declaration of war fueled already widespread bigotry and suspicion toward Japanese American citizens. In fewer than 80 days, the country turned its anger, frustration, and fear inward toward more than 100,000 of its own. Roosevelt passed Executive Order 9066, which empowered the army to treat thousands of Japanese Americans as no group in twentieth century America was treated before or since.

February 19, 1942

Executive Order 9066 starts the roundup of Japanese Americans.

In perhaps the most blatantly discriminatory act on the part of the United States government in the twentieth century, President Franklin Roosevelt issued Executive Order 9066. This order authorized military commanders to establish special geographical zones from which "any or all persons" could be excluded. Fueled by fears of further invasion, espionage, and sabotage following the Japanese attack on Pearl Harbor on December 7, 1941, the U.S. Army used this order to evacuate all persons of Japanese ancestry from the west coast of the United States, interning them in "relocation centers" throughout the Rocky Mountain and Midwest regions.

More than 110,000 persons — nearly half of whom were native born U.S. citizens — were forced to sell their homes and business. The internees — many of whom were children — were crowded onto buses, driven to Assembly Centers, then transported to internment camps in Utah, Arizona, and other central states, where they remained for the duration of the war.

For much of the next four years, thousands of Japanese immigrants and Japanese American citizens endured, as prisoners, incarceration by their fellow countrymen and their representative government.

February 25, 1942

Philip Johnston — the son of a Navajo missionary — demonstrates to Major General Clayton P. Vogel, United States Marine Corps, the effectiveness of the Navajo Code Talkers Program.

Johnston, who had grown up on a Navajo reservation, believed the Navajo tongue could be a code the Japanese would not be able to break. Unwritten and completely unintelligible except to another Navajo speaker, messages could be transmitted from one Navajo to another much more quickly than by using conventional cryptographic equipment and techniques. Furthermore, since perhaps 30 non–Navajo speakers of the language — and none among Japanese — existed in the world, the Code Talkers appeared to be a secure group.

General Vogel heartily approved of the demonstration, recruiting 29 Navajos almost immediately. Many of these Indians had grown up under pressure to speak English; to turn away from their native tongue as part of their assimilation into the mainstream culture. Now, the Marines asked them to use that very same native language as a weapon during the war. In all, more than 200 Navajos were recruited into the Code Talkers' program, earning high praise throughout the war from commanders on all levels.

The Code Talkers played crucial roles in many of the war stages of the Pacific. At Iwo Jima, Major Howard Connor, 5th Marine Division signal officer, was reported as saying, "Were it not for the Navajos, the marines would have never taken Iwo Jima" (www.history.navy.mil). Speaking in their own Navajo tongue, the Code Talkers broadcast critical messages between commanders and front line troops that proved indecipherable by the Japanese.

April 9, 1942

American troops in the Philippines, many of whom are Mexican Americans, are forced by their Japanese captors to undertake the Bataan Death March.

Forced to march more than 100 kilometers from Corregidor Island to the prisoner of war camp at Bataan — with no food or water — more than 10,000 soldiers lost their lives.

Three years later, a dramatic pilgrimage was made to north-central New

Mexico's El Santuario del Chimayo, the holy shrine of Our Lord of Esquip-ulas, the "Black Christ." The New Mexico National Guard — composed largely of Mexican Americans — had been sent to the Philippines just before the war in the Pacific broke out. These New Mexicans had been a large per-centage of the unfortunate participants of the Death March.

Jess Price explains: "They vowed, in the rich tradition of their culture, they would make a Lenten pilgrimage to El Santuario del Chimayo. And they did. Some came in wheelchairs; some on crutches. Some made the trip for many miles on their knees" (Price, p. A4).

For years, survivors of the Death March returned to El Santuario in thankfulness for their lives.

June 3, 1942

In a little-publicized episode during World War II, the Japanese invade the Aleutian Islands almost six months to the day after the attack on Pearl Harbor, Hawaii.

The attacks focused on Attu and Kiska Islands, at the western end of the 1,400-mile island chain, with bombing of Dutch Harbor and Unalaska.

The United States counterattack drove out the Japanese, but not before they had captured a number of Aleuts off Attu Island, transporting them back to Hokkaido, Japan. Meanwhile, newspapers on the west coast of the United States draw great attention to the attacks, warning Americans along the Pacific coast, "We may be next!" However, very little attention was paid to the upcoming fate of the Aleut natives (or Unangan, as they call themselves).

Ostensibly to provide for their welfare, the United States govern-ment — in a joint effort by the military and the Department of the Inte-rior — rounded up Aleut people and relocated them to camps in southeast-ern Alaska constructed from abandoned fish canneries. In total, more than 800 Aleuts were transported to the camps, where they would remain until April of 1945.

Unfortunately, due to a lack of coordination between the military and the Department of the Interior the old canneries were ill-supplied or pre-pared to house human beings, while food and health supplies arrived only sporadically. A letter from two women relocated to a camp at Funter Bay described the conditions they endured:

> We the people of this place want a better place ... to live. This ... is no place for a living creature. We drink impure water then get sick, the children's get skin disease, even the grown ups are sick from the cold. We ate from the mess house and it is near the toilet only a few yards away. We eat the filth that is flying around.

Due to the filth, cold, and disease at the internment camps, away from their own lands and ways of life, one out of ten Aleuts died.

Of the 321 recognized Native American groups in the United States, 210 live in Alaska. They include tribes such as the Aleut, Ingalik, Tlingit, Inupiaq, and the Yup'ik. But like the Japanese invasion of the Aleuts, little recognition is given to these people, outside Alaska.

August 4, 1942

The Bracero program encourages the mass movement of Mexican laborers to the U.S.

The Labor Importation Program — also known as the Bracero program — emerged from a carefully negotiated, bilateral labor agreement facilitated by the secretary of agriculture, Claude Wickard, with the Mexican foreign ministry. Mirroring a similar effort during World War I that brought 20,000 workers north, the Bracero program was supposed to protect the basic human and economic rights of the Mexican worker.

By 1943, however, the American Farm Bureau Federation lobbied for the management aspect of the program to be limited. Mexico complained about poor treatment of its people, but there was nothing it could do to monitor conditions inside the United States. Congress weakly enforced the law and purposely ignored violations of the program ranging from the trampling of basic human rights to the massive influx of illegal immigrants.

The Bracero program reflected the economic realities of the 1940s, when farmers accounted for 22 percent of the entire population of the U.S. (By 1964, when the program officially ended, farmers made up only 6.8 percent of the total population.) Following the Great Depression, the Department of Agriculture maintained its heightened apprehensions about adequate food supply. With the war effort, food procurement was seen as a security measure as well as an economic concern. The Bracero program continued through World War II, into the Korean War, and beyond. It seems, says writer John Ross, that "whenever Washington has gone off to war, it turns to Mexico for manual labor" (Ross, p. 3).

Between 1942 and 1964, four million workers crossed the border to work in the north. American farmers quickly took advantage of the highly skilled but illiterate work force. From the beginning, U.S. agricultural interests lobbied against government regulation and monitoring of living conditions, minimum wages, and various other safeguards put in place on behalf of migrant laborers. Illegal recruitment of workers began in 1954.

In his book *La Raza*, Steven Steiner wrote, "Braceros had been herded like cattle. They had no rights, no protection under our laws. They were not citizens and could not join unions. One word of protest and they could be deported at whim. In the fields, they worked "harder than the beasts of burden" (Steiner, p. 280).

With the demise of the Bracero safety net in 1964, United States farmers became able to use plentiful, willing, if illegal, workers at a dramatically lower cost. Despite a history of hostility toward illegal migrant workers, Americans today often forget that many of these workers were invited by the government and the farming industry beginning almost 60 years ago.

February 1, 1943

The 442nd Regimental Combat Team (RCT), made up entirely of Japanese American troops, is authorized, beginning training landings in Fort Shelby, Mississippi.

The 442nd RCT waged eight campaigns through Italy, southern France, the Rhineland, and central Europe between 1943 and 1945. It was regarded as one of the best assault troops in the army, and became the most decorated unit, for its size and strength, in the history of American military, winning seven presidential citations. The 100th Infantry Battalion of the 442nd suffered so many wounds and deaths that its nickname was "the Purple Heart Battalion."

In one of the true ironies of the war, many of the 442nd RCTs troops had volunteered for enlistment after being relocated in internment camps. The Nisei generation felt compelled to prove their loyalty to the nation in the European theater, even while their relatives in the States languished in interment camps.

The 442nd RCT won 18,143 decorations in all. President Harry S. Truman reportedly told them in July 1946, "You fought not only the enemy, but you fought prejudice — and you have won" (Hull, July 1996).

June 7, 1943

Bands of hundreds of sailors, Marines, and soldiers in southern California range the Hispanic neighborhoods of Los Angeles, looking for young Mexican American men in zoot suits.

When the young men were found, the soldiers beat them, tearing their suits from their bodies. For seven days — from June 3 to June 10 — these so called Zoot Suit Riots expanded, as the military men targeted African Americans and Filipino Americans as well as Hispanic Americans. Hundreds were injured, and the riots left an aftermath of racial hatred in Los Angeles.

Zoot suits — flashy, expensive counterpoints to the cloth rationing common during the war — came to symbolize the rebelliousness of youth. Some elements of the California press used the opportunity to portray Mexican Americans as "Zoot Suiters": unwelcome, unpatriotic foreigners who formed murderous and dangerous gangs. These media techniques set a precedent for the negative media portrayal of teenagers — particularly those of color — through the fifties and beyond.

June 21, 1943

The United States Supreme Court hands down the first of three decisions addressing Executive Order 9066 and its effects on the lives of particular Japanese Americans.

Gordon Hirabayashi, a Japanese-American, had sued the army for imposing an 8 P.M. to 6 A.M. curfew, which Hirabayashi claimed constituted racial discrimination and a violation of due process under the Fifth and Fourteenth Amendments. In the unanimous decision on *Hirabayashi v. United States*, the Supreme Court refused to consider the issue of discrimination and ruled against Hirabayashi, saying the curfew was a justified wartime measure.

However, in December 1944 in the case of *Ex Parte Endo*, the Supreme Court decision prohibited the army from detaining a Japanese American whose loyalty had been established. Misuye Endo who had been detained at the Tule Lake Relocation Center in 1942, challenged her detention. The Court unanimously granted her liberty, stating the order only applied to individuals whose loyalty had not yet been established.

Finally on December 18, 1945, the Supreme Court presented its decision on *Korematsu v. United States*. Fred Korematsu, an American-born citizen of Japanese descent, had run away from his home in Oakland, California, refusing to obey the evacuation order in 1942, again on the grounds that it violated his Fifth and Fourteenth Amendment rights against deprivation of property without to due process. He had been arrested and convicted in 1944.

In its decision, the Court ruled six to three that the military had been justified in relocating the people without individual hearings, due to national security needs.

Justice Frank Murphy, in writing the dissent, railed against the order as "legalization of racism." In its judgment, the Supreme Court upheld the internments. Because, the Court reasoned, "approximately five thousand American citizens of Japanese Ancestry refused to swear unqualified allegiance to the United States," the military had been justified in ordering the evacuation and internment of more than 110,000 Americans.

Neither the Court nor the government would address the unconstitutionality of Executive Order 9066 itself, or acknowledge and redress the injustice, for another five decades.

December 17, 1943

The Chinese Exclusion Repeal Act is passed by the United States Congress, nullifying the Exclusion Act passed in 1902.

The action was taken in response to China's position as an ally during World War II. Congress established a quota of 105 Chinese immigrants per year. This quota would remain until finally abolished in 1965.

April 3, 1944

The United States Supreme Court overturns a Texas Democratic Party policy that excludes African Americans from membership, thus preventing them from voting in the primary elections.

In the case of *Smith v. Allwright*, Lonnie E. Smith, represented by National Association for the Advancement of Colored People attorneys William H. Hastie and Thurgood Marshall, challenged the local party's policy. Smith sued election judge S.E. Allwright for excluding him from voting in the primaries because of his race. Reversing its decision in *Grovey v. Townsend* (1935), the Court declared the party had been acting as an agent of the state and, because the primary could not be considered a private matter, violated the Fifteenth Amendment by discriminating against an African American.

September 18, 1944

Martin Luther King, Jr., meets one of the most influential forces in his life.

On this day, young Martin Luther King, Jr., begins his education at Morehouse College in Atlanta, Georgia. There, King met for the first time Benjamin Elijah Mays, the president of Morehouse College. A towering figure in African American education, Mays was known for his hypnotic voice and powerful bearing. Mays spoke out early and often against segregation and for equal education, greatly affecting King.

Born in South Carolina in 1895, Mays graduated from Bates College in Maine in 1920. He earned his masters' and doctorate degrees at the University of Chicago and was ordained a Baptist minister in December of 1921. After teaching stints at Morehouse College and South Carolina State

College, Mays served at Howard University School of Religion from 1934 to 1940. In 1940, Mays attained the position of president of Morehouse College, which he would hold for 25 years.

Benjamin E. Mays became the first black president of the Atlanta school board. He received more than 30 honorary doctorates and awards, and published several books. An informal advisor to Dr. King, Mays delivered the eulogy at King's funeral on April 9, 1968.

December 28, 1945

The War Bride Act allows thousands of Asian and other foreign-born women newly married to American soldiers to enter the United States.

Overturning decrees of the 1924 Immigrant Quota Act and other immigration restricting measures, the War Bride Act waived visa requirements and provisions of immigration law concerning members of the American armed forces who, during World War II, had married nationals of foreign countries.

Under the provisions of the act, foreign-born wives needed only to present proof of marriage to an American citizen to enter the United States. The act was passed to facilitate "admission of alien spouses and alien minor children of citizen members of the United States armed forces" (www.clements.umich.edu). The war brides era represented the largest migration to the United States since the 1920s. During World War II, an estimated 1 million American soldiers married women from over 50 foreign countries.

January 17, 1946

Malcolm Little is sentenced to eight to ten years for burglary at Charleston Prison in Massachusetts.

While serving his sentence, he learned of the Nation of Islam. He joined the Black Muslims, becoming a devout follower of Elijah Muhammad, and renouncing his slave name to become known as Malcolm X.

Upon his parole in August 1952, Malcolm X became the Black Muslims' most charismatic preacher, encouraging followers to live separately from and to distrust whites. From Temple Seven in Harlem, New York, he incited African Americans to take pride in their own ethnic heritage and to develop a sense of dignity, equality, and even superiority to European Americans.

During the next decade, the Nation of Islam gained scores of followers, mostly due to the inspired oration of Malcolm X. He became a national figure, greatly boosting the visibility of the Nation of Islam and Elijah

Muhammad, while educating a people in the school of black separatism and black power.

July 4, 1946

In compliance with the precepts of the Tydings-McDuffie Act of 1935, the Philippines gains independence from the U.S.

At the same time, both Filipinos and Asian Indians were authorized to become naturalized American citizens. Filipinos, declared ineligible for citizenship in 1933, now were granted an annual immigrant quota of 100. In addition, a small number of Asian Indians were allowed to immigrate.

April 9, 1947

The Congress of Racial Equality (CORE) begins the Journey of Reconciliation, the precursor of the Freedom Rides of the '50s and '60s.

Eight blacks and eight whites set out to test Supreme Court ruling on interstate transportation and segregation by attempting to take a bus ride across the upper South. Four of the journeyers were arrested in Chapel Hill, North Carolina. Three, including Bayard Rustin, were confined to a chain gang, gaining national attention for the organization.

The Congress of Racial Equality had been founded in 1942 in Chicago, Illinois. Originally called the Committee of Racial Equality, it was formed by an interracial collection of University of Chicago students, including James Farmer and George Houser, in cooperation with another group, Bayard Rustin's Fellowship of Reconciliation (FOR). Many of its members had been profoundly influenced by the nonviolent resistance practices of India's Mohandas Gandhi. Nonviolent resistance gestures such as the Journey of Reconciliation, sit-ins, and other demonstrations became the trade mark of CORE. Later nonviolent protests conducted by CORE produced effects of great scope and impact.

April 15, 1947

Jackie Robinson plays his first Major League game.

Before 26,623 fans — including 14,000 African Americans — at Ebbets Field in Brooklyn, New York, Jackie Robinson stepped onto the field for his first Major League baseball game, when the National Leagues Brooklyn Dodgers faced the Boston Braves.

By the time the 1947 season began, Robinson had become accustomed to being on the front line in the struggle for racial justice. He had faced and had been acquitted in a court-martial in 1944, when he refused to go to the back of a military bus that had officially been desegregated under Roosevelt's measures to desegregate the armed forces. Nine judges took just a few minutes to find him not guilty.

After leaving the army, Robinson had signed on with the Kansas City Monarchs in the Negro Leagues, hitting .387 for the season. On October 23, 1945, he signed with the AAA Montreal Royals of the International League, of the Brooklyn Dodgers' farm system. Robinson managed to play well, despite the tension of enduring abuse, insults, and personal threats toward his wife Rachel and himself. Robinson led the Royals to their first league championship.

To facilitate the breaking of the Major League color barrier, Brooklyn Dodgers owner Branch Rickey wanted a man with the courage to refrain from fighting back against the mistreatment he would suffer. As Robinson entered the Major Leagues in 1947, there seemed to be a lifting of the spirits of African Americans, particularly young African Americans. Kenny Washington had actually already broken in with the Los Angeles Rams of the National Football League in 1946. However, because baseball was considered, especially at the time, the National Pastime, Robinson's achievement was considered far more significant. Suddenly anything seemed possible; suddenly, it seemed that people of color might be given the same opportunities as white Americans.

Robinson brought a newfound speed and excitement to the base paths, drawing exuberant crowds who filled great stadiums just to see him. In 1947, he won the *Sporting News* Rookie of the Year Award.

March 26, 1948

Dr. Hector Perez Garcia forms the American GI Forum, which provides competent health care for war veterans refused services because they were considered "Mexicans."

For the remainder of the century, the American GI Forum would be in the forefront of those offering services and advocacy for Hispanic American veterans.

Born in Liera, Tamaulipas, Mexico, on January 17, 1914, Garcia was the son of a college professor and a school teacher. His family moved to Mercedes, Texas, in 1918, during the Mexican Revolution. Garcia worked in the agricultural fields as a young boy, experiencing his first bitter taste of discrimination. But his father encouraged his children to break the stereotypical mode for Hispanic Americans in Texas: "poorly educated, poorly nourished, poorly paid, and poorly treated."

Garcia graduated a valedictorian from high school, then graduated with honor from the University of Texas, deciding to pursue a career in medicine. He attended medical school at the University of Texas Medical School at Galveston.

After the outbreak of World War II, Garcia volunteered for army duty in 1942. He earned a Bronze Star for his service in northern Africa. When Garcia returned to Corpus Christi in 1946, he set up his medical practice in an office next to the Veterans Administration. He quickly learned that other doctors were refusing to see Hispanic Americans, even those who had served in the Pacific. Unable to abide such treatment, Dr. Hector — as he soon would be known — offered to take patients from the VA at $3 per person.

May 3, 1948

The United States Supreme Court issues a decision in *Shelley v. Kraemer*, stating that any state or state court that upholds a discriminatory housing policy is violating the equal protection clause of the Fourteenth Amendment.

A private housing development in St. Louis, Missouri, had made it a policy to discriminate against African Americans, even though there had already been blacks living in the development, some as early as the late nineteenth century. Under the name of Shelley, several black residents brought suit after they bought a parcel in the development, but the state court of Missouri forced their divestment. The petitioners claimed they had been denied equal protection of the law, and had been deprived of property without due process.

The Supreme Court took issue not so much with the private discriminatory policy but with how the Supreme Court of Missouri had upheld and supported it. Chief Justice Fred Vinson wrote, "We hold that in granting judicial enforcement of the restrictive agreements in these cases, the States have denied petitioners the equal protection of the laws and that, therefore, the action of the state courts cannot stand."

Four years earlier, on June 22, 1944, President Roosevelt had signed the Servicemen's Readjustment Act, better known as the GI Bill, to provide funds for housing and education for veterans after the war. While the GI Bill was meant to facilitate the purchase of property by all World War II veterans, race-restrictive covenants impeded the ability of nonwhite veterans to buy housing in the neighborhoods they chose. Many veterans of color were initially forced to find shelter in military barracks, until enough race-restrictive covenants were lifted to allow them to buy homes.

July 9, 1948

Satchel Paige pitches his first Major League game.

The oldest rookie to ever play Major League baseball walked onto the field at Cleveland's Municipal Stadium, before 72,000 fans. Leroy "Satchel" Paige, after playing 22 years in the Negro Leagues, proceeded to pitch his first game for the Cleveland Indians. A legend from the Negro Leagues, Paige entered the game in the fifth inning, pitching two no-hit innings. He won his first game on August 3, finishing with a record of 6–1 for the season.

The promotion of Jackie Robinson to the Brooklyn Dodgers a year before had caused a wave of color to sweep through the stodgy and segregated national game. Earlier that season the Cleveland Indians had brought up Larry Doby, the first African American to play for the American League. In April of 1949, Orestes Minoso signed with the Cleveland Indians, becoming the first black Latino to play Major League baseball. Soon, such names as Roy Campanella, Don Newcombe, Jim "Junior" Gilliam, Willie Mays, and Hank Aaron were listed among the Major Leaguers. These changes were the death knell of the Negro Leagues.

In two years the color line was broken in the National Basketball Association as well. Nat "Sweetwater" Clifton and Chuck Cooper were recruited, respectively, by the New York Knickerbockers and the Boston Celtics; they were two of 12 African Americans to enter the league that year. Within a quarter century, the NBA would be dominated by African Americans, who would take the sport to a level of athleticism and spectacle never known in American sports.

July 26, 1948

President Harry S. Truman issues an executive order barring discrimination in the military.

The order followed two years of constant pressure from A. Philip Randolph and an organization initially called the Committee on Jim Crow in Military Service and Training. In 1947, Truman had called for a peacetime draft but failed to present a provision for the prevention of segregation in the armed services. In response, Randolph's committee had called for blacks to refuse to register for the draft or to serve if called. He eventually testified before the Senate Armed Services Committee, as dissension grew in the African American community. Truman finally relented.

August 7, 1948

Dr. Sammy Lee wins a gold medal at the London Olympics for the ten-meter platform dive, becoming the first Asian American to win an Olympic gold.

Born in 1920 of Korean ancestry in Fresno, California, Lee had grown up in Los Angeles, studying premed at Occidental College and graduating from medical school at the University of Southern California in 1947. Lee remembered the restrictions facing him growing up in Los Angeles. Nonwhites could use the pool at nearby Brookside only one day per week. The pool was then emptied, with fresh water supplied for the next day's swim.

Standing barely five feet tall at the age of 28, Lee won the Olympic gold as well as the bronze medal for the three-meter springboard. He also won gold for the ten-meter platform in 1952, becoming the first male diver to win gold medals in back-to-back Olympics. He went on to coach Bob Webster — who would win the gold in diving in 1960 and 1964 — and Greg Louganis, who would win silver in 1976.

October 1, 1948

The California Supreme Court rules against anti-miscegenation laws in its decision concerning *Perez v. Sharp.*

Andrea Perez and Sylvester Davis had attempted to obtain a marriage license in Los Angeles. W.G. Sharp, the county clerk of Los Angeles, refused, citing Civil Code Section 60 which stated, "No license may be issued authorizing the marriage of a white person with a Negro, mulatto, Mongolian or member of the Malay race."

After spending a considerable amount of effort refuting traditional arguments of the inferiority or the undesirability of various races, the California Supreme Court stated that prohibitions against interracial marriage had been based on racial distinctions that were "by their very nature odious to a free people." Judge J. Traynor stated, "Since the right to marry is the right to join in marriage with the person of one's choice, a statute that prohibits an individual from marrying a member of a race other than his own restricts the scope of his choice and thereby restricts his right to marry."

Judge J. Carter, in his concurrent opinion, wrote, "The rest of the world has never understood and will never understand why and how a nation, built on the premise that all men are created equal, can three times send the flower of its manhood to war for the truth of this premise and still fail to carry it out within its own borders."

Anti-miscegenation laws had a long history in the United States. The first such law is said to have been established in Maryland in 1661. In 1883, a Missouri judge prevented racial intermarriage because he believed — as many did — it to be an authenticated fact that if the children of a black man and a white woman, or a white man and a black woman intermarried, they could not possibly reproduce. Such convictions were used to justify the prohibition of intermarriage well into the last years of the twentieth century.

In the 1950s and 1960s, 14 other states repealed anti-miscegenation laws: Arizona, California, Colorado, Idaho, Indiana, Maryland, Montana, Nebraska, Nevada, North Dakota, Oregon, South Dakota, Utah, and Wyoming. The federal courts, however, took no such stand until nearly 20 years after *Perez v. Sharp.*

March 1, 1950

W.E.B. Du Bois leads a gathering of about 40 Americans in New York to organize the Peace Information Center.

After the days of the Harlem Renaissance, he had resigned from the National Association for the Advancement of Colored People and *The Crisis* in 1934, and turned his attention largely to the burgeoning worldwide peace movement. He attended the founding of the United Nations in 1945 in San Francisco as a consultant. He then organized several conferences on world peace, lectured, edited, and traveled. Du Bois also attended several conferences concerning world peace in Russia, Prague, and Stockholm, at which the "Stockholm Appeal" to abolish the atomic bomb emerged. Inspired by these events, Du Bois and others hoped to organize a peace movement in the United States as well.

In the light of the contemporary paranoia concerning communism, the organization of the Peace Information Center almost immediately drew public derision. Secretary of State Dean Acheson wrote in the *New York Times*, "I am sure that the American people will not be fooled by the so-called 'world peace appeal' or 'Stockholm resolution' now being circulated in this country for signatures. It should be recognized for what it is — a propaganda trick in the spurious 'peace offensive' of the Soviet Union" (www2.pfeiffer. edu).

Du Bois immediately responded through a press release, writing, "The main burden of your opposition to this Appeal and to our offer lies in the charge that we are part of a 'spurious peace offensive' of the Soviet Union? Is it our strategy that when the Soviet Union asks for peace, we insist on war? Must any proposal for averting atomic catastrophe be sanctified by Soviet opposition? Does it not occur to you, Sir, that there are honest Americans who, regardless of their differences on other questions, hate and fear war and are determined to do something to avert it."

The paranoia prevailed, however, leading to Du Bois's eventual indictment, trial, and acquittal on charges of acting as an "unregistered foreign agent" in connection with leadership of Peace Information Center.

April 1, 1950

Dr. Charles Drew, America's preeminent expert on the storage and preservation of blood plasma, bleeds to death after an automobile accident outside of Burlington, North Carolina.

One myth said he would not be admitted to a white hospital, while another version asserts a white doctor tried feverishly to save him. Perhaps the last sight Drew saw is that of the needle extending from a flask of plasma.

Senator Hubert Humphrey, on the floor of the Senate on April 10, 1950, commemorated Drew as "a pioneer in the field of blood plasma [who], as a result of his brilliant research in the field, saved thousands of British and American lives during the war.... Dr. Drew's tragic accident is a profound loss to the whole American community." An editorial in the *Washington Post* said, "He worked ardently to enlarge the meager opportunities for Negro doctors to receive training in American medical schools and hospitals. He will be missed ... by men everywhere who value scientific devotion and integrity."

In September of 1940, at the height of Nazi Germany's blitzkrieg against Britain, Drew had headed the effort to ship plasma to England for the Blood for Britain project for the war efforts. Within a year, he was placed in charge of American Red Cross Blood Bank. He supervised the shipping of plasma to American soldiers during World War II, saving countless lives in the process.

Born in Washington, D.C., in 1904, Charles Drew was an outstanding athlete at Amherst College, then graduated at the head of his class from McGill Medical College in 1933. In 1941 Drew was named professor of surgery at Howard University's teaching and clinical facility, Freedman's Hospital. There, Dr. Drew trained the majority of America's first generation of black surgeons.

Even while he headed the Red Cross drive for blood, the blood banks regularly denied the use of Negro blood for the general banks. They segregated it, using it only for African American victims. Drew assailed the practice, maintaining that all human blood is the same regardless of race.

June 5, 1950

Two United State Supreme Court cases, issuing further challenges to the concept of "separate but equal," are decided on the same day in 1950.

When Heman Sweatt had been refused entrance into the law school at the University of Texas, he had sued in state court. The state court had conceded that Sweatt had been denied equal protection, but had failed to act further and had allowed Texas time to create a black law school. Sweatt had refused to apply to the new school, reasoning its resources would be vastly inferior to the long established university.

In the unanimous decision of *Sweatt v. Painter*, the Supreme Court ordered that Sweatt be admitted to the University of Texas. Chief Justice Fred M. Vinson voiced the decision, saying, "It is difficult to believe that one who had a free choice between these law schools would consider the question close." The Court's contention was based on the premise of equal access and equal protection.

In *McLaurin v. Oklahoma State Regents for Higher Education*, the Supreme Court decided that blacks in state universities could not be segregated after admission. A black student admitted to the doctoral program at the University of Oklahoma nevertheless had been assigned special seats in classrooms and separate facilities in the library and cafeteria. The Court determined that such state-imposed iniquities could not be condoned, because they failed to meet equal protection and access standards by imposing limits on education and professional development.

In questions of housing, education, transportation, and public facilities, the law of the land had begun to determine that "separate but equal" meant always separate, but never equal.

August 28, 1950

Althea Gibson is the first African American to compete in the U.S. Open.

Althea Gibson steps onto Court 14 at Forest Hill Tennis Club in New York, becoming the first African American — male or female — to compete in the United States Open tennis tournament. She soundly defeats Barbara Knapp in straight sets, 6–2, 6–2.

Born to sharecroppers on August 25, 1927, on a cotton farm in South Carolina, Gibson moved to New York in the 1930s. Coach Buddy Walker, of the New York Police Athletic League, introduced her to tennis. Gibson went on to win the New York state championship six times between 1944 and 1950. Finally in 1950, she turned her sights toward a higher goal by applying for entrance into the United States Lawn Tennis Association (USLTA). The all-white association rejected her at every attempt.

Finally Alice Marble, a highly respected former U.S. Open champion, wrote a blistering letter to the July 1950 edition of *American Lawn Tennis* magazine. The message reportedly revealed Marble's embarrassment at the bigotry displayed by the USLTA. One week later, the association granted Gibson admittance.

The impact Gibson had on the sport is immeasurable. Ten years before the emergence of Arthur Ashe, she became the first African American to win at the U.S. Open, in 1957 at Forest Hills. She won the tournament again in 1958. She also became the first African American to win the Wimbledon Championship of Tennis, also in 1957, and the first to win at the French Open.

Gibson's remarkable tennis career spanned 20 years, 100 professional titles, and five Grand Slam titles. She was elected to National Lawn Tennis Hall of Fame in 1971.

Gibson, a splendid athlete, at one point took up golf. Not surprisingly, she became the first African American to earn a Ladies Professional Golf Association card.

September 1, 1950

Gwendolyn Brooks, in winning the Pulitzer Prize for *Annie Allen*, becomes the first black ever cited by the Pulitzer committee.

Born to Keziah Corine Wims and David Anderson Brooks on June 17, 1917, in Topeka, Kansas, Brooks moved to Chicago at the age of four. She had her first poem published at the age of 13.

As an adult, Brooks eventually became a weekly contributor to the *Chicago Defender*. Her writings offered to the nonblack reader insight into the African American culture, with commentary on the impact of prejudice from the inside out. Having won the Midwestern Writers' Conference Award in 1943, Brooks also received the American Academy of Arts and Letters Award, the Frost Award, and the National Endowments for the Arts Award.

She died of cancer at the age of 83 in the year 2000.

September 22, 1950

The first African American receives the Nobel Peace Prize.

On this date, American diplomat Ralph Johnson Bunche learned he had won the Nobel Prize for Peace for his courageous mediation efforts among Israel and the Arab states during the Palestine Conflict. He was the first African American to win that award.

Ralph J. Bunche was born on August 7, 1904, in Detroit, Michigan. His father Fred Bunche worked as a barber serving only white customers, while his mother Olive Johnson Bunche was an amateur musician. When his parents fell sick and died in Albuquerque, New Mexico, in 1916, Bunche and his two sisters moved with their grandmother Nana — who had been born into slavery — to Los Angeles. There, the grandmother courageously raised the three children while working odd jobs to contribute to the household till.

Displaying evidence of intellectual brilliance at an early age, Bunche was named valedictorian at Jefferson High School. He attended the University of California at Los Angeles on an athletic scholarship to study international relations. He continued on to earn a scholarship to Harvard University, eventually earning his master's degree and his doctorate.

Bunche displayed heroic patience and fortitude in facilitating the armistice forged on the island of Rhodes, Greece, in 1949, between the Jews and the Arabs.

March 18, 1952

Rosa Minoka Hill, the second Native American woman in United States history to become a medical doctor, dies in Oneida, Wisconsin.

Born on St. Regis Mohawk Reservation in New York, Rosa Minoka was adopted by a Quaker doctor, who took her to Philadelphia. She graduated from Women's Medical College in Pennsylvania in 1899, sharing a practice with another woman doctor from 1899 to 1904. She married Charles Hill in 1905, and moved to Oneida, Wisconsin; she gave birth to six children. Charles Hill died in 1915, leaving Rosa Minoka Hill to raise the children by herself. She intended to give up medicine to concentrate on family and farm, but neighbors kept coming to her for medical advice. They offered chickens and squash in return for her counsel, as Hill was the only recognized doctor in Oneida.

Soon Hill realized she would need a Wisconsin medical license if she were to continue her practice with any hope of financial success. After years of practicing medicine in Oneida, she took and passed the Wisconsin State Medical Exam at the age of 58, becoming a pioneer in medicine for Native Americans and American women. Hill combined her knowledge of Western medicine with respect for traditional native healing techniques, using herbs as easily as Western techniques and encouraging her patients to try both until one worked.

Two years after her death, a monument was erected in her honor, reading, "Physician, Good Samaritan, and Friend of People of all religions in this community, erected to her memory by the Indians and white people."

June 30, 1952

Congress enacts the McCarran-Walter Act, which President Harry S. Truman had vetoed as inhumane, discriminatory, and inconsistent with democratic ideals; Congress overrides the veto by one vote.

The act added new provisions to the Immigrant Quota Act of 1924, including allowing the naturalization of the Issei, the first generation of Japanese immigrants. It also lifted the ban on all immigrants from Asia, although it maintained a very low quota.

The act was authored in part by Senator Patrick A. McCarran of Nevada, who two years previous had sponsored the Subversive Activities Control Act, which required the registration of all Communists with the attorney general. A provision of the McCarran-Walter Act — with which Truman had contended — allowed the Immigration and Naturalization Service to exclude "possible subversives" and to permit the deportation of aliens who engage in activities seen as "prejudicial to the public interest" (Kohn, p. 200). This act emerged during the McCarthy Era, when the anxiety bred by Senator Joseph McCarthy over communism in the United States ran at an all-time high.

June 11, 1953

Amos 'n' Andy is pulled from the Columbia Broadcasting System after three years of broadcasting.

Critical pressure from groups such as the National Association for the Advancement of Colored People forced it off the air. However, it remained in syndication until 1966, despite ever-growing criticism during the expanding civil rights movement.

Amos 'n' Andy depicted classic examples of prejudice and ethnic stereotyping. It had started as a radio show in 1925, created in "black voice" by white actors Freeman Gosden and Charles Correll. At one point, the two had donned blackface in 1930, to make an *Amos 'n' Andy* movie called *Check and Double Check*.

The show opened on CBS TV in the summer of 1950. Like the radio show, the television production concerned itself with the comedic situations encountered by main characters Andy Brown and Amos Jones, played by Spencer Williams, Jr., and Alvin Childress.

In syndication, *Amos 'n' Andy* proved extremely popular in the South. However, the Urban League assessment was, "The show depicts the Negro as a foot-shuffling, handkerchief head. The station owners who run it are going to catch hell, and the sponsors of the show will not sell to the Negro market" (Mitz, p. 31).

Alvin Childress, who played Amos Jones, countered the comments of critics by saying, "What its detractors fail to mention is that it was the very first time we saw a few blacks playing professionals — judges, doctors, lawyers" (Mitz, p. 30). For better or worse, *Amos 'n' Andy* was the first situation comedy starring black actors.

August 1, 1953

The United States Congress passes Concurrent Resolution 108, Public Law 280, implementing the Termination and Relocation phase of the Indian Reorganization Act (IRA) of 1934.

Determining that the Reorganization Act had failed due to the same incompetence and corruption that plagued the administration of the Dawes Act, the Bureau of Indian Affairs commenced the Termination and Relocation phase. Funding for the IRA quickly decreased, causing bankruptcy and painful dislocation among the tribes.

More importantly, the act removed government recognition of 61 tribal communities, including the Flatheads, the Hoopa, the Klamath, the Osage, the Potawatomi, and the Menominee. More than 12,000 individual Native Americans suddenly became ineligible for government assistance, while more than 2.5 million acres of Indian land were removed from protected status.

October 5, 1953

Earl Warren — former governor and attorney general of California — is sworn in as chief justice of the United States Supreme Court, appointed by President Dwight D. Eisenhower.

The Warren court — as it came to be known — would be recognized as one of the most progressive of high courts, its justices numbering among the most prestigious and influential in United States history: Hugo Black, Felix Frankfurter, William O. Douglas, Harold H. Burton, Tom C. Clark, John M. Harlan, and William Brennan would be listed among them.

For the next 16 years, the Warren court was challenged by stirring civil rights cases, in turn challenging the laws of the land, in the development of sweeping civil rights and due process legislation.

January 11, 1954

For the first time, the United States Supreme Court recognizes Mexican Americans as a class of people separate from whites, suffering profound discrimination.

In the case of *Hernandez v. Texas*, Peter Hernandez was a Mexican American convicted of the murder of Joe Espinoza in Jackson County, Texas. The conviction had come from a jury with no member of Mexican descent, although many qualified potential jurors of the ethnicity lived in the county. The Texas Court of Criminal Appeals had upheld the verdict of the trial court. Hernandez sued, asserting he had been deprived of equal protection under law because he had not been tried by a jury of his peers.

Acting upon a writ of certiorari, the Court ruled that Hernandez had proved that those of Mexican descent constituted a separate class in Jackson County. In their presentation, Hernandez's attorneys demonstrated common community distinctions between Mexicans and whites in Jackson County. Mexican children had been segregated in schools until just prior to the decision. Hernandez's team showed that at least one restaurant had displayed a sign saying "No Mexicans served." Toilets had been regularly segregated.

The Court ruled Hernandez had to also prove systematic discrimination in the jury selection system in Jackson County. He did. Chief Justice Earl Warren, in the Court's opinion, wrote, "It taxes our credulity to say that mere chance resulted in there being no members of this class among the over six thousand jurors in the past 25 years."

The Court ruled that, indeed, because he had not been tried by a jury of his true peers, Peter Hernandez had been denied the equal protection and due process guaranteed by the Fourteenth Amendment.

The Hernandez case was the first to distinguish Mexican Americans as separate class of people, subject to discrimination. Prior to this, Texas had only distinguished between whites and Negroes. The case paved the way for Hispanic Americans to use legal means to attack all types of discrimination throughout the United States. In addition, *Hernandez v. Texas* was the first United States Supreme Court case to be argued and briefed by Mexican American attorneys.

May 17, 1954

In what is undoubtedly the most staggering blow to the antiquated concept of "separate but equal," the United States Supreme Court unanimously declares racial segregation in public schools to be unconstitutional in the case of *Brown v. Board of Education of Topeka, Kansas*.

In the fall of 1951, eight-year-old Linda Brown's father, the Reverend Oliver Brown, had tried to enroll her in Summer Elementary School, a few blocks from home, instead of having her go to her segregated school, a mile away through a railroad switchyard. The Topeka, Kansas, school board said no. Linda Brown had the wrong color skin. Other Topeka parents with similar experiences joined Brown in the request by the National Association for the Advancement of Colored People for an injunction forbidding segregation in Topeka schools.

The United States District Court for the District of Kansas heard the case in June of 1951. Although sympathetic to the notion that segregation had a detrimental effect on the education of nonwhite children, the court decided to uphold the precedent of *Plessy v. Ferguson*, apparently since it had not been overturned in 55 years.

The case was presented to the Supreme Court by the NAACP chief counsel, the future justice Thurgood Marshall. The Court heard the case on December 9, 1952, could not decide, then heard it again on December 7–8, 1953. Finally, the Court reached a decision.

In expressing the opinion of the court, Chief Justice Earl Warren pondered, "Does segregation of children in public schools solely on the basis of race, even though the physical facilities and other 'tangible' factors may be equal, deprive the children of the minority group of equal education opportunities? We believe that it does.... We conclude that in the field of public education the doctrine of 'separate but equal' has no place. Separate educational facilities are inherently unequal." Warren reportedly understood the severe importance of the case and asked the other eight for a unanimous decision to present to the American people a united and unwavering front.

At once voiding the "separate but equal" stance of *Plessy v. Ferguson*, the decision substantially invalidated 56 years of Jim Crow laws. The decision that "separate but equal facilities are inherently unequal," violating equal protection under the Fourteenth Amendment, became a solid precedent for the desegregation and civil rights movements for the next 50 years.

The reaction in the Southern states was expectedly volatile. Southerners feverishly vowed to preserve the "Southern" way of life; fiery crosses burned over Texas and Florida. Southern politicians stumped to preserve segregation, while random Ku Klux Klan violence broke out throughout the Southern states.

On May 31, 1955, the Court followed up *Brown v. Board of Education* by issuing what has become known as "Brown II." In the final decision of *Brown v. Board of Education*, the Supreme Court tried to deal with the implementation of integration set forth in its initial declaration. However, the Court set extremely vague criteria for the states, announcing the compliance with the new desegregation policy should proceed with "all deliberate speed."

While *Brown v. Board of Education* did not immediately abolish the segregation of other public facilities, nor immediately desegregate schools, it opened the flood gates for a river of litigation, all aimed at nullifying the "separate but equal" discrimination practices that had for so long guided numerous aspects of American life.

July 4, 1954

A racial atrocity changes the life of a Mississippi publisher.

As evidence that all white folks in the South did not share the bigoted point of view, the life of editor and publisher Hazel Brannon Smith changed when she witnessed the unjustified shooting of a black man for making noise on a public highway in Holmes County, Mississippi. From this point on, she became a fierce, uncommon advocate for racial justice in the deep South.

Hazel Brannon was born in Gadsen, Mississippi, and studied journalism at the University of Alabama. After graduation, Brannon borrowed $3,000 to purchase four local weekly newspapers. She married Walter D. Smith, who became her business manager. They settled down for what Brannon Smith expected to be a quiet, prosperous life, running her publications free of controversy.

Following her personal epiphany, Smith quietly supported the *Brown v. Board of Education* decisions, even though this opposed her Southern upbringing. She wrote scathing criticism of the county sheriff in the newspaper: "The vast majority of Holmes county people are not rednecks who look with favor on the abuse of people because their skins are black. Mr. Byrd as Sheriff has violated every concept of justice, decency, and right in his treatment of some of the people of Holmes County" (Ware, p. 304).

She continued to editorialize in this blistering manner. Sheriff Byrd sued her for libel. The local jury awarded Byrd $10,000, but the United States Supreme Court later overturned the verdict.

Hazel Brannon Smith regularly attacked bigots, defending those who had been oppressed by the bigotry. Brannon Smith spoke for law and for the emerging civil rights movement. Her periodicals covered society events in the black community as well as the white, showing the enlightened face of a new, emerging South.

Brannon Smith quickly became a target for the white Citizens' Council in Holmes County. Rejected by many of her Mississippi peers, she endured three decades of boycotts, threats, crosses burning on her front lawn, and even the bombing of one of her offices.

Despite the opposition, Brannon Smith continued to run several newspapers in Mississippi. Since she owned the only printing presses in town, she remained solvent despite protests, canceled subscriptions, and boycotts. In 1960, she started printing the *Mississippi Free Press*, a pet project of Mississippi NAACP leader Medgar Evers. Although vilified in her home county, Brannon Smith gained recognition for her courage and articulation worldwide. In 1964, she won the Pulitzer Prize for the *Lexington Advertiser*, for her "steadfast adherence to her editorial duty in the face of great pressure and opposition."

July 15, 1954

General Joseph Swing, new commissioner for the Unites States Immigration and Naturalization Service and Border Patrol, begins Operation Wetback.

Swing had accompanied John "Black Jack" Pershing in his 1916 quest into Mexico to capture Pancho Villa. Now retired, Swing's goal was to capture and deport the increasing number of illegal Mexican immigrants coming across the United States border, the flood north that had been initiated in part by invitation under the Bracero program.

Begun in Texas, the operation discovered more than 1 million immigrants. At the same time, Mexican Americans and legal immigrants faced oppression from government agents as well as individuals. Thousands of United States citizens of Mexican descent were arrested and detained. The INS allowed deportation hearings for only a small fraction of those captured. In some case, American-born children of Mexican descent were deported along with the parents. Agents regularly stopped "Mexican-looking" individuals and asked them for identification.

In the face of complaints from both the United States and Mexico about the new police state, Operation Wetbacks faded away by the fall of 1954.

January 7, 1955

Marian Anderson becomes the first black soloist to play the Metropolitan Opera of New York City.

Famous conductor Arturo Toscanini praised her voice as one "that comes once in a hundred years." Three years after the Met performance, Anderson became a delegate to the United Nations.

September 23, 1955

Roy Bryant and J.W. Milam are found not guilty of the murder of Emmett Till.

It had taken the jury less than an hour to return the verdict. One Mississippi white reportedly said, "Why all the fuss over a dead 'nigger' in the Tallahatchie ... that river's full of niggers" (Oates, p. 62).

A 14-year-old African American from Chicago named Emmett Till, while visiting relatives in Greenwood, Mississippi, had been captured by three white men, members of the Ku Klux Klan. They would claim Till had whistled at a white woman. His body was found flung into the Tallahatchie River with 70-pound cotton gin fan tied to his neck with barbed wire. During the funeral, Till's mother insisted on an open casket so the whole world could see what had been done to her son.

Three years previous Jeremiah Reeves, a young drummer in an all–Negro high school band in Montgomery, Alabama, had been accused of raping a white woman. An all-white jury found him guilty and sentenced him to hang. After five years of legal intervention by the National Association for the Advancement of Colored People, Reeves was executed. The NAACP had cited numerous examples of brutality inflicted upon black women by white men, with no consequences to the attackers.

While the civil rights movement had begun to make large strides in the United States, incidents such as these provided reminders that there was a long way to go.

December 1, 1955

In perhaps the century's best example of how one individual can make a difference, Rosa Parks, a 43-year-old Montgomery, Alabama, seamstress, is arrested after refusing to give up her seat to a white passenger, James Blake.

When the bus driver threatened to have her arrested, she reportedly said, "Let the cops come." Later, she wrote, she thought "how you spent your whole life making things comfortable for white people" (Parks, p. 116).

Two uniformed officers hustled Parks down to the police station, charging her with violating the city bus ordinance that required black bus passengers to give up their seats for white passengers. Although her throat was dry, they did not let her drink from the whites-only fountain.

Parks was not just an average passenger; she was an impeccable woman, "a most unassuming instigator" (Buchanan, *Historic Places of Worship*, p. 195). She had been active in the National Association for the Advancement of Colored People for 12 years, fully abreast of the civil rights issues on which the Association worked. Those who knew her regarded Parks as honest, smart, morally clean, and holding the respect of the community. The reason Montgomery authorities chose to pick a fight with her can perhaps never be known. One observer outside the courthouse would be overheard saying, "They've done messed with the wrong one now" (Parks, p. 133).

E.D. Nixon, the current head of the Brotherhood of Sleeping Car Porters and legal counsel for the local NAACP office, represented her in court. It was the first time a Negro would be charged with violating the segregation code.

On December 2, Parks was charged in municipal court with disobeying the segregation ordinance and fined $14. Nixon could not believe the good fortune — and the ignorance of the Montgomery officials — that presented him with a federal court test case. Nixon filed an appeal, refusing to pay the fine, taking the first step on the road to the Supreme Court.

That night Martin Luther King, Jr., presided over the first meeting of what would be called the Montgomery Improvement Association (MIA), a name suggested by Ralph Abernathy, pastor of the First Baptist Church. Held at the Dexter Avenue Baptist Church in Montgomery, the meeting was called to organize a bus boycott for the purpose of putting economic and political pressure on the city's segregation policies.

The bus boycott began Monday, December 5. Students hitchhiked to Alabama State, while men and women walked as much as 12 miles to their jobs. Mules, horse-drawn buggies, and sympathetic drivers — black and white — replaced the empty buses as transportation. The Montgomery Bus Boycott was one of the most dramatic demonstrations of nonviolent protest in the history of American race relations.

December 5, 1955

As the American Federation of Labor (AFL) merges with the Congress of Industrial Organizations (CIO), A. Philip Randolph is named the first African American vice president of the AFL-CIO.

With desegregation of federal jobs and the war industries, more than 1.5 million blacks had become union members. Randolph continued to work for the benefit of all workers of color, trying to force the end of discrimination within the labor movement. His influence over the minority work forces would have profound effects on the civil rights advances to come.

March 12, 1956

In response to the 1954 Supreme Court decision of *Brown v. Board of Education of Topeka, Kansas,* 101 Southern members of the United States Senate and House of Representatives sign the "Southern Manifesto on Integration."

In what appeared to be a last-ditch, mass effort to resist desegregation of the schools, the Southern representatives called the Court decision "a clear abuse of judicial power" and urged the use of "all lawful means to bring about a reversal of the decision which is contrary to the Constitution."

The manifesto continued, "The unwarranted exercise of power by the court, contrary to the Constitution, is creating chaos and confusion in the states principally affected. It is destroying the amicable relations between the white and the Negro races that have been created through ninety years of patient effort by the good people of both races. It has planted hatred and suspicion where there has been heretofore friendship and understanding."

In Brown II, the Court had commanded the states to implement integration with "all deliberate speed." After the rebuffs of the Southern Manifesto, the Court would soon lose patience for the issue.

February 3, 1956

Under a storm of protest from the white students and surrounding community, Autherine Juanita Lucy becomes the first African American to enroll in the University of Alabama.

Her entrance into the university became possible because of a court order obtained by the National Association for the Advancement of Colored People. The court order, granted on June 29, 1955, restrained the university from rejecting her application because of race.

Upon entering the university, Lucy immediately faced death threats, and fellow students pelted her with eggs and other objects. Lucy required a police escort to get safely to class. People traveled from all over the state to protest her admission.

After that first day of admission, the university suspended her, ostensibly for her safety and that of her fellow students. When the NAACP filed a contempt of court suit, they lost, causing Lucy's eventual expulsion.

Autherine Juanita Lucy was born on October 5, 1929, one of ten children of Minnie and Milton Lucy. She had earned a Bachelor of Arts degree in English in 1952 from the all-black Miles College in Fairfield, Alabama. After her expulsion from the University of Alabama, Lucy received several offers from universities in Europe to study at no cost. Back home, however, she could not find work as a teacher because of the notoriety she had achieved.

Lucy finally moved to Texas, where she met the Reverend Hugh Foster. She resided in the Lone Star state for 17 years, bore five children, and eventually found work as a substitute teacher. She returned to Alabama in 1974.

In 1988, two University of Alabama teachers invited her to speak to a class about her experiences. Several members of the faculty finally worked to get her expulsion expunged.

Finally, in 1989, Lucy returned to the University of Alabama to earn a master's degree in elementary education. At the same time, her daughter Grazia entered the university to get a bachelor's degree in corporate finance. Mother and daughter received their degrees together in 1992.

April 10, 1956

While performing at a concert in Birmingham, Alabama, popular singer Nat King Cole is attacked by a group of white men.

While Cole was singing his fourth song before an all-white audience at the Birmingham Municipal Auditorium, six armed men approached the stage. One of the assailants lunged toward Cole's feet, causing the microphone stand to fall and strike Cole in the face. The attack created a melee, as the police converge upon the attackers. Ultimately, all six instigators were arrested, but the incident would haunt Cole for years.

As a prominent African American entertainer in the 1940s and 1950s, King had been subjected to numerous incidents of racial prejudice. In a musical career that spanned more than 30 years, Cole was often criticized for not taking a more militant stand for justice and equality.

Born in Montgomery, Alabama, on March 17, 1919, Nathaniel Adams Coles moved to Chicago when he was four. His father Edward was a Baptist minister, while his mother Perlina raised four brothers and one sister alongside Nathaniel. At age 12, Nathaniel took his first formal piano lessons.

Nathaniel attended Wendell Phillips High School in Chicago, where he developed his talents in music and athletics, so much so that teams within the Negro Leagues showed interest. By then he had developed an interest in jazz, watching and listening to groups coming to the south side of Chicago to play.

He joined the Solid Swingers as pianist in the 1930s, recording several songs through Decca's Sepia Series of "race records." In 1937 Cole joined a revue called *Shuffle Along*, which toured much of the country, ending up in Los Angeles. Cole remained in Los Angeles, becoming a regular performer at the Century Club.

In 1938, he joined with guitarist Oscar Moore and bassist Wesley Prince to form the King Cole Trio, as he became Nat King Cole. The trio recorded some "race records" with famed vibraphone player Lionel Hampton in 1941.

Soon, Cole's career began to veer away from his jazz roots into popular form of music. He signed a recording contract in 1943 with burgeoning Capitol Records. Over the years his more popular hits have included "The Christmas Song," "Nature Boy," "Mona Lisa," "Unforgettable," "Too Young," "Answer Me, My Love," "Those Lazy, Hazy, Crazy Days of Summer," and "Ramblin' Rose."

The National Broadcasting Company premiered *The Nat King Cole Show* in November 1956, but the variety show lasted only a year. Cole was the first African American to host a network variety show, just as he had been the first to host his own radio program. Still, advertisers demonstrated great reluctance to sponsor a show featuring a black performer, believing it to be economically disadvantageous. Despite such experiences, Cole did not lash out against the injustice of the times, nor did he refuse to perform at segregated venues. Instead, Cole believed showing goodwill and exhibiting talent would be more effective in providing opportunities for black performers than formal protests. "I can't settle the issue...," Cole once said, " but I can help to ease the tension by gaining the respect of both races all over the country."

Nat King Cole died on February 25, 1965, of lung cancer, after a lifetime of smoking. He was inducted into the Rock and Roll Hall of Fame in 2000 for his remarkable influence on popular music.

November 13, 1956

The United States Supreme Court orders an end to Montgomery bus segregation, declaring the practice unconstitutional.

On December 21, African Americans in Montgomery, Alabama, returned to the buses, legally able to sit anywhere they wished. The boycott to attain that right had lasted 380 days. It cost the Montgomery Improvement Association $225,000 in legal fees and expenses, while cutting $250,000 in revenues from the city bus company.

January 3, 1957

Dalip Singh Saund is elected to the House of Representatives from the twenty ninth Congressional District in Westmoreland, California; he is the first Asian Indian elected to Congress.

Born in Amritsar, India, on September 20, 1899, Dalip Singh Saund was educated at the University of Punjab and immigrated to the United States in 1920. Attending the University of California at Berkeley, Saund received both his Master of Arts and Ph.D. degrees in mathematics in 1922.

Saund began his work career as a lettuce farmer, then was a chemical fertilizer distributor in California's Imperial Valley from 1930 to 1953. After becoming a United States citizen in 1949, Saund won election as judge of the Justice Court, Westmoreland Judicial District, County of Imperial, in less than a year. However, because he had not been a citizen more than a year, the seat was denied. One year later, he was elected to the same court in 1952.

Saund became a delegate to Democratic national conventions in 1952, 1956, and 1960, while winning the congressional seat in 1957. After serving three terms, his career as a congressman ended in 1963. Saund died on April 22, 1973, in Hollywood, California. He is interred at Forest Lawn Cemetery in Glendale.

August 7, 1957

Martin Luther King, Jr., calls 115 African American leaders to Montgomery to form the Southern Christian Leadership Conference (SCLC).

The purpose of the SCLC was to bring the "Montgomery Way"—meaning nonviolent, civil protests on a grassroots level—specifically to communities across the South.

One of the SCLC's primary initial efforts was a Southern voter registration drive called Crusade for Citizenship, to be launched on Lincoln's birthday, 1958. Bayard Rustin, one of the founders of both the Fellowship of Reconciliation (FOR) and the Congress on Racial Equality (CORE) joined in the drive.

September 9, 1957

The United States Congress begins to march in step with the grassroots movements, as it passes the Civil Rights Act of 1957, protecting the voting and other civil rights of African Americans, as well as other Americans.

The act created the Civil Rights Commission to prosecute civil rights violators and to seek federal injunctions to protect civil rights.

Three years later, on May 6, 1960, Congress passed the Civil Rights Act of 1960, providing criminal penalties for obstruction of school desegregation. Designed to strengthen the Civil Rights Act of 1957, the measure also provided the Department of Justice with access to voting records, provided desegregated education for the children of military personnel, and provided court-appointed referees to assure the registration of black voters.

September 24, 1957

Federal troops are sent to ensure black students' entrance to Little Rock High School.

In perhaps the most inadvertently progressive act of his presidency, Dwight D. Eisenhower announced on national television that he had ordered federal troops to Little Rock, Arkansas, in support of the United States Supreme Court mandate for desegregation of public schools, as ruled in the decision of *Brown v. Board of Education of Topeka, Kansas.*

On September 2, Arkansas governor Orville Faubus had posted 270 men from the Arkansas National Guard outside Little Rock Central High School. Their duty was to prevent nine black adolescents from entering the previously all-white high school. From this point forward, Elizabeth Eckford, Ernie Green, Melba Pattillo Beals, Gloria Ray Karlmark, Minnijean Brown, Carlotta Walls LaNier, Terrence Roberts, Jefferson Thomas, and Thelma Mothershed-Wair would collectively become known as the "Little Rock Nine."

Adhering to a court order, Governor Faubus finally withdrew the troops, leaving the protection of the children to a small group of reluctant police. On September 23, the students returned to enter the high school. Witnessed on national television, the students were met by an angry, jeering mob, who spat and cursed at them. At one point, a mob overcame the police barricade, but the Nine managed to get away safely.

To this point, the president had not wanted to interfere in what he saw strictly as a state matter. Finally on September 24, however, Eisenhower acted. Declaring "mob rule cannot be allowed to override the decisions of our courts," Eisenhower federalized the Arkansas National Guard and dispatched 1,000 troops from the 101st Airborne Division.

He was the first president since Andrew Johnson in the Reconstruction to use federal troops to protect the rights of African Americans. More concerned about enforcing federal law than protecting children, Eisenhower sent the troops to maintain peace and order, to defend presidential authority, and to uphold the law of the land — not necessarily to enforce desegregation. Of course, the president's actions outraged many Southern whites.

Eight of the Little Rock Nine remained at Central High the entire year, enduring the abuse. Arkansas NAACP president Daisy Bates became their mentor, and Ernie Green became the first African American to graduate from Central High School in Little Rock, Arkansas.

January 18, 1958

A clash between the Lumbee Indian tribe and the Ku Klux Klan breaks out in Robeson County, North Carolina.

The KKK had burned a cross on a number of lawns in the community, including that of a Lumbee woman, presumably because she had married a white man. The Klansmen had announced their plans to hold a membership rally in a field outside Maxton in Robeson County.

Between several hundred and 1,000 armed Lumbee tribesmen showed up at the rally site to demonstrate to the Klan how unwelcome they were. Many African American men of the community offered to lend their support as well. There was a confrontation, in which heated words were exchanged. Wild shots were fired, but the only casualty was a light bulb that was shattered by a stray bullet. The Klansmen scattered in the dark, apparently abandoning their flags and other paraphernalia as they sprinted for safety in the woods.

The incident made national headlines, with *Life* magazine carrying two separate articles on the subject. Photographs of the Indian men standing over the Klansmen's belongings accompanied the stories. Fervent letters — mostly in support of the Lumbee effort — poured in from all over the country. The Ku Klux Klan was reportedly never seen in Robeson County again.

June 30, 1958

The State of Alabama, in an attempt to curtail the activities of the National Association for the Advancement of Colored People, tried to compel the association to reveal the names and addresses of statewide members.

Fearing reprisals against its members, the NAACP refused Alabama's request, and the state filed an equity suit, enjoining the association from conducting further business.

The United States Supreme Court, in the case *NAACP v. Alabama*, ruled that an organization is not required to reveal its membership as a condition for doing business. The Court further ruled that Alabama's requirement was a violation of the constitutional rights of the membership to lawfully associate around common beliefs.

Justice John Harlan, in delivering the opinion of the court, wrote, "It is hardly a novel perception that compelled disclosure of affiliation with groups engaged in advocacy may constitute as effective a restraint on freedom of association as the forms of governmental action in the cases above were thought likely to produce upon the particular constitutional rights involved. This Court has recognized the vital relationship between freedom to associate and privacy in one's associations."

The State of Alabama had asked the NAACP to produce bank statements, deeds, leases, and other records, as well as the names of its members. The organization complied with the former requests, but drew the line when asked for names. The NAACP attorneys felt, and the Supreme Court agreed, that such a disclosure would severely curtail its membership from assembling to carry on the business of the NAACP.

September 3, 1958

Martin Luther King, Jr., is arrested in Montgomery, Alabama, charged with loitering and refusing to obey a police officer.

He had accompanied Ralph Abernathy, pastor of the First Baptist Church, to the Montgomery County Courthouse, where Abernathy was involved in a court case. A guard at the courthouse refused King entrance. As a fray ensued, the two policemen twisted King's arm behind him, frisked him and kneed him, called him several names, choked him, spun him around, kicked him, then locked him in a cell. The myopic policemen had no idea who he was.

The story quickly reached the national media, complete with photos. Police commissioner Clyde Sellers compounded the situation by saying the treatment meted to King was typical of the treatment given to prisoners at the county courthouse. Sellers made the case go to trial.

On September 5, with the national press crowding the courthouse, King was charged a fine of $10 and court costs, or 14 days in jail. King chose jail, reading a statement in court: "Your honor, I could not in good conscience pay a fine for an act that I did not commit, and above all for brutal treatment I did not deserve. I also make this decision because of my deep concern for the injustices and indignities that my people continue to experience.... The time has come when perhaps only the willing and nonviolent acts of suffering by the innocent can arouse this nation to wipe out the scourge of brutality and violence inflicted upon Negroes who seek only to walk with dignity before God and Man" (Oates, p. 136).

The entire episode provided great theater, revealing for the American people the kind of abuse African Americans experienced daily in courthouses throughout the country.

Commissioner Sellers ended up paying King's fine himself, to thwart what he saw as a King publicity stunt.

September 20, 1958

Martin Luther King, Jr., is stabbed by a black woman outside the National Broadcasting Company studios in New York.

King was rushed to Harlem Hospital, where physicians had to remove a rib and part of the breast bone to extract the knife blade. King would recover.

The news of the attack flashed throughout the world. Thousands of notes, letters, and telegrams poured into the hospital from all over the world. One particular letter from a white woman read, "Your voice is the only true voice of love today & we hear, we hear.... Please don't lose faith in us 'whites,' there are so many of us who are good & pray for your triumph" (Oates, p.139).

Meanwhile, the same month, King's book *Stride Toward Freedom* was released through Harper and Row publishers. Hailed by critics and the public, the book is in part a narrative about the bus boycott, in part autobiography, in part an argument for nonviolence and racial change. Eighteen thousand advance copies were sold, with total sales amounting to 60,000 in the United States, Great Britain, Sweden, India, and Japan.

September 29, 1958

The United States Supreme Court unanimously decides in *Cooper v. Aaron* that attempts by the governor or the legislature of Arkansas to resist court-ordered desegregation are unconstitutional.

The Court held that the constitutional right of children to be protected against segregation superseded the state's right to uphold segregation. This decision supported the Court mandate in *Brown v. Board of Education of Topeka, Kansas*, to end segregation in public schools.

Arkansas had argued it was not bound by the Supreme Court's decision in *Brown v. Board of Education*, since it was not a party to the original suit. The state also argued that the governor of Arkansas had as much right to interpret the Constitution as the Supreme Court.

In an unusual step to emphasize the importance of the remarks, all nine justices signed the shared opinion in *Cooper v. Aaron*, as the Supreme Court reasserted itself as the ultimate interpreter of the Constitution. The opinion further reads: "State support of segregated schools through any arrangement, management, funds, or property cannot be squared with the [Fourteenth] Amendment's command that no State shall deny to any person within its jurisdiction the equal protection of the laws. The right of a student not to be segregated on racial grounds in schools so maintained is indeed so fundamental and pervasive that it is embraced in the concept of due process of law."

The *Cooper v. Aaron* case marked the end of the Supreme Court's period of waiting, declared in Brown II, for the states to implement desegregation with "all deliberate speed." The Warren court now began handing down a stream of decisions facilitating integration of American schools.

December 1, 1958

The musical play *Flower Drum Song* opens at the St. James Theater in New York City.

Written by Oscar Hammerstein II and Joseph Fields, with music by Richard Rodgers and Oscar Hammerstein II, the musical was based on the novel by C.Y. Lee. Among the lesser known of the Rodgers and Hammerstein musicals, its story is set in San Francisco's Chinatown. The first musical to present Chinese Americans in a reasonable light, it concerns the generation gap between the Old World and the New World. The film version, released in 1961 by Universal-International, starred Nancy Kwan and Jack Soo.

August 21, 1959

Hawaii becomes the fiftieth state of the Union.

Soon after, Daniel Inouye was elected to the House of Representatives for the new state. In three years, he was elected to the Senate, holding the position for the next 40 years. Inouye was the first Japanese American elected to the Senate.

Born in Honolulu, Hawaii, in 1924, Inouye had grown up with dreams of becoming a doctor. But in March 1943, he enlisted in the United States Army's 442nd Regimental Combat Team. While fighting in 1945 near San Terenzo, Italy, with the 422nd, Lieutenant Inouye lost his right arm to a grenade, ending his hope for a career in medicine. After spending 20 months in army hospitals, he returned home a captain, with a Distinguished Service Cross, a Bronze Star, a Purple Heart with cluster, and 12 other citations and medals.

After attending George Washington University Law School, Inouye returned to Hawaii, where he broke into politics with stints in the Territorial House of Representatives and the Territorial Senate of Hawaii.

February 2, 1960

Lunch counter sit-ins start a movement.

Four black students from A&T College in Greensboro, North Carolina, marched into a Woolworth's department store. They sat at the lunch counter, refusing to leave unless served. Inspired by their courage, hundreds of students — black and white — assailed the counter for the next week. The demonstration was reminiscent of the CORE sit-ins engineered in the forties and fifties, except that this particular incident drew a great deal of media attention in newspapers and on television. The Greensboro Woolworth's counter event inspired similar protests across the country, ushering in an era of celebrated college student sit-ins.

July 3, 1960

Muddy Waters brings the blues to the Newport Jazz Festival at Newport, Rhode Island.

His famed Chicago blues band featured Otis Spann on piano, Pat Hare and Jimmy Rogers on guitar, Francis Clay on drums, and James Cotton on harmonica. Waters was the first blues performer to play at the famed music festival, introducing his extraordinary brand of music to a largely white audience. One year previous, the same brilliant blues band had been the first of its kind to play at Carnegie Hall in New York City.

Born McKinley Morganfield in April of 1915 in Rolling Fork, Mississippi, he changed his name presumably because he like to play in the muddy Mississippi. As a child he worked as a farm laborer, taking up the harmonica at the age of 13. Four years later he began to play guitar, imitating the popular "bottleneck" style of guitar accompaniment. He began playing at all venues, from juke joints to company picnics, perfecting his unique instrumental and vocal styles.

Waters moved to Chicago in 1943, where in 1948 he began his recording career while working as a truck driver. The pioneer of the Chicago blues scene, Waters' innovative use of guitar amplification brought a new sound to American music. Among his ground-breaking, classic records were "I Can't Be Satisfied," " I Feel Like Going Home," "Got My Mojo Workin,'" and "Rollin' Stone"— the song from which British band the Rolling Stones would take its name.

His particular brand of music influenced everyone from the Beatles to Bob Dylan and the Rolling Stones. Waters died in his sleep on April 30, 1983.

April 9, 1961

Rita Moreno is named Best Supporting Actress at the Academy Award ceremony for her portrayal of Anita in Leonard Bernstein's *West Side Story*.

Born Rosita Dolores Alverio in Humacao, Puerto Rico, in 1931, Moreno was the first actress to win the Oscar (*West Side Story*, 1961), the Tony Award (*The Ritz*, 1975), the Emmy Award (*The Muppet Show*, 1977; *The Rockford Files*, 1978), and a Grammy Award (Sound track to *The Electric Company*, 1972).

Five years previous, Anthony Quinn had won the Oscar for his portrayal of Vincent Van Gogh in *Lust for Life*. Quinn had also won in 1952 for the role of Emil Zapata's brother in *Viva Zapata!*

May 4, 1961

The Congress of Racial Equality (CORE) organizes the Freedom Rides, patterned after the Journey of Reconciliation in 1945.

Despite Supreme Court decisions in 1946 and 1961 (*Boynton v. Virginia*) that outlawed the segregation of buses, trains, and stations, Southern bus terminals remained adamantly segregated. The Freedom Rides featured two buses, with CORE passengers determined to test bus terminals between Washington, D.C., and New Orleans to determine the level of integration.

The first Freedom Ride included seven black riders and six white passengers. When it arrived in Anniston, Alabama, on Mother's Day, an angry mob surrounded the bus, setting it on fire while severely beating the riders. The second bus made it to Birmingham, only to be met by a mob of Klansmen, who beat them with pipes, bats, and chains.

The Freedom Rides drew national media attention, as Attorney General Robert Kennedy tried to work behind the scenes to support the Freedom Riders. Meanwhile, badly beaten, the Riders canceled the remainder of the trip and flew to New Orleans. But on May 20, the Freedom Rides were taken up by student activists from the newly formed Student Nonviolent Coordinating Committee (SNCC).

Organized in April 1960 by Ella Baker — director of the Atlanta chapter of the Southern Christian Leadership Conference — the SNCC was composed of activists in more than 50 high schools and colleges in the South. The SNCC emphasized a more aggressive, militant style than King's Southern Christian Leadership Conference, relying more on grassroots, group-oriented protests.

The next Freedom Ride was organized in Birmingham, headed for Montgomery. Among the riders was John Lewis, future leader of the SNCC and future United States congressman from Georgia. In Montgomery, the students were met by a thousand armed whites who beat them with pipes and clubs, with no police in sight. Martin Luther King, Jr., flew to Montgomery to be with them as the violence increased. Finally, Robert Kennedy sent federal marshals and the Alabama National Guard to quell the outbursts.

Despite reluctance from King and other organizers, the Freedom Rides continued through the South through the summer of 1963. Hundreds of riders were arrested and jailed. Meanwhile, the extreme violence of Southern white assailants, and the indifference shown by local police and government entities — under the glaring scrutiny of the media — caused a national outcry.

Ultimately, the Freedom Rides and organized sit-ins tolled the passing bell for Jim Crow policies in Southern bus facilities. At the request of Robert Kennedy, the Interstate Commerce Commission issued regulations, effective November 1961, to integrate transportation facilities throughout the South.

December 11, 1961

In the case of *Garner v. Louisiana*, the United States Supreme Court decides that a group of black protesters, simply by sitting at a segregated lunch counter, had not disturbed the peace as the State of Louisiana had asserted.

The Court ruled that since the protesters had behaved in an orderly manner, they had not violated Louisiana's breach of peace statute. The Court ruled furthermore that the lower court's ruling had been in violation of the Fourteenth Amendment.

Justice John Marshall Harlan said that even though the demonstrations had been over the owner's objections, the public had a constitutional right to conduct a sit-in in an enterprise that operated in the public interest and domain.

July 24, 1962

A court decision in favor of Martin Luther King, Jr., inflames a violent chain of events.

The Fifth Circuit Court of Appeals overturned an injunction granted four days earlier by U.S. district judge J. Robert Elliot, an avowed segregationist, enjoining Martin Luther King, Jr., and other civil rights activists from all forms of civil disobedience. That night, in Albany, Georgia, the pregnant wife of a movement leader was knocked unconscious by a sheriff's deputy, who kicked her so hard she miscarried. By nightfall, 2,000 blacks rioted, fighting police with bottles and stones. The governor sent in 12,000 National Guard troops to restore order. King's efforts for integration were upended by the violence.

October 2, 1962

United States Marshals, armed with a federal court order, accompany James Meredith, an Air Force veteran, as he attempts to enroll at the University of Mississippi at Oxford.

Governor Ross Barnett and a cadre of state troopers turned them away, as a mob of white students chanted, "Glory, glory segregation," to the tune of the "Battle Hymn of the Republic."

After futile attempts by President John F. Kennedy to work with the governor, Meredith and the federal marshals finally attempted to enter again. Gunfire broke out among the white resistors. In the ensuing battle, several were killed and 375 injured. President Kennedy dispatched federal troops, restoring order. Meredith was finally enrolled, but marshals continued to escort him to class, where white students repeatedly refused to sit near him. Meredith graduated from the institution in 1964.

Two years later, Meredith published his first book, *Three Years in Mis-*

sissippi, in which he recounts his experiences at Ole Miss. In 1966 he engaged in his own "March Against Fear" from Memphis, Tennessee, to Jackson, Mississippi, to demonstrate against the physical violence experienced by African Americans on a daily basis. During the march, he was shot by a sniper and hospitalized. Civil rights leaders such as Martin Luther King, Jr., and Stokely Carmichael took up the march for him, with Meredith rejoining 20 days later.

March 21, 1963

The movie version of Harper Lee's classic novel, *To Kill a Mockingbird*, premieres in Mobile, Alabama.

Although Lee's home town of Monroeville had campaigned for the premiere, the film played in Mobile until March 27, then appeared in Monroeville the following week. Lee was on hand for the premiere.

It was unlike any major motion picture released before. Lee's story follows the family and neighborhood of attorney Atticus Finch as he labors to defend a black man in an Alabama town, falsely accused of the rape of a white woman. Told from the point of view of Finch's six-year-old daughter, Jean Louise "Scout" Finch, the book and subsequent movie would become staples in American schools. *To Kill a Mockingbird* would often provide an elementary student's first introduction to the concepts of racial justice, misunderstanding, and prejudice.

Nelle Harper Lee was born in Monroeville, Alabama, on April 28, 1926. The youngest of four children born to Amasa and Frances Lee, she attended Huntington College from 1944 to 1945. She studied law at the University of Alabama from 1945 to 1949, then studied one year at Oxford University in England. She moved into an apartment in New York City in the 1950s and worked as an airline clerk.

Lee submitted the "Mockingbird" manuscript to publisher J.B. Lippincott Company in 1957. She spent another two and half years rewriting it before its eventual publication. Although she subsequently had articles published in *Vogue* and *McCall's* magazines, *To Kill a Mockingbird* turned out to be her only published book. Nevertheless, as a tribute to the story's power and importance in American literature, Harper Lee won the 1960 Pulitzer Prize for Literature. Following the publication, the Alabama legislature passed a resolution congratulating Lee for her success. In 1966, Lee was named by President Lyndon Johnson to the National Council for the Arts.

The film starred Brock Peters as Tom Robinson, Mary Badham as Scout, Robert Duvall as Boo Radley, and Gregory Peck as Atticus Finch. Peck won the 1962 Academy Award for Best Actor for the film.

April 16, 1963

Martin Luther King, Jr., issues the "Birmingham Manifesto," demanding that all lunch counters, restrooms, department and variety stores, and drinking fountains in downtown Birmingham, Alabama, be desegregated.

He insisted that Negroes be hired in local business and industry, and that a biracial committee be established to work out a schedule for desegregation in other areas of city life. The subsequent series of demonstrations and the responses by the Birmingham establishment would be called "the battle for the soul of Birmingham."

Police Commissioner Eugene "Bull" Connor had stood as the primary embodiment of the Southern opposition to King's campaign in Birmingham. Connor had just been defeated by Albert Bothwell for mayor of Birmingham. However, Connor had refused to vacate his commissioner's office, saying he had been elected to that post to serve through 1965.

King's corps staged a series of nonviolent sit-ins and demonstrations, attracting a horde of media to witness the escalating fracas. King had faced some opposition among local blacks, who complained about the outsider while wanting to give mayor-elect Bothwell a chance. Nevertheless, the demonstrations commenced, directly violating a state injunction against conducting such protests. Finally, King himself was jailed by Commissioner Connor on April 12.

While holed up in his cell, King composed his "Letter from Jail," subsequently considered one of the greatest pieces of literature produced by the civil rights movement. In the letter, which would be circulated in hundreds of periodicals throughout the country, King expounded on the importance of the Birmingham intervention, quieting the protests of the local clergy against the outsider's "untimely and disquieting" demonstrations (Oates, p. 224).

"We have waited for more than 340 years for our constitutional and God-given rights," King wrote. "The nations of Asia and Africa are moving with jet-like speed toward gaining political independence, but we still creep at a horse and buggy pace toward gaining a cup of coffee at a lunch counter. Perhaps it is easy for those who have never felt the stinging darts of segregation to say 'Wait.' But when you have seen vicious mobs lynch your mothers and fathers at will and drown your sisters and brothers at whim; when you have seen hate filled policemen curse, kick, and even kill your black brothers and sisters; when you see the vast majority of your twenty million Negro brothers smothering in an airtight cage of poverty in the midst of an affluent society; when you suddenly find your tongue twisted and your speech stammering as you seek to explain to your six-year-old daughter why she

can't go to the public amusement park that has just been advertised on television ... when your name becomes 'nigger,' your middle name becomes 'boy'
... then you will understand why we find it difficult to wait" (Oates, p. 224).

King was at last released from jail on April 20, as the protests continued. Finally on May 2 and 3, D-Day came to Birmingham. Thousands of
school children joined their parents and other adults to march in the streets
of Alabama city. More than 900 children were arrested, prompting local
police to use school buses to transport them. Finally, fire hoses and police
dogs were turned on the crowd, all before the unblinking cameras of a global
media. Cries of indignation broke out across the land and around the world.

On May 5, with more than 3,000 young people on a prayer pilgrimage to the Birmingham jail, the protesters were once again faced with fire
hoses. This time, for whatever reason, the firemen refused to turn them on.
By May 6, more than 3,000 African Americans were confined inside the
Birmingham jails, which were full and unable to handle any more. Condemned in the world media, with the city's economy suffering, Birmingham
businessmen decided to negotiate with King. On May 10 an accord was
reached. Within 90 days, Birmingham — long considered the staunchest bas-
tion of segregation in the South — integrated its lunch counters, its restrooms, its fitting rooms, its drinking fountains.

June 12, 1963

Mississippi NAACP leader Medgar Evers is assassinated in Jackson,
Mississippi, by a white supremacist named Byron De La Beckwith, in front
of Evers' Jackson home.

Born in Decatur, Mississippi, Evers had earned his bachelor's degree at
Alcorn State University. Mississippi's best known civil rights champion, Evers
served on the state staff of the National Association for the Advancement of
Colored People from 1954 to 1963.

The assassination of Medgar Evers occurred the day after President John
F. Kennedy had addressed the nation on the subject of civil rights, an address
many civil rights supporters considered too late in coming. Appealing to the
consciences of all Americans, particularly those of the Southern whites,
Kennedy said, "The heart of the question is whether all Americans are to be
afforded equal rights and equal opportunities.... We say we are the land of
the free. We are, except for Negroes. The time has come for America to
remove the blight of racial discrimination and fulfill her brilliant promise"
(Oates, p. 245).

The death of Evers seemed to be the Southern segregationists' answer.
Ten days after the murder, police arrested Beckwith; his fingerprints were

found on the murder weapon. Beckwith was tried by all-white juries twice; neither jury reached a verdict, and the charges were dropped. Finally, new-found evidence reopened the case in 1989. Before a jury composed of eight African Americans and four whites, Beckwith was finally convicted.

August 27, 1963

W.E.B. Du Bois dies in Accra, Ghana, in Africa, where he would be given a state funeral.

Having become a communist, he had grown discouraged by the war-mongering of the United States, renounced his citizenship, and moved to Ghana earlier that year.

Sixty years previous, Du Bois had insisted that African Americans — as well as all Americans — had basic rights that did not have to be proven or earned but must be considered inalienable. He seemed to time his death well: the next day was to be the March on Washington — an event that would probably not have happened had his philosophy not influenced so many Americans.

With the death of Du Bois, there appeared to be a passing of the torch.

August 28, 1963

At the pinnacle of the 1960s civil rights movement, Dr. Martin Luther King, Jr., delivers his profoundly stirring "I Have a Dream" speech.

The moment came at the end of the March on Washington for jobs and freedom. A. Philip Randolf— the current vice president of the AFL-CIO who had dreamed of a massive march on Washington 22 years previous — had helped to organize the unprecedented event to reinforce the effective-ness of African Americans working together toward a common goal.

On the steps of the Lincoln Memorial, King addressed more than 250,000 listeners, including celebrities such as Sammy Davis, Jr., Ossie Davis, Lena Horne, Harry Belafonte, and Josephine Baker. Before a mes-merized crowd, King's voice boomed vigorously:

> I say to you today, my friends, that in spite of the difficulties and frustrations of the moment, I still have a dream … I have a dream that one day this nation will rise up and live up to the true meaning of its creed: "We hold these truths to be self-evident — that all men are created equal."
>
> When we let freedom ring, when we let it ring from every village and every hamlet, from every state and every city, we will be able to speed up the day when all God's children, black men and white

men, Jews and Gentiles, Protestants and Catholics, will be able to join hands and sing in the words of the old Negro spiritual, "Free at last! Free at last! Thank God Almighty, we are free at last!" [Oates, p. 261].

September 15, 1963

Four young African American girls — Denise McNair, 11, and Cynthia Wesley, Carole Robertson, and Addie Mae Collins, all 14 — are killed by a bomb that explodes at the Sixteenth Street Baptist Church in Birmingham, Alabama.

Four hundred had been gathered for Sunday worship when the explosion tore a hole in the side of the church. While the community searched the rubble, not one white government representative came to the church to offer condolences or even to observe.

Ku Klux Klansman Robert Edward Chambliss was arrested, but no charges were leveled, and he was set free. In 1976, the case was re-opened by Alabama attorney general Bill Baxley. The subsequent trial led to the conviction of Chambliss 13 years after the incident.

November 22, 1963

President John F. Kennedy is assassinated at 12:30 P.M., during a motorcade in downtown Dallas, Texas.

In shadow of the Texas School Book Depository building, in a sequence of six to eight seconds, Kennedy was hit by at least one bullet in the back, the neck, and the back of the head. Texas governor John Connelly was struck in the shoulder, the wrist, and the leg. The president was raced to Parkland Memorial Hospital four miles away.

The unforgettable November 25 funeral march in Washington D.C., the first event of its kind broadcast on national television, united a nation in its grief. Millions of viewers were riveted to their black and white sets. Although Kennedy had been, in the opinion of many civil rights advocates, too slow and cautious in his work for civil rights, the assassination may have destroyed an important symbol of youth and possibilities.

Two days later, on November 27, Lyndon Baines Johnson assumed the office of president of the United States. Addressing Congress for the first time, Johnson pledged to continue the policies of Kennedy, particularly in the area of civil rights. "No memorial oration or eulogy," Johnson would say, "could more eloquently honor President Kennedy's memory than the earliest possible passage of the civil rights bill for which he fought so long" (Kohn, p. 169).

December 1, 1963

Malcolm X implies racist motives for the assassination of President Kennedy.

Nine days after the death of President Kennedy, Malcolm X addresses a crowd of seven hundred at the Manhattan Center. When someone asks him thoughts on the assassination of the president, Malcolm X utters his now famous phase, "Chickens coming home to roost never make me sad; they've always made me glad" (Perry, p. 241). On the day of the assassination, Malcolm X had characterized Kennedy as a segregationist, calling his brother Kennedys the "KKK." At the Manhattan Center, Malcolm X espoused themes of vengeance from Allah, who he said would wreak justice on white America.

In the wake of the battle for the soul of Birmingham, Malcolm X — drawing a young audience growing increasingly impatient with what was seen as incremental progress by King and his followers — had stepped up his rhetorical criticism of the Baptist preacher. He railed against the Birmingham project and King's popularity, saying, "The white man pays Reverend Martin Luther King, subsidized Reverend Martin Luther King, so the Reverend Martin Luther King can continue to teach the Negroes to be defenseless" (Perry, p. 237). In one fiery speech, he said, "You don't have a peaceful revolution. You don't have a turn-the-other-cheek revolution. There is no such thing as a nonviolent revolution.... Revolution is bloody. Revolution is hostile. Revolution knows no compromise. Revolution overturns and destroys everything that gets in its way" (Perry, p. 237).

Malcolm X intensified his black separatist stance, calling King's reliance on help from the federal government like "asking the fox to protect you from the wolf" (Oates, p. 252). He continued to attract followers who felt a more aggressive, militant stance should be taken to secure civil rights for African Americans.

Malcolm X offered an alternative voice to King, embracing African culture and heritage, and seeking to separate from white America rather than to find a way to live within it. Malcolm X preached that Southern whites were actually morally superior to Northern whites because at least they were "honestly racist."

His statements about the newly venerated, martyred Kennedy, however, turned out to be a line some said he should not have crossed. Even for Elijah Muhammad, who had often uttered the phrase "white devils," the vilification of the fallen president by Malcolm X was a public relations fiasco the Nation of Islam could not afford. Muhammad censured his most popular disciple, forbidding him to speak publicly for 90 days.

March 9, 1964

In the case *New York Times Company v. Sullivan*, the United States Supreme Court upholds the rights of free speech and press over a state's power to award damages in a libel suit brought on by a public official.

L.B. Sullivan, an elected commissioner in Montgomery, Alabama, had sued the *New York Times* for publishing an advertisement alleging that Alabama election officials had harassed black civil rights workers.

The Court unanimously decided that the First and Fourteenth Amendments to the Constitution assured Americans the right to criticize the official conduct of public officials. The Court stated that such criticisms, even if they contained factual errors, would not be punishable unless malice could be proven.

Justice William J. Brennan, in his opinion for the unanimous court, wrote, "We consider this case against the background of a profound national commitment to the principle that debate on public issues should be uninhibited, robust, and wide-open, and that it may well include vehement, caustic, and sometimes unpleasantly sharp attacks on government and public officials ... erroneous statement is inevitable in free debate," he continued, adding that even false statements must therefore "be protected if the freedoms of expression are to have the breathing space that they need ... to survive."

New York Times Company v. Sullivan was regarded as a landmark decision in relation not only to the issue of free speech but to the right of all Americans to openly debate the elements of civil rights and racial equality.

April 16, 1964

At the Academy Awards presentation at Santa Monica Civic Auditorium, Sidney Poitier wins the Best Actor Oscar for *Lilies of the Field*.

Poitier captured the award for his charming role as handy man Homer Smith, who meets a group of refugee nuns from Germany and helps them to build a chapel in the desert of Arizona. Poitier was the first African American to win the Best Actor award.

Born in Miami in 1924 of Bahamian parents, Poitier was raised in the Bahamas, coming to the United States without a penny to his name. Although his career was full of racially-charged roles, he won the Oscar in 1964 for a role that could have been played by anyone — of any cultural background. Perhaps due to his arrival at the right time in history, along with his personal charisma and charm, Poitier was the first African American to receive widespread acclaim for his acting ability alone.

Two movies Poitier made later in the decade would consummately reflect the life and times of the sixties.

May 21, 1964

Completing the pilgrimage required by his faith, Malcolm X visits Mecca, Saudi Arabia, the spiritual center of Islam.

He met Prince Faisal of Arabia, who criticized the Black Muslim movement. Malcolm X decided to follow Sunni Islam, adopting the name el-Hajj Malik el-Shabazz. At the same time, Malcolm X decided to break away from Elijah Muhammad's Nation of Islam, forming his own group, the Organization of Afro-American Unity.

Even prior to the pilgrimage, the growing rift between Malcolm X and Elijah Muhammad had become a chasm. Malcolm X had resented Muhammad's nonpolitical stance, believing African Americans must become politically active to change the landscape of society. He also had seen Muhammad's alleged premarital sexual activity and greed as antithetic to his Islamic beliefs.

The pilgrimage seemed to soften the perspective of Malcolm X, who adopted a more forgiving tone, rejecting the idea that all whites are devils. He also began taking a more conciliatory tone toward Martin Luther King, Jr.'s nonviolent approach to civil rights. A year later, when he and King visited Selma, Alabama, at the same time, Malcolm X sent a message through King's wife, Coretta, saying, "I want Dr. King to know that I didn't come to Selma to make his job difficult. I really did come thinking I could make it easier. If the white people realize what the alternative is, perhaps they will be more willing to hear Dr. King" (Oates, p. 341).

His new more conciliatory demeanor turned previous followers away, while angering former fellow members of the Nation of Islam.

July 2, 1964

The United States Congress passes the strongest civil rights legislation since the Reconstruction.

The Civil Rights Act of 1964 prohibited discrimination in all public accommodations, including hotels, gas stations, restaurants, and theaters. In establishing the Equal Employment Opportunity Commission, the act also prohibited hiring, firing, or otherwise discriminating in the workplace based on race, religion, or sex. It also ensured standardized state voting qualifications.

September 1, 1964

San Francisco Giants reliever Masanori Murakami becomes the first Japanese player in major league history.

He posted a record of 5–1, with a 3.43 earned run average. After he pitched two seasons, his family convinced him to return to the Japanese League.

January 20, 1965

At his inauguration as president of the United States following his landslide election, Lyndon Baines Johnson reiterates his campaign goal of creating a "Great Society" based on justice, liberty, and union, addressing the plight of the minorities in America.

"In a land of great wealth," he said, "families must not live in hopeless poverty. In a land rich in harvest, children must not go hungry. In a land of healing miracles, neighbors must not suffer and die unattended. In a great land of learning and scholars, young people must be taught to read and write."

February 21, 1965

Malcolm X is assassinated at a rally in the Audubon Ballroom, Harlem, New York.

Having known of his imminent death, Malcolm X nonetheless had insisted on attending the rally unprotected by New York's police. His wife Betty Shabazz — whom he had married in 1958 — sat among the audience.

According to police reports, Black Muslim Thomas 15X Johnson perforated his chest with shotgun pellets, while fellow Black Muslims Norman 3X Butler and Talmadge Hayer pumped his body with pistol fire. The three Nation of Islam members were identified as the killers, although the general consensus alleged that many more entities might have been involved.

The Nation of Islam was indicted as the force behind the murder, as Black Muslims condemned Malcolm X as a hypocrite and a traitor for his criticisms of Elijah Muhammad. Others pointed to a conspiracy involving police, the Federal Bureau of Investigation, and the Central Intelligence Agency. Still others indicted drug dealers, and even leftist communist groups. In any case, the result remained the same: the death of America's prophet for black power and black separatism.

Shortly after his death, Grove Press released *The Autobiography of Malcolm X*, written by future *Roots* author Alex Haley. This book would eventually sell millions of copies worldwide.

In summarizing the impact of Malcolm X, another biographer, Bruce Perry, writes: "Malcolm X fathered no legislation. He engineered no stunning Supreme Court victories of political campaigns. He scored no electoral triumphs. Yet, because of the way he articulated his followers' grievances and anger, the impact he had upon the body politic was enormous. He mobilized black America's dormant rage and put it to work politically. He made clear the price white America would have to pay if it did not accede to black America's legitimate demands. By transforming black fear into white fear, he irrevocably altered America's political landscape" (Perry, p. 380).

March 7, 1965

On what would come to be known as Bloody Sunday, more than 500 people leave for a silent march, one of many taking place over six weeks in and around the central Alabama city of Selma, in support of voting rights for blacks.

The 50-mile march was to stretch from Selma, Alabama, to Montgomery, Alabama, along Highway 80, known as Jefferson Davis Highway. Led by a future congressman and current leader of the SNCC, John Lewis, the marchers left Brown Chapel to be confronted by Dallas County sheriff James Clark, with his deputized posse and state troopers, wearing gas masks and hardhats. After ordering the marchers to disperse, the troopers attacked them with billy clubs and tear gas. Lewis had his skull fractured, as "they shoved the front ranks back like dominoes ... hammered women and men alike" (Oates, p. 348). Troopers chased African Americans through the neighborhoods of Selma, leaving 70 hospitalized.

Newspapers and televisions stations flashed the story of Bloody Sunday in Selma, shaking the nation more than any previous incident, even more than Birmingham. Thousands of civil rights supporters in cities across the county poured into the streets, condemning the brutality in central Alabama.

On March 15, President Lyndon Johnson — the former schoolteacher from Texas — vehemently addressed Congress concerning the violence in Selma, and the issue of voting rights for African Americans. "There must be no delay, or no hesitation, or no compromise," Johnson declared. "What happened in Selma is part of a far larger movement ... the effort of American Negroes to secure for themselves the blessings of American life.... Their cause is our cause, too. Because it's not just Negroes, but really it's all of us who must overcome the crippling legacy of bigotry and injustice.... And we shall overcome" (Oates, p. 355). He went on to say, "Should we defeat every enemy, double our wealth and conquer the stars, and still be unequal to this issue, then we will have failed as a nation and people" (Krebs, *New York Times*, p.13).

Meanwhile, Martin Luther King, Jr., called upon clergy from around the country to descend on Selma on March 21, to complete the march attempted on March 7. King left Selma with a throng of 3,200; the crowd swelled beyond 25,000 in Montgomery. After tramping through central Alabama for four days, King and Ralph Abernathy led the March 26 tour through the state capital, with 4,000 National Guard and United States Army troops protecting them. The huge throng descended on the state capital to present Governor George Wallace with a petition calling for equal voting rights and the end to police brutality. It was the largest demonstration ever held in the state of Alabama.

Although Wallace never met with them, the protest did not go unheeded. On August 6, 1965, the United States Congress passed landmark legislation designed to enforce the Fifteenth Amendment, called the Voting Rights Act of 1965. The act suspended the use of literacy, educational, moral and other tests in areas where they had been used to deny the right to vote on the basis of color or race. These provisions went a long way toward removing obstacles to registration and voting that faced all minorities — particularly those regarding illiteracy in English. The act also authorized federal examiners to register voters in such areas, providing criminal penalties for intimidating, threatening, or coercing any person for voting or attempting to vote. It also abolished the poll tax.

In 1966, the Supreme Court upheld the constitutionality of the Voting Rights Act in *South Carolina v. Katzenbach* and *Katzenbach v. Morgan*.

August 11, 1965

The Watts riots flare in Los Angeles.

On a steamy southern California evening, a white policeman pulled over a young black man for drunk driving in the Watts district of east Los Angeles, California. An angry crowd gathered, quickly growing louder and angrier as it incited the police officer. The patrolman called for reinforcements, which were met with bottles and stones. The crowd grew into a mob, and then the situation exploded.

The Watts neighborhood resembled many inner-city, mostly nonwhite communities throughout the country. Poverty, high crime, unemployment, and widespread substance abuse characterized the district. In the wake of civil unrest throughout the country, fueled by the assassination of Malcolm X and other black leaders, inner-city residents had seemed to grow increasingly impatient and militant in the quest for civil rights. Add the heat wave drenching southern California in August of 1965, and the area had become a tinder box just waiting for a match.

The next night, a mob of thousands formed; hostile, angry, and soon beyond control. Molotov cocktails exploded along with the full-blown street rebellion. Looters roamed through storefronts, grabbing weapons with which to fire on police and firefighters. The mob frenzy overwhelmed the situation, and soon the Watts riots erupted in flames amid calls for Black Power.

For six days the rioting continued, leaving much of the district in rubble and ashes. Thirty-four people were killed and more than 1,000 injured; there was $35 million in damage. Finally, the Watts area was sealed off by 4,000 National Guardsmen sent in to control the rioting.

The Watts riots were the predecessors for mob violence throughout the West and Northeast in the following four years. In June of 1966, for example, following the shooting of a youth by a policeman, the Puerto Rican community rioted for two days in Chicago. The violence led to an airing of grievances by the community on issues of housing, education, and discrimination. The mayor's administration apparently listened to the grievances, appointing a member of the Puerto Rican community to the Committee on Human Relations.

At one time or another the cities of Newark, New Jersey; Detroit, Michigan; Hartford, Connecticut; San Diego, California; Philadelphia, Pennsylvania; and Springfield, Massachusetts also erupted in violence, as African Americans and other people of color displayed the displeasure at their social plight. In more than 100 riots between 1965 and 1968, more than 8,000 were killed or injured.

Reflecting the more militant generation of civil rights leaders, Floyd McKissick was named head of the Congress of Racial Equality, while Stokely Carmichael became chairman of the Student Nonviolent Coordinating Committee. McKissick, an attorney from North Carolina, advocated the need for African Americans to attain political and economic power on their own.

Stokely Carmichael, however, had just begun to exert his influence on the country. Born in Trinidad in 1941, he had grown up in Harlem, graduating from Howard University in 1964. He would make his famous "Black Power" speech in the midst of James Meredith's March Against Fear in 1966. A student of Malcolm X, he vehemently deplored the nonviolence movement as ineffective and actually supportive of the white man's oppressive policies. He went on to write *Black Power* in 1967, with Charles Hamilton, and become prime minister of the Black Panther Party in 1968.

September 15, 1965

I Spy premieres on the National Broadcasting Company, with Bill Cosby — as Alexander Scott — becoming the first African American to co-star in a dramatic series.

The show aired from 1965 to 1968, launching Cosby's extraordinary career on American television. To NBC's surprise, only three local affiliates — Savannah, Georgia; Albany, Georgia; and Daytona Beach, Florida — refused to air the series.

The role of Alexander Scott proved important to the evolving portrayal of African Americans on television. It revealed a mature and capable man in an important position, in an international setting. It depicted an African American male as a romantic figure, presenting, in one episode, the first kiss between a black man and an Asian woman. Alexander Scott appeared as an intelligent, sophisticated, cosmopolitan individual. Bill Cosby won three Emmy Awards for his portrayal, helping to create the possibility of other such roles on television.

September 16, 1965

Cesar Chavez, along with Dolores Huerta, organizes the successful Delano grape strike, the first national boycott of table grapes in the country.

On September 8, Filipino workers had demanded better wages, walking out on the Delano, California, area grape growers. More than 5,000 workers walked off their jobs in the protest, which included a 340-mile march in 1966 from Delano to Sacramento. Soon afterwards, the United Farm Workers were recognized by the AFL-CIO.

In 1962, Chavez and Huerta — known for her protests against the Bracero program and against toxic pesticides that threatened farm workers — had founded the National Farm Workers Association, the predecessor to the United Farm Workers union. From Delano, the UFW drew international attention to the plight of migrant farmers.

Through nonviolent strategies such as protests, pickets, strikes, and public fasts, Chavez and the UFW raised national awareness concerning issues such as nondiscrimination, better pay, and better working conditions for the farm laborer, a mainstay of United States agriculture for most of the twentieth century.

The UFW's renowned symbol, the black and red eagle, was designed by brother Richard Chavez, with the colors chosen by Cesar. The image of the eagle, along with the slogans *Huelga* (strike) and *Viva La Causa* (Long live our cause), became associated with the UFW worldwide.

In 1968, Chavez conducted the first of his public fasts, attracting the national media and further raising consciousness over his cause. Going 25 days with only water, Chavez repeated the gesture in 1972, living 24 days with only water.

October 3, 1965

Immigration quotas based on national origin are ended.

President Lyndon Johnson, in the shadow of the Statue of Liberty, signed into law the Immigrant Act of 1965, also known as the Hart-Celler Act. Designed by bill sponsor New York congressman Emanuel Celler, the legislation ended the national quota system set up by the Immigrant Quota Acts of 1921 and 1924.

The old system had designated certain numbers of immigrants to be allowed from certain countries of origin. The new system primarily focused on work skills and family reunification, giving preference to relatives of American citizens. For the first time, the act set annual ceilings of 120,000 immigrants from the Western Hemisphere, while it set a limit of 170,000 from the rest of the world. The new system also favored permanent resident aliens with special job skills, particularly in occupations for which there was an insufficient labor supply.

The Hart-Celler Act signified the beginning of a significant immigration of Asian Indians to the United States, particularly those in the high technology electronic industries. After the passage of the Hart-Celler Act, more than 96,000 Asian Indians immigrated to United States. Between 1870 and 1965, about 19,000 had come to America from India.

September 8, 1966

Star Trek brings interracial interaction to television.

Perhaps as a positive omen of a hopeful future, the dramatic science fiction television series *Star Trek* debuted on the National Broadcasting Company, offering the American television audience its first prime time multiracial cast. This cast featured George Takei as the Japanese Mr. Hikaru Sulu, Nichelle Nichols as Lt. Nyoto Uhura from Africa, James Doohan as Lieutenant Commander Montgomery Scott, Walter Koenig as Russian ensign Pavel Chekov, and Leonard Nimoy as the extraterrestrial Mr. Spock.

One particular episode further shattered previous taboo areas on television. In "Plato's Stepchildren"—which aired November 22, 1968—the characters portrayed by Nichelle Nichols (Lt. Uhura) and William Shatner (Captain Kirk) engaged in television's first black-white kiss. The episode generated the greatest volume of fan mail to date for the series, the vast majority of which showed enthusiastic support for the scene.

The series—the creative masterpiece of Gene Roddenberry—continued for more than 37 years, in the forms of dramatic television and movie spin-offs. With its multiracial, multispecies cast, the series provided Americans with a positive glimpse into the future. The show not only depicted the characters as complex, feeling, capable individuals but presented them in mature, intelligent, and some times romantic relationships with each other. More importantly, a primary theme of the *Star Trek* phenomenon projected a future in which race — indeed, species — is simply not a discriminatory factor. In the earth of *Star Trek*, racism, nationalism, poverty, illiteracy — all social plagues of the sixties — have become obsolete ideas from a distant, often disturbing past.

September 9, 1966

Bruce Lee stars as Kato, the valet to the Green Hornet, in the television series of the same name.

Van Williams starred as the masked crime fighter, who pursued villains in a souped-up Chrysler Imperial dubbed "Black Beauty." *The Green Hornet* was a radio show from 1936 to 1952 and a movie serial in the 1940s. The television version played two seasons before being canceled by ABC TV.

The Green Hornet was America's first exposure to Bruce Lee, born Lee Siu Loong in 1940. Though brief in duration, the series provided a vehicle for display of the beauty and skill of Lee's art. Lee appeared in other television shows before beginning his movie career in 1969 in the movie *Marlowe*. Lee went on to star in three 1973 martial arts classics, *Fists of Fury*, *Way of the Dragon*, and *Enter the Dragon* — which many consider the greatest martial arts film of all time.

Bruce Lee died of a brain aneurysm on July 20, 1973, at Queen Elizabeth Hospital in Hong Kong. He was buried at Lake View Cemetery in Seattle, Washington. Rumors swirled for years concerning the circumstances of his death. After his death, his following reached unprecedented numbers.

April 25, 1967

Five thousand copies of *The Black Panther*, the newspaper for the Black Panther Party, appear on the streets of Oakland, California.

Merely two mimeographed sheets of paper stapled together, the first issue explored the death of Denzil Dowell, 22, who had died from a policeman's bullet in Richmond, California. The newspaper set the tone for the emerging activist organization.

The Black Panther Party for Self Defense had been formed by black activists Bobby Seale and Huey Newton in Oakland in October 1966 to monitor police treatment of blacks and to protect blacks from police actions considered to be brutality. The name was soon changed to simply the Black

Panther Party (BPP). David Brothers established a branch in Brooklyn and Lumumba Shakur opened an office in Harlem. Soon, other centers emerged in cities including Philadelphia, Chicago, Newark, Omaha, Denver, New Haven, San Diego, and Los Angeles. Over the years, 28 Panthers and 14 police would die in panther-police encounters.

The forte of the Black Panther Party lay in its mass organizing and propaganda techniques. Through mediums such as *The Black Panther*, symbols such as the clenched black fist became popularized. The party spread its revolutionary black nationalist ideology through media campaigns, rallies, speaking tours, slogans, posters, leaflets, cartoons, and buttons. Unfortunately, the organization could never establish a solid funding base, and many of its leaders and members became corrupted away from its original pure ideals.

Bobby Seale, the original chairman of the party, lost his bid for mayor of Oakland in 1973. After joining the Black Panthers in 1966, Leroy Eldridge Cleaver published *Soul on Ice*, in which he preached the doctrine of black power. He ran for president as a member of the Peace and Freedom Party in 1968, but then fled to Algeria in 1968 following a shooting incident in California. He returned in 1980, facing arrest for parole violation. Incarcerated until 1985, Cleaver sought a Republican nomination for Senate in 1986.

Huey Newton met his fate in Oakland in 1989.

April 28, 1967

Muhammad Ali is stripped of his World Heavyweight Championship in boxing after refusing to register for the selective service.

Muhammad Ali had refused induction into the army, instead registering as a conscientious objector, following the precepts of his recent conversion to the Nation of Islam.

After winning a gold medal at the 1960 Olympic Games in Rome, Ali entered heavyweight boxing under his birth name of Cassius Clay. He beat Sonny Liston in 1964 to gain the title of Heavyweight Champion of the World. He retained the championship the next year by defeating Liston again.

Inside the ring, Ali personified the rare attributes of speed, size, and footwork, along with flamboyance and a streak of mischievousness to beat his combatants. He taunted his opponents and showboated for the audience, all the while unleashing a furious combination of blistering jabs and uppercuts to devastate his adversaries.

Outside the ring, his charisma and showmanship drew the attention of audiences and media alike. He demonstrated, however, a courage of convic-

tion perhaps unexpected. Many turned on him after he adopted the Nation
of Islam as his religion, then refused to participate in an already controversial, unpopular war. After being stripped of the title, Ali was convicted of
draft evasion, fined $10,000, and sentenced to five years in prison. His insight
and his integrity prevailed, however, and in 1971 the United States Supreme
Court overturned his conviction.

Meanwhile, after obtaining a boxing license from New York State while
still waiting for his appeal, Ali returned to the ring in 1970, defeating Jerry
Quarry in three rounds. After two spectacular bouts with Joe Frazier, he
regained his heavyweight title in 1974 by knocking out George Foreman. In
1975 he defeated Frazier again in a classic bout that was known as "the Thrilla
in Manila."

Muhammad Ali came to be regarded as the greatest boxer of all time,
having gained the heavyweight crown three separate times. More importantly, he became an ambassador of black pride, an inspiration for anyone
standing for an individual conviction. His became the most recognized face
in the world, even when ravaged in later years by Parkinson's Disease. In
short, he was deemed, by fans and media alike, as "The Greatest."

June 12, 1967

The United States Supreme Court declares laws against interracial marriage unconstitutional in its decision in the case of *Loving v. Virginia*, overturning miscegenation laws in Virginia and 15 other states.

Judge Leon Bazile of the Virginia Superior Court had sentenced Richard
and Mildred Loving to one year in prison for their interracial marriage, a
violation of Virginia law. The Lovings had challenged the conviction and
the case eventually reached the Supreme Court. Their attorney, William
Marutani, became the first Japanese American of the Nisei to argue before
the Supreme Court.

The United States had a long history of anti-miscegenation laws, beginning with the first passed in Maryland in 1661. In all, 30 states had passed
such laws, with 16 keeping those laws on the books until 1967. A dozen other
states kept those laws into the 1970s, while one — Alabama — kept a formal,
official ban on interracial marriage until November of 2000.

September 11, 1967

Ethnic studies pioneer Ronald Takaki offers the first-ever African American history course at the University of California at Los Angeles.

In particular, Takaki offered the ground-breaking course "The History of Racial Equality" at a time when college students had begun clamoring for the development of ethnic programs. Takaki also dove into the work of the Black Student Union, as well as activities for Asian and Hispanic students. Ironically — and perhaps because of this work — Takaki was refused tenure at UCLA, instead joining the ethnic studies faculty at the University of California at Berkeley.

Born on April 12, 1939, in Honolulu, Hawaii, of Japanese American ancestry, Takaki earned a doctorate in history at UC Berkeley in 1967. After a teaching stint at the College of San Mateo from 1965 to 1967, Takaki joined the faculty of UCLA in 1967.

Takaki worked to provide a voice for those not normally represented in Anglo-centric accounts of history. He wrote several books, particularly involving the adaption of Asian immigrants into mainstream American society. Takaki appeared on many television shows including *The Today Show, Good Morning, America,* and the *MacNeil/Lehrer News Hour.* His work led to his membership in the prestigious Society of American Historians.

October 2, 1967

Thurgood Marshall is appointed justice of the United States Supreme Court, the first African American to attain such a lofty position.

He became known for his "sliding scale" approach to the interpretation of equal protection under the Fourteenth Amendment, revealing a particular sensitivity to the impact of cold law upon the plight of the poor. He was noted, for example, for his position in the case *Furman v. Georgia,* in which he saw capital punishment as an instrument of vengeance no longer viable, appealing only to base instincts. He injected a dose of real-world experience into the sometimes distant realm of constitutional law.

November 7, 1967

Carl Stokes becomes the first black mayor of a major United States city.

After serving three terms in the Ohio House of Representatives, he was elected mayor of Cleveland, then the eighth largest city in America. Stokes served two terms, from 1967 to 1971.

Stokes was elected reportedly because of his ability to negotiate differences between the black vote and the conservative white vote. However, he lost his popularity due to the growing animosity between black protesters and the Cleveland police. The racial conflicts overshadowed the gains he had made within the Cleveland infrastructure. Stokes declined a campaign for a third term, but went on to work as a reporter, a labor lawyer, and a municipal court judge.

Carl Stokes paved the way for future African American mayors for Atlanta, Detroit, New Orleans, Los Angeles, and other important cities.

January 2, 1968

The Elementary and Secondary Education Act, Title VII, is passed by the United States Congress, enacting the first federally mandated bilingual education programs.

The new law required that children who did not speak English be instructed in two languages, and that teachers be trained, materials developed, and research conducted to assist these children.

Congress appropriated more than 7 million dollars for the execution of the act, a figure that would reach 100 million in 1979. The initial funds supported 76 pilot projects serving 27,000 students.

However, the act proved the beginning of a long, rocky road. Despite efforts to bring education in languages other than English, bilingual education faced barriers as states' movements against immigrants increased. Through the 1970s and particularly the 1980s, a majority of states considered — and many passed — ordinances declaring English the official state language. Ironically, this occurred at a time when the world marketplace faced a growing need for multilingual abilities.

In 1978, Congress passed an amendment to the 1968 act making funds available for transitional programs only, forsaking the maintenance of languages other than English. In 1986, 73 percent of the voters in California passed Proposition 63, the first Official English measure passed by ballot initiative. Two years later, however, the Ninth United States Circuit Court of Appeals struck down English-only rules in the workplace, in the case of *Gutierrez v. Municipal Court.*

February 29, 1968

The National Advisory Commission on Civil Disorders, appointed by President Lyndon Johnson and headed by Illinois governor Otto Kerner, releases a report on the wave of riots that struck American inner cities between 1965 and 1967.

The Kerner Commission Report revealed that, despite civil rights legislation and desegregation efforts, little had been done to address issues of housing, employment, education, and quality of life for African Americans in the United States. The report concluded the country was "moving toward two societies, one black, one white — separate but equal." It also claimed white racism to be the primary cause of black unrest. The Kerner report further asserted that a "compassionate, massive, and sustained" program of national action would be required to remedy the situation. No such program ever emerged (Kohn, p. 176).

April 4, 1968

At the Motel Lorraine in Memphis, Tennessee, Martin Luther King, Jr., is assassinated.

King had come to Memphis to lend his aid to a striking garbage workers' demonstration that had turned violent. The night before, King had addressed the crowd at the Mason Street Temple in an emotional speech addressing rumors of threats to his life. His words remained confident, upbeat, and prophetic.

By this time, King's leadership in the civil rights movement had somewhat waned. More militant groups had begun to question the continued relevance of his leadership, while the Federal Bureau of Investigation's J. Edgar Hoover reportedly had made him the subject of constant surveillance and harassment.

On the evening of April 4, King stopped in front of room 306 of the motel to chat with friends. He was accompanied by Jesse Jackson, Ralph Abernathy, and Hosea Williams. At 6:01 P.M., a shot rang out, as a bullet ripped through the right side of King's jaw, severing his spinal cord. James Earl Ray, a drifter with a long criminal record, shot him with a 30.06 Remington Gamester rifle from a rooming house across the street.

King was pronounced dead at St. Joseph's Hospital in Memphis at 7:05 P.M. Within 24 hours, riots broke out in more than 100 cities, requiring more than 75,000 federal troops and National Guardsman to patrol the streets throughout the country.

President Lyndon B. Johnson declared April 7 a national day of mourning, while Ralph Abernathy and Coretta Scott King led a silent memorial march through the streets of Memphis. On April 9, nearly 100,000 mourners gathered in and around Ebenezer Baptist Church in Atlanta, Georgia, to pay tribute to the fallen leader.

April 10, 1968

The Academy Awards honors two controversial 1967 movies starring Sidney Poitier.

Both movies — though very different in style and subject — seemed to reflect and define the racial movements of the late sixties. The Columbia Pictures release of *Guess Who's Coming to Dinner?* coincided almost perfectly with the United States Supreme Court's decision to declare bans on interracial marriage unconstitutional in *Loving v. Virginia*. Poitier starred with screen immortals Spencer Tracy and Katharine Hepburn in a film about interracial marriage. Among other contentious scenes, the film featured the movies' first interracial kiss. Although in retrospect the film seems charming if not overtly challenging, in 1967 the subject still raised many eyebrows.

William Rose won the Oscar for his intelligent script, and Hepburn captured the Oscar for Best Supporting Actress. Poitier played the near perfect suitor Dr. James Prentice, who wins over bigotry — both overt and covert — while winning over the parents of Joey Drayton. However, he was passed over even for nominations at the Oscars. Stanley Kramer directed, while the old on-screen chemistry of Tracy and Hepburn carried much of the film. It was Tracy's last performance, as he died ten days after completing the picture.

The second film, United Artists' *In the Heat of the Night*, contained what was perhaps Poitier's defining role, the Philadelphia detective Virgil Tibbs. In this steamy detective thriller set in Sparta, Mississippi, Poitier shared the screen with Rod Steiger as Sheriff Bill Gillespie. Steiger's performance earned him the Academy Award for Best Actor. *In the Heat of the Night* won the 1967 Best Picture Award, the first detective film accorded such an honor. Again, Poitier was passed over on Oscar night, but his role and the movie's poignant themes opened future doors for other actors in movies of similar themes.

April 11, 1968

The United States Congress enacts the Civil Rights Act of 1968, intended to end housing discrimination based on race, color, religion, or national origin.

Passed in the wake of the assassination of Martin Luther King, Jr., the act prohibited discrimination in federal housing, in private housing units greater than four units, and in single-family dwellings. It also prohibited discrimination in the financing of housing and in brokerage services.

August 10, 1968

In a bizarre attempt to usher in a period of black-white revolt throughout America that he called Helter Skelter, Charles Manson and his Family of Four murder seven residents of wealthy Beverly Hills in three days.

Los Angeles police found the mutilated bodies of Sharon Tate (wife of film director Roman Polanski), hairdresser Jay Sebring, Polish screenwriter Voytek Frykowski, coffee heiress Abigail Folger, and Steve Parent at Tate's Beverly Hills residence at 1050 Cielo Drive. They later found supermarket chain owners Leno and Rosemary LaBianca at their own home 12 miles away. A total of 102 stab wounds had been inflicted upon the victims.

A lifelong criminal from the age of 13, the 34-year-old Manson had also become a fanatical follower of the British rock group The Beatles. Manson reportedly derived many of his delusional prophecies through bizarre interpretations of Beatles lyrics — particularly from the 1968 LP known as the White Album — and the Book of Revelation in the Bible. He believed the Tate-LaBianca murders would be blamed on African Americans, spawning a massive interracial war. This uprising would divide and destroy much of the white population, leaving the blacks as the "establishment," who in turn would be ruled by Manson. Manson and his Family would then repopulate the white race on earth, using the black population as servants.

Manson's prophecies fell quite a bit short of fulfillment. Arrested at Barker Ranch in Death Valley on October 12, 1969, Manson and his Family faced a highly publicized Los Angeles trial from July 24, 1970, to November 21, 1971. In the end, the jury found Manson — along with Patricia Krenwinkel, Tex Watson, Leslie Van Houten, and Susan Atkins — guilty of the Tate-LaBianca murders. They were all sentenced to life in prison. Manson himself was denied parole ten times.

October 16, 1968

John Carlos and Tommie Smith stand on the winners' blocks at the Summer Olympics in Mexico City, fists held high in silent protest.

Carlos and Smith had finished first and third respectively in the 200-meter run. Having received their medals, they stood silently, raising fists covered in black gloves, presenting the Black Power salute to protest racism in the United States.

Prior to the commencement of the nineteenth Olympiad, there had been talk of an Olympic boycott by African American athletes in solidarity with the civil rights struggles. A poll of United States athletes revealed that 65 percent supported the gesture of Carlos and Smith. The United States Olympic Committee, however, did not appreciate what they saw as an inappropriate stance. They feared opening a Pandora's Box of international protest. The image of the racers, of course, was broadcast worldwide. Within 30 hours, the two athletes were thrown off the team by the USOC.

October 28, 1968

Luis Walter Alvarez learns, at the age of 48, that he has become the first American-born Hispanic to win the Nobel Prize in Physics.

One of the United States' most distinguished physicists, Alvarez won the Nobel for his work in the detection and identification of subatomic particles while designing the first proton linear accelerator.

Born on June 13, 1911, in San Francisco, Alvarez had earned his bachelor's degree and Ph.D. at the University of Chicago. Most of his work took place at the University of California, Berkeley, where he served on the faculty from 1936 until his death in 1988. A pioneer as well in the fields of physics, astrophysics, ophthalmics and vision optics, geophysics, and air navigation, some of his best work took place at the prestigious Lawrence Livermore National Laboratory. Alvarez also served on the Manhattan Project with Dr. J. Robert Oppenheimer in Los Alamos, New Mexico. Alvarez was aboard the *Great Artiste,* which accompanied the *Enola Gay* on the fateful day of August 6, 1945. Alvarez was among the collection of scientists to observe and monitor the detonation of the atomic bomb called Little Boy, which exploded 1,850 feet above Hiroshima, Japan, during World War II. Three days later, the bomb called Fat Boy was dropped on Nagasaki, Japan, essentially ending World War II, while ushering in the atomic age.

In addition to the Nobel Prize, Alvarez won the Collier Trophy in 1946, the Scott Medal in 1953, the Einstein Medal in 1961, and the National Medal of Science in 1964 — the first U.S. Hispanic to win each of these awards.

June 9, 1969

The United States Supreme Court decides for the defendant in the case *Brandenburg v. Ohio,* thus protecting the concept of free speech except when it can be demonstrated that such speech represents a clear threat of violence.

Clarence Brandenburg had led a group of 12 hooded men, who burned a cross and hurled epithets at Jews and African Americans. The Supreme Court ruled that free speech and the free press are protected against state intervention by the constitution "except where such advocacy is directed to inciting or producing imminent lawless action and is likely to incite or produce such action" (Hall, p. 85).

November 20, 1969

One hundred Native Americans disembark on Alcatraz Island in San Francisco Bay, claiming "the Rock" as Indian land.

The group, calling themselves "Indians of All Tribes," represented nations including the Mohawk, Shoshone-Bannock, and Chippewa. Once settled on the island, the Indians of All Tribes established schools for children, started a newspaper, and arranged for food and health care. They remained on Alcatraz for 19 months, until the government realized the occupation was intended to be permanent. The authorities cut off food and water in May 1970, and federal marshals stormed the island in May of 1971.

Alcatraz Island had closed as a federal maximum-security penitentiary in 1963. For six years following the closure, Native Americans had claimed, under the Treaty of Laramie of 1868, that they could reclaim the land. Four members of the Sioux tribe had captured the island in March of 1964. On November 11, 1969, a group of 14 college students had held it for 19 hours.

March 25, 1971

Representatives of the Congressional Black Caucus (CBC) meet with President Richard M. Nixon to outline the political agenda for African Americans.

Thirteen representatives from the United States House of Representatives, who had joined forces to form the Congressional Black Caucus in 1969, presented 60 recommendations for government action on both domestic and foreign issues.

The CBC had arisen to give special focus to issues and concerns affecting millions of underrepresented African American citizens. The representatives included some of the most important names in civil rights: Shirley Chisholm, William Clay, Sr., George Collins, John Conyers, Ron Dellums, Charles Diggs, Jr., Walter Fauntroy, Augustus Hawkins, Ralph Metcalf, Parren Mitchell, Robert Nix, Charles Rangel, and Louis Stokes.

Many of the goals of the CBC concerned the legacy of economic and political servitude that characterized the history of African Americans. With an ever-growing body of local, state, and national political representatives, the Congressional Black Caucus led the struggle for political power among minorities.

One of the most concrete of the CBC goals was to have African Americans comprise at least ten percent of the membership of the House of Representatives. At the time of its formation, ten percent would have been 45 members. As of the year 2000, 35 representatives came from an African American heritage. All belonged to the Congressional Black Caucus.

July 6, 1971

Louis Armstrong dies of a heart attack at his home in the Corona area of New York, two days after his claimed birthday. (He had actually been born on August 4, 1901.)

Tributes poured in from all over the world, including from President Richard M. Nixon, who said, "His talent and magnificent spirit added richness and pleasure to all our lives."

Duke Ellington, one of his contemporaries in the emergence of jazz as a major force in American entertainment, said, "He is the epitome of jazz and always will be. He is what I call an American standard, an American original."

Armstrong's final performance had been the previous February, part of a two-week engagement at the Waldorf-Astoria hotel in New York. He had recently been discharged from Beth Israel Medical Center, after receiving treatment for heart and kidney ailments.

In the 1920s, Armstrong had helped to introduce jazz to Chicago and New York through his incomparable coronet playing. He became affectionately known as "Satchmo."

He later fell out of favor with many young people, as more modern purveyors of jazz emerged on the music scene. Many interpreted his onstage demeanor as that of a happy-go-lucky Uncle Tom. In his later years he had been an unofficial ambassador of good will for the State Department, traveling to Africa, the Middle East, and Latin America, drawing great crowds as he went. In 1966, his rendition of "Hello Dolly" had topped the charts, becoming the top record and album of the year (Krebs, *New York Times*, 1971).

December 17, 1971

Ramona Acosta Banuelos is named treasurer of the United States, the first Hispanic woman ever to hold a presidential cabinet post.

Born in Miami, Arizona, Banuelos had actually faced deportation during the Depression. In 1944, she returned to the United States to open a Los Angeles tortilla business. There she had been recognized as Outstanding Business Woman in 1969. She was appointed U.S. treasurer during the first presidential term of Richard Milhouse Nixon.

March 25, 1972

President Nixon boosts Equal Employment powers.

To expand the United States government's powers against discrimination in employment, President Richard Nixon signed into law the Equal Employment Opportunity Act, which strengthened the Equal Employment Opportunity Commission. The measure gave the Commission the power to bring lawsuits in federal district court to enforce the provisions of the

Civil Rights Act of 1964. It expands the protection of the 1964 act to state and local government, small businesses, and additional educational institutions.

The Equal Employment Opportunity Commission eventually enforced rights and protections encompassed in the Age Discrimination in Employment Act of 1967, the Rehabilitation Act of 1973, and the Americans with Disabilities Act of 1990. These acts combined to prohibit discrimination and harassment on the basis of race, color, religion, sex, national origin, disability, or age.

June 29, 1972

The United States Supreme Court acknowledges the disproportional number of executions imposed upon and carried out against African Americans in its decision in *Furman v. Georgia*.

Justice William O. Douglas denounced the racial injustice of capital punishment, concluding that the death penalty had disproportionately been applied to poor and socially disadvantaged convicts. Douglas thus equated the Eighth Amendment with equal protection values. In a 5–4 decision, the Supreme Court struck down the death penalty as a violation of the Eighth Amendment, which abolished cruel and unusual punishment.

In its arguments, the Court declared that state statutes had allowed arbitrary discretion in sentencing, a freedom "pregnant with discrimination" and thus violating constitutional guarantees of equal protection under the law. Justice William Brennan declared that it was a "denial of human dignity for the State arbitrarily to subject a person to an unusually severe punishment that society ... does not regard as acceptable and that cannot be shown to serve any penal purpose more effectively than a significantly less drastic punishment."

July 26, 1972

An article on the front page of the *New York Times* reveals the details of the Tuskegee Syphilis Study, "one of the most outrageous abuses of trusting patients in medical history" (Jean, p. 1).

From 1932 to 1972, 600 African American males had unwittingly been recruited for a study of the course the disease syphilis would take if left untreated. Three hundred ninety-nine of the participants had actually contracted syphilis; the others were used as the control group. But instead of offering the inflicted compassionate treatment, the researching doctors allowed the disease to spread, telling the subjects they simply suffered from "bad blood." Even though penicillin had proven to be an effective treatment by the 1950s, these men continued to receive no care, suffering the devastating effects of tumors, blindness, deafness, paralysis and — in the case of nearly 100 — death.

The study came to light after the Centers for Disease Control in Atlanta investigated the study in 1969.

In 1925, the Advisory Council of the Milbank Fund had provided funds for the research. The subjects of the research came primarily from Macon County, Alabama; poor, uneducated, naïve, they were offered food, clothing, and shelter in exchange for participation in the study. The participants were never told of the syphilis, only of the "bad blood."

The United States Public Health Services Department took over the study in 1932, under the direction of Dr. J.R. Heller, although the Milbank Fund continued paying $50 apiece for burials. The study continued until 1972, with two surgeons general retaining full knowledge of the experiment. Still, no one made any effort to stop it. Offering no remedy, the study merely conducted periodic examinations, then autopsies after death to determine the effect of the disease on the body.

Many would contend that the experiment cast a long shadow of distrust over the relationship between African Americans and the biomedical research community: "It is argued that the Study is a significant factor in the low participation of African Americans in clinical trials, organ donation efforts, and routine preventive care" (www.med.virginia.edu, p. 1).

Despite this 40-year abuse of the doctor-patient relationship, and despite a $10-million settlement to the survivors and their families, no formal apology was ever issued until 1997, when President William J. Clinton apologized to the five surviving victims of the experiment, in a solemn ceremony at the White House.

October 24, 1972

With diabetes and heart disease riddling his once magnificently athletic physique, Jack Roosevelt "Jackie" Robinson dies at 7:10 A.M., at the age of 53.

Only ten days earlier, he had thrown out the first pitch at the World Series, which featured the Oakland Athletics and the Cincinnati Reds.

Funeral services transpired on October 29, at Riverside Church in Harlem, where Robinson's body lay in state. More than 2,500 mourners attended, including labor leader A. Philip Randolph, boxing great Joe Louis, basketball star Bill Russell, baseball legends Hank Greenberg and Henry Aaron, several members of Robinson's old Brooklyn Dodgers team, and New

York governor Nelson Rockefeller. Tributes poured in from around the world, hailing the determined breaker of civil rights barriers.

Robinson was survived by Rachel, his wife of 29 years, his daughter Sharon, and his son David. His oldest son, Jackie Jr., had died the year before in an automobile accident.

Unwavering and fiery virtually to the end, Robinson had still been advocating an African American Major League baseball manager. The moment would come three years after Robinson's death, when former Cleveland and Baltimore star Frank Robinson became manager of the Cleveland Indians.

In his later years, Robinson had thrown his support behind several upcoming African American political leaders, particularly the former disciple of Martin Luther King, Jr., the Reverend Jesse Jackson. Robinson considered Jackson a most viable and dedicated leader.

Later, Robinson's wife Rachel summarized the life, volatile and tested by fire, from which her husband had finally found rest. "Nobody could hurt him again," she said. "He wouldn't hear the name-calling. He would only hear the cheers and somehow I could fantasize my own little story about where he was and how he was doing and let him rest in peace" (Ward and Burns, p. 427).

In his legendary career, Robinson had been named the National League's Most Valuable Player in 1949 and had been voted into the Baseball Hall of Fame in 1962 — the first African American at Cooperstown. In 1984, President Ronald Reagan posthumously awarded Robinson the Medal of Freedom, the nation's highest civilian honor.

February 26, 1973

A demonstration at the Pine Ridge Indian Reservation in South Dakota explodes into violence among the Sioux tribe; the incident would become known as Wounded Knee II.

A corrupt tribal government had conspired with the United States government to take away mineral rights from the Sioux in early 1970. Protesters banned from the reservation requested the intervention of the American Indian Movement (AIM), the Native American advocacy group founded in 1968.

Begun in Minneapolis, the purpose of the AIM was to confront issues affecting Native Americans such as welfare, police brutality, slum housing, low employment rates, racist and discriminatory policies of county welfare systems, and questionable behavior of the federal government. For the next 35 years, AIM worked to advance the cause of Native Americans throughout the country, hosting protests and conferences and doing advocacy work.

On February 27, a 54-car caravan arrived at Pine Ridge, carrying more than 200 activists. By dawn, the protesters found themselves sealed in by roadblocks and surrounded by government agents. On March 11 traditionalists, led by Oglala head Frank Fools Crow, poured into Wounded Knee. For 71 days, government troops harassed the protesters, firing half a million rounds into the group, killing two and seriously wounding 15 others. By May 3, 563 were arrested, with 185 indicted on such benign charges as interfering with postal inspectors and trespassing. Only 15 were actually convicted. The American Indian Movement leader, on the other hand, faced 37 felony charges. After three years and more than a million dollars in legal costs, he was cleared of all charges.

The harassment of tribe members and the AIM continued. In 1975, despite all the protests, the Oglala tribe president turned over more than 76,200 acres of Sioux land to the federal government.

The disaster is reminiscent of Wounded Knee I, which had transpired on December 29, 1890, at the same reservation. In that incident, more than 250 Teton and Yankton Sioux were killed by United States soldiers. The tribes had been practicing the Ghost Dance — ritual dance of hope, developed by Southern Paiute medicine man Wovoka — which had been banned by the secretary of the interior. Many Sioux, and those of other tribes, believed that the dance would eventually cause the white man to disappear from the native lands. The Native Americans at Pine Ridge had gathered in a great circle to perform the dance. The dancers were filled with great emotional exhilaration and ecstasy, some actually falling into unconsciousness. Sadly, the bigoted, frightened soldiers opened fire on the Ghost Dancers.

November 19, 1973

The United States Supreme Court decides the case of *Espinoza v. Farah Manufacturing Company*, distinguishing between "national origin" and "citizenship" in employment opportunity.

Mrs. Espinoza had applied for a job as a seamstress with Farah Manufacturing Company in San Antonio, Texas. The company refused her employment because she was not a United States citizen like her husband. A district court in Texas had found in favor of Espinoza, relying on an Equal Employment Opportunity Commission guideline banning discrimination based on citizenship. The court of appeals reversed the decision, and the Supreme Court upheld the court of appeals' determination, arguing the distinction between citizenship and national origin.

The Supreme Court reasoned that since federal employees were required to be citizens, Congress did not intend the concept of national origin to include citizenship. The Court also reasoned that Farah had not discriminated against Espinoza based on national origin, given its employment track record. Ninety-six percent of Farah employees were of Hispanic background, while 97 percent of those had been engaged in the same kind of work for which Espinoza had applied. Furthermore, the person hired in Espinoza's place had come from a Hispanic background, but was also a citizen.

The Court therefore reasoned that Farah discriminated not on national origin, but on citizenship, which is not protected by law.

The Court decides the case by an 8-to-1 margin, with Justice William O. Douglas the lone dissenter. In his opinion Douglas wrote, "Mrs. Espinoza is a permanent resident alien, married to an American citizen, and her children will be native-born American citizens.... The majority decides today that in passing sweeping legislation guaranteeing equal job opportunities, the congress intended to help only the immigrant's children, excluding those 'for whom there is no place at all.' I cannot impute that niggardly an intent to Congress."

April 8, 1974

Henry "Hank" Aaron breaks baseball's most coveted record, held by George "Babe" Ruth for 39 years.

Off a fast ball from Los Angeles Dodgers pitcher Al Downing, Aaron hit his 715th home run, more than any other man to play Major League baseball.

As he neared the record in the 1973 and early 1974 seasons, Aaron had endured merciless taunts, particularly at his own ball park in Atlanta. "I didn't expect the fans to give me a standing ovation every time I stepped onto the field," Aaron said later, "but I thought a few of them might come over to my side as I approached Ruth. At least, I felt I had earned the right not to be verbally abused and racially ravaged in my home ballpark" (Aaron, p. 231).

As Aaron drew closer to the legendary mark, the incidents of derogatory and threatening mail increased. "Dear Nigger," one letter read, "Everybody loved Babe Ruth. You will be the most hated man in this country if you break his career home run record." Another correspondence said, "Dear Mr. Nigger: I hope you don't break the Babe's record. How do I tell my kids that a nigger did it?" (Aaron, pp. 230–231).

Once the press publicized the kind of horrible letters Aaron had been receiving, however, thousands of letters of support began to pour in. One young person wrote, "Dear Mr. Aaron, I am twelve years old, and I wanted to tell you that I have read many articles about the prejudice against you. I really think it's bad. I don't care what color you are. You could be green and it wouldn't matter. These nuts that keep comparing you in every way to Ruth are dumb. Maybe he's better. Maybe you are. How can you compare two people 30 or 40 years apart? You can't really. So many things are different. It's just some people can't stand to see someone a bit different from them ruin something someone else more like them set. I've never read where you said you're better than Ruth. That's because you never said it! What do those fans want you to do? Just quit hitting?" (Aaron, p. 242).

Although Aaron and Ruth were compared and contrasted all through the 1973 and 1974 seasons, they could not have been more different. Aaron, the former Negro League player who had signed with the Milwaukee Braves in 1959, was a quiet, contemplative individual, in marked contrast to the Babe's flamboyant, boyish style. Ruth had loved the limelight, while Aaron cherished his privacy and his quiet. Ruth had changed the game, but as for Aaron, he was just "a player who simply kept swinging longer and more effectively than all the others" (Aaron, p. 228).

Hank Aaron kept swinging for two more years, eventually retiring with 755 home runs, the most in any Major League baseball career. In his fabled tenure, he appeared in 24 All-Star games, more than anyone else in history.

September 12, 1974

Racial desegregation of public schools begins in South Boston, following an order by United States district judge Arthur Garrity ordering integration in Boston public schools.

Unfortunately, this involved the busing of poor black children from the Roxbury and Dorchester districts to primarily poor Irish South Boston.

On the morning of the twelfth, school buses were scheduled to transport 20,000 students, but only a small percentage actually rode the bus the first day. Bringing remembrances of racial confrontation in the deep South, the busing encouraged confrontation between black residents of Roxie and the Irish neighborhood of South Boston, or Southie.

Violence eventually erupted in both neighborhoods, against both groups. South Boston High School was closed after a black teen stabbed a white teen, causing 1,500 white parents to trap the black student inside the school. Racial epithets were muttered and stones were thrown as mounted police escorted the yellow school buses into the neighborhoods.

The busing of school children raised the question of whether it made sense to transport students many miles from their homes simply to integrate them. Some characterized the issue as pitting equality of opportunity against a call to community. Others objected to the frailty of progressive social experiments continually carried out on the backs of the poor.

February 25, 1975

The death of a leader divides the Nation of Islam.

When Elijah Muhammad died, the 500,000-member-strong Nation of Islam — which had brought Malcolm X to America, helping to change black America's attitude — was rendered into pieces between Muhammad's son Warith Deen Muhammad and other factions, particularly that of a calypso singer from Massachusetts, whom Malcolm X himself had brought into the fold.

Warith Deen led his followers down a path that more closely followed orthodox Sunni Islam, abandoning the path of black separatism. In 1976, Warith Deen Muhammad's faction became the World Community of Al-Islam in the West; it placed greater emphasis on American patriotism and global solidarity. In 1980 the faction became the American Muslim Mission, which eventually filed for bankruptcy in 1986.

Of the splinter groups, the most notable was that led by Louis Far-rakhan. Born Louis Eugene Walcott in New York, Farrakhan had been re-cruited by Malcolm X. He changed his slave name in 1965 for Louis Haleem Abdul Farrakhan, becoming a compelling and fiery speaker in his own right.

Upon splitting from Warith Deen Muhammad's group, Farrakhan kept the name Nation of Islam. A charismatic leader, Farrakhan claimed 50,000 followers in 1988, inspiring African Americans to demonstrations reminis-cent of the early sixties. Farrakhan also stirred controversy around his appar-ent negative attitudes toward whites and Jews, an attitude he claimed was falsely attributed to him.

December 4, 1975

Stanford University removes the word "Indians" from the names of its sports teams, in deference to protests from Native Americans.

Instead, they adopt the name "Cardinal." For years, Native Americans had objected to the use of mascots that they believed developed and perpet-uated racial stereotypes of Native Americans. As one of the top universities in the country, Stanford helped set a new standard.

Stanford had actually originally adopted the name "The Cardinal" in 1971, dropping it in 1972. After a series of student referendums and votes in which the pros and cons were thoroughly debated, the issue was finally resolved at the end of 1975. Stanford University adopted "The Cardinal" for perpetuity.

Other institutions that changed their names included Dartmouth ("Indians" to "Big Green"); Siena College ("Indians" to "Saints"); and Saint

Mary's College, Minnesota ("Red Men" to "Cardinals"). In addition, several universities — including Marquette, Mankato State, the University of Oklahoma, and Saint John's — dropped their mascots, which also reportedly trivialized Native Americans.

June 25, 1976

The United States Supreme Court rules that private educational institutions cannot refuse admission to African Americans solely because of their race.

The parents of Michael McCrary and Colin Gonzales had sued Russell and Katheryne Runyan, who operated a private school in Arlington, Virginia. In deciding *Runyan v. McCrary et al.* on a 7–to–2 basis, the court declared that the school violated the Civil Rights Act of 1964 by refusing the opportunity of education solely because of race.

January 8, 1977

Pauli Murray is ordained the first black female priest of the Episcopal Church, at the age of 62.

Born in Baltimore, Maryland, orphaned, and raised by two aunts in Durham, North Carolina, Murray attended Hunter College in New York. She became well acquainted with racial and sexual discrimination, being denied admittance to the University of North Carolina in 1938 because of race, and to Harvard because of gender. Murray persevered, attaining her law degree at Howard University in 1944, then her master's in law at the University of California at Berkeley.

From her college days, Murray seemed to make a lifelong commitment to eradicating Jim and Jane Crow. She participated with the Congress of Racial Equality in sit-ins in lunch counters in Washington, D.C., in the 1940s, and she was an original founder of the National Organization for Women. She was named Woman of the Year by *Mademoiselle* magazine in 1947 and became author of *Proud Shoes: Profile of an American Family* in 1956. She went on to write many other books and also poetry.

In Murray there was a synthesis of advocacy for women and for African Americans.

January 23, 1977

The American Broadcasting Company (ABC) begins its eight-day presentation of *Roots*.

As the series progressed, it drew the largest viewing audience of any dramatic program presented on American television. Written by Alex Haley, the author of *The Autobiography of Malcolm X*, *Roots* depicted the history of the author's family from tribal Africa to the post–Civil War era.

For the first time, an American television audience watched the developing legacy of an African American family; many were exposed to the harsh reality and human poignancy of black history for the first time. The series starred some of television's most luminary figures, such as LeVar Burton, Ben Vereen, Ed Asner, Harry Rhodes, Lloyd Bridges, and Sandy Duncan. The production won an unprecedented 37 Emmys and became the subject of educational and entertainment attention for years to come.

June 28, 1978

In a nationally polarizing case involving reverse discrimination, the United States Supreme Court, in *Regents of the University of California v. Bakke*, orders that Allan P. Bakke be admitted to the University of California Medical School at Davis.

The Court concluded that the school's racial quota plan proved inflexible and unjustifiably biased against white applicants like him. At the same time, confusingly, the Court upheld the constitutionality of college affirmative action admissions programs, which strove to give blacks and minorities redress for past discrimination.

The University of California at Davis had utilized a quota system among its medical school applicants, setting aside approximately 15 percent of the slots in medical school for disadvantaged students. Allan Bakke had sued the university because his grade average had exceeded that of some of the "disadvantage students" who had been admitted. The California Supreme Court had struck down the university's program, ordering Bakke's admission. But the United States Supreme Court, in an unusual tactic, both affirmed and reversed the California Supreme Court's ruling.

The university had defended its special admissions system by saying it fulfilled four distinct purposes in creating equal opportunity in education: 1) The system reduced the traditional historic deficit of minorities in medical schools; 2) it countered the effects of societal discrimination; 3) it increased the number of physicians in underserved communities; and 4) it facilitated the educational benefits that flow from a diverse student body.

In its ruling, the Court responded by asserting there had been no evidence to show the policies exercised by the university achieved the purposes touted. The justices stated that the preference of members of any one group for no reason other than race or ethnic origin is discrimination for its own sake, thus strictly forbidden by the Constitution. The Court also insisted that the government had no compelling interest in helping one group while harming another, again asserting no evidence could be seen that showed such a program actually provided more physicians within disadvantaged communities.

The one argument the Court could not easily dismiss was the advantage racial diversity brought to the education process. Such an assertion has been a crucial part of cases involving equal access to education since *Brown v. Board of Education*. Therefore, the Court agreed that the University of California had a compelling interest to take some consideration of race in its application system. At the same time, however, the Court decided the special admissions program was invalid under the Fourteenth Amendment equal protection clause, ordering that Bakke was entitled to the injunction allowing his admission to the university.

November 4, 1979

Iran Hostage Crisis begins when a mob of 450 cuts the chains on the gate to the United States embassy in Tehran, pushing back the Marine guards.

The mob took 66 embassy staff as hostages, then demanded the return of the Shah Mohammed Reza Pahlevi to Iran from his medical asylum in a New York hospital. The next 444 days would be a declaration of vengeance against the United States, the nation called "The Great Satan."

The Ayatollah Ruhollah Khomeini — the amply-bearded, humorless Muslim cleric — seized control of what he now considered a theocracy. Born in 1901, he had seen the rise of the Shah, who seized control of Iran in 1921. After falling out of power in the late forties, the Shah was reinstated by a CIA-led coup in 1953. The new government brought rights to women and increased urbanization and industrialization, in an administration more popular outside Iran than inside. The Shah's regime also resorted to harsh repression and brutality, as another Third World nation was introduced to the American Way, in turn rejected when the Ayatollah came to power.

The Iran Hostage Crisis began a backlash against perceived Iranians and Iran-Americans living in the United States, as well as those perceived to be of Middle Eastern origins. Both the American public and the government turned on these individuals, who became victims of hate crimes, and many hopeful immigrants had their visas revoked. Suddenly, those of Middle Eastern ethnicities faced reprisals from neighbors suddenly driven to hate by the events in Tehran.

This kind of backlash would be replayed in 1987, during the Gulf War, and in 2001, after the September 11 World Trade Center attack.

December 8, 1979

Edith Spurlock Sampson, the first African American woman judge in America, dies.

She had been appointed to the Chicago municipal court in 1962.

Born in Pittsburgh, PA, c. 1901, Sampson attended John Marshall Law School in Chicago while working as social worker. After failing the Illinois bar exam, Sampson attended and graduated from Chicago's Loyola University Law School, the first woman of any culture to do so. A pioneering African American woman, she served as a United Nations delegate in 1950 as well as a member-at-large of the North Atlantic Treaty Organization (NATO). Sampson was the first African American woman to hold either of those posts.

July 2, 1980

The United State Supreme Court issues a decision in the case of *Fullilove v. Klutznick*, in which the court upholds the validity of federal minority hiring quotas.

It ruled that the Public Work Employment Act, which set aside 10 percent of its available funds for contracts awarded to minority-owned businesses, was constitutional. The decision rejected the assertion by nonminority businessmen that the act constituted reverse discrimination. It ruled, essentially, that the federal government had been authorized to remedy past injustices in discrimination through legislative measures.

March 1, 1981

Perhaps symbolic of the growing Hispanic power within American business, Roberto C. Goizueta is named chief executive officer and chairman of the board of Coca-Cola.

In 1996, Goizueta would be named the leading entrepreneur on the Hispanic Business Rich List, listing the top 11 Hispanic businessmen whose personal wealth exceeded $100 million.

Born on November 18, 1931, in Havana, Cuba, Goizueta started out working for a Coca-Cola affiliate in Havana in 1954. He had already received his Bachelor of Science degree in chemical engineering at Yale University. Leaving Cuba a year after the Castro revolution in 1959, Goizueta soon worked as a chemist for the soft drink giant, gradually climbing the managerial ladder.

Under Goizueta's direction, Coca-Cola introduced the lucrative Diet Coke to the consumer market, but also unleashed the New Coke debacle in

1985. During his regime, Coca-Cola's stock market value as a company exploded from 4 billion to 150 billion in 15 years.

Goizueta died of lung cancer in 1997.

March 21, 1981

Henry Hays, the son of a ranking official in the Alabama Ku Klux Klan, sets out for revenge.

The day before, the jury in the trial of Josephus Andersonan — a black man charged with killing a white police officer — had been able to reach no verdict. While cruising angrily about Mobile, Alabama, Hays and a cohort James Knowles kidnapped 19-year-old Michael Donald. They abducted the young man at gunpoint and took him forcibly by car to the next county, where they mercilessly beat him, finally lynching him from a tree near the Hays home.

The brief investigation by local police erroneously determined that Donald had been murdered over a drug deal. Buelah Mae Donald, knowing her son had not been involved in drugs, was determined to find justice. She contacted the Reverend Jesse Jackson, who highlighted the shameful incident by organizing a protest against the failed police investigation. Thomas Figures, assistant United States attorney in Mobile, persuaded the Federal Bureau of Investigation to send agent James Bodman to southern Alabama.

Bodman convinced Knowles to confess, and he testified against Hays. The jury sentenced Knowles to life in prison, then sentenced Hays to death.

With the help of Morris Dees and Joseph J. Levin of the Southern Poverty Law Center, Beulah Mae sued the United Klans of America in 1987. The all-white jury held the Ku Klux Klan responsible for the murder of Donald, ordering it to pay 7 million dollars in damages. This award bankrupted the Klan, forcing it to hand over all its assets, including those in the national headquarters in Tuscaloosa. Beulah Donald became owner of the building, which she eventually sold for $52,000.

Hays was executed on June 6, 1997, after a long legal struggle. It was the first time a white man was executed for a crime against an African American since 1913. At that time, authorities hung two white outlaws after they shot and killed an African American cockfight trainer in northern Alabama.

The case of Michael Donald illustrated the violence of the bigotry that still burned in the hearts of some Americans despite gains in civil rights. It also demonstrated the substantial advances in the system of justice for persons of color, as well as the reduction of the influence of the Ku Klux Klan.

June 23, 1982

Vincent Chin dies of injuries sustained during a vicious attack with a baseball bat four days earlier, outside a fast food restaurant in suburban Detroit.

On June 19, 1982, a fight erupted outside of Fancy Pants, where Vincent Chin had celebrated his bachelor party. Chin was to be married nine days later. Autoworkers Ronald Ebens and Michael Nitz allegedly assaulted Chin because they thought he was Japanese; they blamed the Japanese for the struggling United States auto industry.

The altercation broke up, but Ebens and Nitz found Chin outside a fast food restaurant 20 minutes later. Ebens beat Chin with a baseball bat, striking him on the leg. Then, as Nitz held Chin down, Ebens crushed his skull. For the next four years, the wheels of injustice would roll right over the case.

On March 16, 1983, Wayne County judge Charles Kaufman found Ebens and Nitz guilty of manslaughter only. Ultimately, Kaufman sentenced each to three years' probation, a $3,000 fine, and $780 in court fees. During the trial, the prosecuting attorney was not present; neither Chin's mother Lily nor any prosecution witnesses was called to testify.

In November of 1983 — following an FBI investigation — Ebens and Nitz were indicted on charges of violating Chin's civil rights, and for conspiracy. In June of 1984, Ebens was found guilty of violating Chin's civil rights. He was sentenced to 25 years in prison, but was released on $20,000 bond. Nitz was cleared on both charges.

Two years later, in September 1986, Eben's conviction was overturned by a federal appeals court on a legal technicality: an attorney for a group called American Citizens for Justice — formed by Asian Americans in response to the Chin case — was accused of improperly coaching prosecution witnesses.

Bowing to intense public outcry, the Justice Department ordered a retrial in a new venue, Cincinnati, Ohio. However, in May of 1987, the Cincinnati jury cleared Ebens of all charges. In July of 1987, a civil suit ordered Ebens to pay $1.5 million to Chin's estate as part of a court-approved settlement. But Ebens disposed of his assets and fled the state. He has yet to pay a dime of the settlement.

Vincent Chin's mother, Lily Chin — disgusted and outraged by the country's legal system — left the United States, returning to her native village in Guangzhou province in China. She died there on June 9, 2002. However, her son's legacy was a rallying point for Asian American equality and justice for many years.

April 12, 1983

Democrat Harold Washington defeats Republican Bernard Epton to become the first African American mayor of Chicago, Illinois.

During the campaign, Washington managed to capture 51.5 percent of Chicago voters, gaining support particularly from blacks, Hispanics, and middle class whites. The mayoral campaign deeply divided the city, as Washington faced severe opposition from the conservative white electorate.

A native born Chicago resident, Harold Washington was the son of an attorney and a Democratic precinct captain. Washington attended Roosevelt College in Chicago, obtaining his law degree at Northwestern University Law School. Washington served as arbitrator for the Illinois Industrial Commission, as state legislator, and as Democratic precinct captain, then as a United States congressman.

By 1990, African American mayors had been elected in all of the following major American cities: Carl B. Stokes (Cleveland, Ohio, 1967); Richard G. Hatcher (Gary, Idaho, 1967); Ernest "Dutch" Morial (New Orleans, Louisiana, 1978); Tom Bradley (Los Angeles, California, 1973); Marion Barry (Washington, D.C., 1978); Dave Dinkins (New York, New York, 1990); Coleman Young (Detroit, Michigan, 1974); and Maynard Young, Andrew Young, and Bill Campbell (Atlanta, Georgia, 1973–2001).

April 19, 1983

More than 100 black students protest in front of the administration building at the University of Mississippi at Oxford, which still uses the Confederate flag as a symbol of the university.

The protest came in response to activity the night before, when several hundred white students had waved the flag while singing "Dixie" in front of the black fraternity house on campus.

For more than a year, black students had vocally objected to the flag, the song "Dixie," and the mascot "Col Reb." They denounced the symbols as representative of a time that supported the institution of slavery. White supporters of the flag characterized the flag as a symbol of their history and heritage.

On April 20, Chancellor Porter Fortune announced that the flag would no longer be used as a school symbol. However, black students continued to object, arguing that the ruling did not ban the individual use of these symbols, which were still supported by a substantial part of the white student population.

The debate of the place of the Confederate flag in Southern states continued on college campuses, in state houses, and in courthouses well into the new millennium.

August 30, 1983

The orbiter shuttle *Challenger* blasts off on its third mission from the Kennedy Space Center in Florida. On board is Guion S. Bluford, Jr., the first African American NASA astronaut in space.

The *Challenger* completed 98 orbits, launched a satellite, and conducted several onboard experiments before landing at Edwards Air Force Base in California five days later.

Born November 22, 1942, in Philadelphia, Pennsylvania, Bluford graduated from Pennsylvania State University in 1964 with a Bachelor of Science degree in aerospace engineering. He graduated with distinction from the Air Force Institute of Technology in 1974, then earned a doctorate in 1978. Bluford also earned a master's degree in business administration at the University of Houston, Clear Lake, in 1987. Bluford completed pilot training at Williams Air Force Base in Arizona. Subsequently, he flew 144 missions during the Vietnam War. He became an astronaut for the National Aeronautics and Space Administration in August 1979.

By the time Bluford left NASA in July 1993, he had logged more than 688 hours in space, including four space shuttle missions. He won numerous awards in Vietnam and as an astronaut. He also accepted the NAACP Image Award in 1983.

September 17, 1983

Vanessa Williams is crowned Miss America, the first African American to win the title.

That same year, a controversy erupted over a photo layout of her that appeared in *Penthouse* magazine. However, Williams triumphed over the adversity, pursuing a successful career in movies, television, and the recording industry.

Vanessa Williams's parents — both music teachers — influenced her early years. Born in Millwood, New York, and attending Syracuse University, Williams majored in musical theater.

Following the *Penthouse* fiasco, Williams was signed by Mercury/Wing records for her first album *The Right Stuff* in 1988. She released several singles including "Save the Best for Last," which eventually topped the charts.

Williams went on to receive two NAACP Image Awards, seven Grammy Award nominations, and a number of New York Music Awards.

January 2, 1984

Oprah Winfrey premieres on *A.M. Chicago*, the title of which would be changed to *The Oprah Winfrey Show* in a little more than a year.

Winfrey's show competed well with that of Windy City talk show icon Phil Donahue. After one full year *The Oprah Winfrey Show* was playing on 120 channels, attracting 10 million viewers. At one point, the cattlemen of America shuddered when she said she would stop eating beef. Her endorsement of any book virtually assured its place as a best seller.

Winfrey's life and fabled career seemed to be the perfect subject matter for the medium that she has made her own. Born in 1954 to unwed teenage parents in Kosciusko, Mississippi, Winfrey lived with her grandmother for the first six years of her life. She then moved to Milwaukee to live with her mother, Vernita Lee, for the next seven years. During her time in Milwaukee she was sexually molested and raped. In response to her pain Winfrey rebelled, got into trouble, and eventually ended up in a detention home at the age of 14. She became pregnant, giving birth to a stillborn child. At that point, she vowed to reclaim her shattered life.

Winfrey moved to Nashville to live with her father Vernon Winfrey, who apparently set the proper limits she needed to turn her life around. Winfrey landed her first job at a radio station in Nashville, while studying broadcasting at Tennessee State University. She won several local pageants, including "Miss Black Nashville" and "Miss Tennessee."

After college Winfrey moved to Baltimore, where for eight years she hosted a talk show called *People Are Talking*. She then moved to Chicago. Her radiance on TV attracted the attention of Steven Spielberg, who cast her in the film *The Color Purple*, with Whoopi Goldberg and Danny Glover. Her motion picture debut as Sofia earned her an Academy Award nomination.

Oprah Winfrey received a Doctor of Humane Letters degree from Morehouse College in Atlanta, Georgia, the alma mater of Dr. Martin Luther King, Jr. In return, she donated a million dollars to the all-male college, a gift to be used to educate 100 African American males. By this time in her storied career, Oprah Winfrey was the wealthiest black woman in America, by some accounts more powerful and influential than the president.

July 17, 1984

Jesse Jackson, candidate for president of the United States, addresses the Democratic National Convention in San Francisco.

Minister, negotiator, advocate, Jackson had recently organized the Rainbow/Push Coalition, an advocacy group of poor and disenfranchised persons of all colors throughout the United States.

Born in Greenville, South Carolina, in 1941, Jackson joined the civil rights movement through Martin Luther King, Jr.'s Southern Christian Leadership Conference. Ordained a Baptist minister in 1968, he served as executive director of the SCLC from 1967 to 1971. In the 1970s, he pushed to the forefront of American politics, appearing to have the greatest chance of any African American of being elected president.

In his remarks in San Francisco, Jackson told the Democratic Party, "America is not like a blanket, one piece of unbroken cloth, the same color, the same texture, the same size. America is more like a quilt — many patches, many pieces, many colors, many sizes, all woven and held together by a common thread — the white, the Hispanic, the black, the Arab, the Jew, the woman, the native American, the small farmer, the business person, the environmentalist, the peace activist, the young, the old, the lesbian, the gay, and the disabled make up the American Quilt" (www.wake america.com).

September 20, 1984

The Cosby Show, destined to become one of the most popular television shows in the United States, premieres on the National Broadcasting Company (NBC).

The situation comedy starred Bill Cosby as Dr. Heathcliff Huxtable, a successful obstetrician who wryly parents a family of precocious children with his beautiful attorney wife, Clair, played by Phylicia Rashad. The Huxtable children featured Lisa Bonet as Denise, Malcolm-Jamal Warner as Theo, Tempestt Bledsoe as Vanessa, Keshia Knight Pulliam as Rudy, and Sabrina Le Beauf as Sondra.

Cosby, born in Philadelphia in 1937, had already starred in the groundbreaking series *I Spy* with Robert Culp. His previous successes in television, movies, radio, nightclubs, and stage had made him one of America's premier performers, but *The Cosby Show* solidified his position as an entertainment icon.

Although the show featured an African American cast, it did not focus on many of the stereotypes that permeated other ethnic situation comedies. Although the episodes sometimes explored topics of importance to the African American culture, they mostly featured situations based on Cosby's stand-up comedy routine, highlighting confounding family dynamics that are resolved through love and gentle humor.

Audiences of all demographics loved the show, which stood at the top of the Nielson ratings for most of its eight seasons. *The Cosby Show* made the TV room the place to be on Thursday nights.

January 7, 1985

Public Television station WNET in New York broadcasts the short film *Ballad of an Unsung Hero*, the true story of the man who first brought Spanish-language radio to the United States.

Radio station KMPC in Los Angeles had broadcast the first Spanish language radio program in America. Pedro J. Gonzalez — a former telegraph operator for Pancho Villa, who had come to the United States to escape the hardships of Mexico — began hosting a program called *Los Madrugadores,* meaning "the Early Risers." *Los Madrugadores* aired every morning from 4:00 A.M. to 6:00 P.M. until 1934. Gonzalez also organized a band by the same name, destined to become the first popular Mexican American group in the United States.

The radio program was carried from Los Angeles on a 100,000-watt signal, which could be heard throughout the Southwest. Gonzalez often used the broadcast as a platform for protesting the treatment of Mexican Americans and Mexican immigrants in the United States.

In 1934, he was sent to San Quentin Prison on trumped-up rape charges. He served only six years of his 50-year sentence and was deported to Mexico, where he resumed his radio career. He eventually returned to the United States and died in Lodi, California, in 1995 at the age of 99.

January 12, 1986

Franklin Chang-Diaz becomes the first Hispanic American astronaut in space.

Speaking in Spanish to television viewers from onboard the space shuttle *Columbia*, he announced, "The view is spectacular." Throughout the mission, he became the eyes and ears of the Hispanic American community, providing commentary and explanation for a Spanish-speaking audience for the first time in NASA history. This was the first of six successful space shuttle flights in which Chang-Diaz would participate between 1986 and 1998.

Born and raised in San Jose, Costa Rica, Chang-Diaz was the grandson of a Chinese immigrant to the Central American country. He immigrated to the United States in 1969, where he studied mechanical engineering at the University of Connecticut. In 1977, Chang-Diaz received a Ph.D. in physics from the Massachusetts Institute of Technology (MIT). The National Aeronautics and Space Administration chose him for the space program in 1980.

January 20, 1986

The birthday of slain civil rights leader Martin Luther King, Jr., is celebrated officially for the first time.

It was three years since President Ronald Reagan had signed the legislation designating the third Monday of January — King's birthday — as a national holiday. King's birthday became the first national holiday created since 1948 (Memorial Day). It also became only the second national holiday commemorating an American (George Washington), and the first national holiday honoring a person of color.

The road to the national holiday had been an arduous, 18-year process. The first proposal to so honor the Reverend King came four days after his assassination, from Michigan congressman John Conyers. In March of 1970, Conyers and Representative Shirley Chisholm of New York announced a hearing to study the creation of the holiday, after Congress was deluged with petitions carrying 6 million signatures in favor of the holiday. Despite objections by Senator Jesse Helms (R-NC) and other conservatives in Congress, the House of Representatives and the Senate both approved the measure in 1983.

African Americans — and other holiday supporters — expressed irritation that many businesses — including the New York Stock Exchange — remained open on Martin Luther King, Jr.'s Birthday for many years after it became a national holiday. However, schools, federal and state employees, and most banks and city services came to observe the day.

November 6, 1986

The United States Congress passes the Immigration Reform and Control Act of 1986, which eases regulations and allows — at least, superficially — illegal United States residents to seek amnesty.

The bill had been originally introduced in 1982 as the Simpson-Mazzoli Bill — named for its co-sponsors, Senator Alan Simpson (R-WY) and Congressman Romano Mazzoli (D-KY). After revisions, the measure offered amnesty for such residents who entered the country before January 1, 1982, by giving them temporary residence for 18 months before they could apply for permanent residence. It also imposed civil and criminal sanctions on employers who knowingly hired or helped aliens not allowed to work in the United States.

Many critics saw the act as merely a means to identify the thousands of undocumented individuals otherwise untraceable by the Immigration and Naturalization Service. As a result of the act, more than 3 million persons — mostly immigrants from Mexico and El Salvador — stepped out from the shadows of illegal immigration to gain amnesty and permanent residency in the United States. The amnesty process — fraught with fear, misinformation, and consternation — caused substantial anxiety throughout much of the Hispanic community. Untold numbers of undocumented individuals — who either knew or suspected they would not qualify for amnesty — remained underground, unwilling to risk identification and deportation.

The outcome of the act seemed to be another plodding bureaucracy that would rarely enforce employer sanctions. An entire black market in phony documents — Social Security cards, permanent resident cards, birth certificates — emerged, enabling employers to keep undocumented workers, who were allowed to remain — tentatively — in the country.

April 6, 1987

A baseball executive reveals lingering prejudice against blacks in management.

An inebriated-looking Al Campanis, vice president of the Los Angeles Dodgers, appeared on NBC's *Nightline* with Ted Koppel. In a public relations disaster for the Dodgers, America gained a useful glimpse into some of the archaic thinking that still infected baseball. Campanis — a one-time teammate with Jackie Robinson on the Montreal Royals — implied that blacks in general "may not have some of the necessities" for front office management in baseball. Campanis went on to bumble through the interview: "I have never said that blacks are not intelligent, many of them are highly intelligent, but they may not have the desire to be in the front office. I know that they have wanted to manage, and some of them have managed. But they are outstanding athletes, very good, gifted, and they are wonderful people. And that's all I can tell you about them" (Burns, p. 452).

The Dodgers fired Campanis within 24 hours.

Until that point, only three African Americans — Frank Robinson, Larry Doby, and Maury Wills — had ever managed a major league team. No African American had ever held a top-level, front office job.

July 3, 1987

Wilma Pearl Mankiller is elected chief of the Cherokee Nation of Oklahoma, the second largest Native American tribe at more than 140,000 members.

As one of the Five Civilized Tribes, based in Tahlequah, Oklahoma, the

Cherokee had played an integral role in the history of the United States. The first woman to ever hold the position, Mankiller had been elected deputy principal chief in 1983. In 1985, she became interim chief in 1985 by appointment of the Bureau of Indian Affairs, when Chief Ross Swimmer resigned. In 1991, she would win her second term, garnering 83 percent of the vote, serving for ten years in total.

In her inaugural speech in 1985, Mankiller spoke of the anticipation of change: "I think there is a bit of nervousness in the Cherokee Nation," she said. "I think any time there is change, people wonder what's going to happen.... I like what's going on at the Cherokee Nation. There will be very little change. The only thing that will change is that there will be more of an emphasis on the development of the economy."

Born in Rocky Mountain, Oklahoma, in 1945, Mankiller was subject to rural and urban poverty, both in her home state and in California. She relocated to the Hunter's Point district of San Francisco as part of the Bureau of Indian Affairs program in 1956. She earned a degree in social work at San Francisco State College, becoming intensely interested in Indian Affairs with the Native American occupation of Alcatraz in 1969.

Wilma Mankiller overcame male chauvinism inside and outside the tribe, then used her position to be a successful organizer of grassroots programs for betterment of the environment and the social situation of Native Americans. As chief, she made education and health care — typically women's concerns — fresh tribal priorities.

Mankiller was elected to the National Women's Hall of Fame in 1993 and earned the Presidential Medal of Freedom in 1998.

April 15, 1988

Warner Brothers Pictures releases *Stand and Deliver*, the first major Hollywood movie whose script, direction, performance, financing, and production was accomplished by Hispanic Americans.

The award-winning, well received theatrical film found a second life through wide distribution among American schools and educational institutions.

The movie depicted the true-life story of Bolivian-born Jaime Escalante, the first Hispanic teacher to be the subject of a Hollywood film. Escalante had perfected a method for teaching advanced mathematics at Garfield High School in East Los Angeles. Escalante — played by Edward James Olmos — is portrayed working to prepare his poverty-stricken, inner-city students for entrance to some of the most elite American colleges. The movie also starred Lou Diamond Phillips, Ramon Menendez, and Rosanna de Soto.

The true-life Escalante received the White House's Hispanic Heritage

Award in 1989, as well as the American Institute for Public Service's Jefferson Award in 1990. He went on to star in a series of classroom programs called *Futures* for the Public Broadcasting System, honored with many awards.

August 10, 1988

The United States Congress authorizes the Civil Liberties Act of 1988.

Signed by President Ronald Reagan, the act authorized reparations for Japanese Americans interned during World War II. Payments of $20,000 per surviving internee were provided the following year. The purpose of the act was, in part, "to apologize on behalf of the people of the United States for the evacuation, internment, and relocations of such citizens and permanent residing aliens."

The Civil Liberties Act was the culmination of the reversals and reparations made in the wake of Executive Order 9066, issued by President Franklin Delano Roosevelt in 1942. The order sent more than 110,000 Japanese Americans to internment camps.

Fred Korematsu had been a young man in 1942 when he ran away from his home in Oakland, California, trying to escape evacuation to an internment camp. That same year, Gordon Hirabayashi had sued the army for imposing an 8 P.M. to 6 A.M. curfew, which Hirabayashi claimed constituted racial discrimination and a violation of due process under the Fifth and Fourteenth Amendments. Both men lost their original Supreme Court cases, but sued again in 1983 for vindication on a charge of "prosecutorial misconduct." A federal court vacated Korematsu's conviction, expunging his criminal record. The court also struck down Hirabayashi's conviction for refusing to obey the evacuation order, but declined to reverse the curfew violation.

These cases amply illustrate the racist fervor of World War II, as well as the change of attitude that had transpired since.

By 1999, more than 82,250 persons of Japanese ancestry received more than $1.6 billion in reparation money. On February 5, 1999, the Office of Redress Administration of the United States Justice Department closed, as the ten-year administration of the Civil Liberties Act of 1988 ended. With it also closed one of the darkest chapters in American history, at least in the matter of federal financial redress.

August 21, 1988

Cesar Chavez completes his 36-day Fast for Life, intended to demonstrate his noncooperation with supermarkets that promoted and sold California grapes.

Chavez considered his fasts a personal spiritual exercise, a method of purification and strengthening. He also used the publicity to demonstrate the importance of the issue at hand, as a heartfelt prayer to the American people for those in the farm worker movement.

Starting July 16, 1988, Chavez consumed nothing but water. When Chavez ended his fast, the Reverend Jesse Jackson took it up for three more days. Other popular figures joining in the fast included the Reverend J. Lowery, president of the Southern Christian Leadership Conference; actors Edward Olmos, Emilio Estevez, Martin Sheen, and Danny Glover; actresses Whoopi Goldberg and Julie Carmen; singer Carly Simon; and Kerry Kennedy, daughter of Robert Kennedy.

October 17, 1988

The United States Congress enacts the Indian Gaming Regulatory Act, paving the way for individual tribes to operate gambling facilities on tribal land.

The act, which established the National Indian Gaming Commission, sought to strike a balance between the interests of the tribes and the interests of the states within whose borders the reservations existed. Many tribes viewed the act as a significant step to allow the procurement of money to meet the service and infrastructural needs of the tribes.

Historically, while state law did not dictate what was permissible within a reservation, Public Law 280 allowed states to prohibit gambling within a reservation only if gambling had been completely prohibited within the state. In *Cabazon v. State of California*, the United States Supreme Court decided that if a state allowed gambling in certain forms during certain events — such as charitable activities — those forms of gambling would be allowed on Indian reservations as well. Thus, the floodwaters were opened to gaming facilities on tribal lands.

Gambling provided a means by which tribes could raise funding, further enabling them to function as independent entities, autonomous of the United States government. Detractors complained of the kinds of seedy elements gambling dens would attract, thus dragging down the tribal function rather than building it up. Supporters responded by saying gambling had been a part of the Native American way of life for centuries and would be a viable alternative to dependence on the federal government. Others, tongues firmly in cheeks, would say providing gambling for the white man would be a way for the tribe to make money, while exerting a certain covert reprisal against European Americans for all they had taken from the tribes.

August 22, 1989

Black activist Huey Newton, the former minister of defense for the Black Panther Party, is gunned down in Oakland, California, by a reputed drug dealer trying to make a name for himself.

The good-looking, charismatic Newton had become the virtual poster boy for Black Panther Party; America never had the chance to know the man beyond the angry image of a clenched fist, the personality of varying and sophisticated tastes.

Newton exemplified a more human side of the Panthers, as active in providing food and medicine to the needy as in clashing with the authorities. Huey Newton was a classically trained concert pianist and a fervent fan of Vincent Price movies; he had boasted an affinity for MacBeth's soliloquy.

After an arrest and manslaughter conviction in 1968, he was released from prison in 1974. In 1973, Newton fled the United States to avoid another arrest, finally returning to Oakland in 1977. By then, the Black Panther Party had dissolved, with most of its leadership dead, jailed, or in exile.

Despite its problems, the mercurial Black Panther Party was an organization unlike any other in the history of the United States. It had highlighted and focused attention on the needs and power of African Americans in the time of their emergence into the forefront of American culture.

October 1, 1989

Colin Powell becomes the first African American appointed to the post of chairman of the Joint Chiefs of Staff for the armed forces.

At 53, Powell was the youngest man ever to serve in the post, and the highest ranking African American in the history of the United States military. Serving in the post under President George Bush, Powell was later appointed as the first African American secretary of state under Bush's son, George W. Bush.

Colin Luther Powell was born in New York City on April 5, 1937. The son of Jamaican immigrants, a clerk and a seamstress, Powell joined the Reserve Officers Training Corps at City College of New York, which won for him a commission of 2nd Lieutenant in the United States Army. Powell served in Vietnam beginning in December of 1962, where he was wounded twice. He earned both the Purple Heart and the Soldier's Medal.

Returning from Vietnam, Powell earned a master's in business administration at George Washington University in Washington, D.C. During the Reagan administration, he became special military advisor to Defense Secretary Caspar Weinberger.

Colin Powell provided a counterpoint, centrist philosophy within the conservative administrations of Reagan and Bush, often advising caution over immediate retribution, while emphasizing restraint and coalition building. Powell has presented something of a paradox, a peace-loving career military man, a black man in a conservative establishment.

In 1995, Powell wrote his memoirs, *My American Journey*, which topped the *New York Times* bestseller list.

January 13, 1990

Lawrence Douglas Wilder is elected governor of Virginia, the first African American to be elected the chief executive of a state in American history.

Pinckney Benton Stewart Pinchback had served as acting governor of Louisiana for a month in 1872, but only to succeed Governor Henry Clay Warmoth, who had been impeached.

For Wilder, the governor's office became the pinnacle of a successful and controversial political career in Virginia. After election as a state senator for Virginia in 1970, Wilder worked to make Martin Luther King, Jr.'s birthday a state holiday. Wilder also launched a blistering attack on the state song, "Carry Me Back to Old Virginny." Wilder spoke out against the song's numerous references that proved detrimental and derisive to African Americans. Elected lieutenant governor in 1986, Wilder became the first African American to hold that post as well. He became an avid supporter of women's rights, particular a woman's right to choose an abortion.

Lawrence Douglas Wilder was born in Richmond, Virginia, in 1931. He was named for the famous abolitionist and advocate Frederick Douglas and pioneer poet Paul Laurence Dunbar. After graduating from Armstrong High School, Wilder earned a Bronze Star for heroism during the Korean War. He received a bachelor's degree in chemistry from Virginia Union University plus a law degree from the Howard University School of Law in 1959. He went on to open a lucrative legal practice in Richmond, where he developed his flamboyant, fashionable, and successful style.

June 27, 1990

Nelson Mandela, now free, visits Atlanta.

On this date, Nelson Rolihlahla Mandela, deputy president of the African National Congress, the very embodiment of the struggle for freedom in South Africa, visited Atlanta, Georgia, as part of a ten-day tour of the United States. Mandela came on a mission to convince Americans to maintain the sanctions against the white-minority government in South

Africa, as well as to raise international awareness of South Africa's apartheid system of government.

Mandela had just been released from Victor Verster Prison on February 11, after spending more than 28 years in prison. As a leader of the African National Congress — banned for years within South Africa — Mandela had constituted the *Umkhonto we Sizwe*, a fortified nucleus preparing for the armed struggle against the white South African government. After traveling abroad to seek support for his cause, he was arrested upon returning to South Africa. Initially charged with illegal exit of the country, incitement to strike, then later sabotage, Mandela was sent to prison on a life sentence. But as his sentence continued over the years, Mandela became a symbol of resistance to the oppression of South African apartheid.

Included among the highlights of the tour of Atlanta was a ceremony in which Mandela placed a wreath at the tomb of Martin Luther King, Jr. He received honorary degrees from several black colleges. He addresses a gathering of 50,000, mostly African American onlookers. During a rousing speech, Mandela drew on the memory and ideals of Martin Luther King, Jr., echoing the words, "Let freedom ring, let us all acclaim now. Let freedom ring in South Africa. Let Freedom ring wherever people's rights are trampled upon."

The next day, on June 28, Mandela traveled to Detroit, where he met Rosa Parks, the matron of the Montgomery Bus Boycott.

In 1991, Nelson was elected president of the African National Congress, which would conduct a national conference for the first time in nearly 40 years. In 1993, he received the Nobel Peace Prize, a year after the officially-sanctioned apartheid system of government in South Africa collapsed. One year later, in May of 1994, he was elected president of South Africa.

March 3, 1991

In a traffic stop that will galvanize a nation, 25-year-old Rodney King, an African American, is stopped and viciously beaten by Los Angeles police officers.

The intoxicated King had led officers on a high speed chase and resisted arrest when he finally stopped. Part-time plumbing salesman George William Holliday, from his nearby apartment, captured the subsequent events on an 81-second video tape.

The video depicted the beating of King by four L.A. police officers: Laurence Powell, Theodore J. Briseno, Timothy E. Wind, and Sergeant Stacey C. Koon. The video showed that 17 other officers at the scene had stood by, apparently merely watching the incident. The altercation left King on the ground, semiconscious after the policemen reportedly rained 56 blows on King's body, beating him with their clubs, kicking him with their feet. The video tape flashed through the electronic media for months to come, spurring furious debate over police brutality, racially motivated violence, and the power of home video. Many African Americans asserted that the brutality depicted was the kind of treatment blacks regularly received in the hands of law enforcement.

The Los Angeles County district attorney dismissed all charges against King four days later. Instead, charges of police brutality were leveled against the four police officers.

August 1, 1991

The 1990 United States Census reveals a Native American population of just under 2 million, an 800 percent increase from the 250,000 Native Americans documented in 1910.

For the first time since European Americans landed on the shores of eastern North America, Native American numbers began to approach those estimated for the seventeenth century.

According to census findings, the states containing the largest Native American populations included Oklahoma (252,000), California (236,000), and Arizona (203,000). The federal government now recognized 210 Native American tribes inside Alaska, and 321 outside.

April 21, 1992

Antonia C. Novello, the first woman and the first Hispanic American to serve as surgeon general, delivers a speech in Los Angeles addressing what she considers the most pressing health issues of the 1990s.

Two years previous, she had been appointed to the post of surgeon general by President George Bush.

Born in Fahardo, Puerto Rico, in 1945, Novello was sickly as a child, which may have motivated her toward a career in health care. She received her bachelor's degree and her medical degree at the University of Puerto Rico, completing her internship and residency at the University of Michigan Medical Center at Ann Arbor. She went to work for the National Institute of Health (NIH) in 1978 while completing her master's degree in public health at John Hopkins University. After serving the NIH in various capacities for 12 years, Novello was chosen by President Bush to succeed C. Everett Koop as surgeon general.

Novello was in the second of her three years as surgeon general when she made the speech. She was already known as an outspoken advocate for health issues involving people of color, children, teens, and woman. She often spoke out against the campaigns of the tobacco and alcohol companies that targeted young audiences. Images such as "Joe Camel" from Camel cigarettes particularly disgusted her. She clearly admonished such advertisements in her address.

April 29, 1992

The verdict of the jury serving on the superior court trial of four Los Angeles police officers for police brutality against motorist Rodney King is returned. All four defendants are acquitted, touching off the worst racial riot of the century.

The trial of *California v. Powell, et al.* had lasted more than three months. So many persons had seen the video captured by George Holliday of the 1991 beating of Rodney King that Judge Stanley Weisberg had found it difficult to select an impartial setting. Finally, he set the trial in Simi Valley, Ventura County, even though the incident had occurred in Los Angeles. The jury — composed of ten European Americans, one Asian American, and one Hispanic American — included no African Americans.

During the trial, attorneys for the defendants picked apart Holliday's video frame by frame, countering the seemingly overwhelming visual evidence of brutality. Attorneys for the defendants also asserted that the use of beatings and electrocutions had become more prominent within the force, following the ban on choke holds imposed by the City of Los Angeles. This ban followed the 1983 United States Supreme Court case *City of Los Angeles v. Lyons.*

Los Angeles v. Lyons had involved a black man who had been placed in a choke hold by a police officer during a routine traffic inspection. Although at that time the Supreme Court had decided against the plaintiff, the case had brought to light the questionable strategies employed by Los Angeles police. The City of Los Angeles subsequently banned the use of choke holds by its officers.

In the end, the Simi Valley jury — after deliberating for seven days — astonishingly acquitted all four officers.

The remarkable decision, broadcast throughout the media, touched off riots throughout Los Angeles. Beginning in South Central Los Angeles, the melees spread throughout the city, creating the worst scene of civil unrest in the century, more destructive than the Watts riots in 1965. In disturbing video footage that would also blaze across the airwaves, bystander truck driver Reginald Denny was dragged out of his truck and beaten on an east Los Angeles street. Several businesses, most run by residents of Korean descent, became targets of the wrath. One hundred fifty fires raged across greater Los Angeles, burning well into the next day. Looters raided stores. Six thousand National Guard troops joined policemen, sheriffs, and the highway patrol in attempts to quell the rage. The rioting left 50 dead, eight shot by police, and more than 2,000 injuries. Eighteen hundred firefighters battled the blazes, which caused more than 1 billion dollars in damage.

Other demonstrations erupted in cities such as Oakland, California, and Atlanta, Georgia, as thousands expressed their outrage at what appeared to many a clear miscarriage of justice.

January 24, 1993

Thurgood Marshall, the first African American Supreme Court justice and a stalwart attorney for the National Association for the Advancement of Colored People during its most trying times, dies at the age of 84.

Appointed to the Supreme Court in 1967 by President Lyndon Johnson, Marshall served on the highest court for 24 years, retiring in 1991 due to deteriorating health.

Marshall received national attention as the chief attorney for the plaintiff in the landmark case of *Brown v. Board of Education of Topeka, Kansas.* He served on the United States Court of Appeals from 1961 to 1965. He became well known for his insightful dissents as well as a biting sarcasm often trained on presenting attorneys and fellow justices alike. Above all, Thurgood Marshall became a preeminent icon of people of color, equal justice and civil rights in America.

April 4, 1993

Ellen Ochoa — born in Los Angeles of a Mexican-born father and an American mother — embarks upon a nine-day mission aboard the Space Shuttle *Discovery,* thus becoming the first Hispanic woman to serve as an astronaut.

Ochoa had first applied to the space program in 1985, eventually placing among the top 100 candidates. In January 1990, she numbered among 22 candidates (out of an original 2,000 applicants) admitted to the Johnson Space Center in Houston, Texas. Ochoa graduated from the training program in July 1991.

Ochoa was born in Los Angeles, California, on May 10, 1958. Her father, Joseph Ochoa, had been born in Mexico and had met Roseanne Deardorff in the United States. After Ellen's father left the family in 1969, Rosanne raised Ellen, her sister, and three brothers by herself. Ellen excelled at math in high school and became an accomplished classical flautist.

Ochoa graduated as valedictorian from San Diego State University, majoring in physics. She continued her education, earning her master's degree in engineering in 1981, then a Ph.D. in the same field in 1985.

Ochoa became a gifted researcher at Sandia National Laboratories in Albuquerque, New Mexico, as well as at the NASA Ames Research Center in Mountain View, California. She held three patents on optical processing. Ochoa participated in several other shuttle missions following her initial 1993 flight, receiving numerous awards for her work. These awards included the Outstanding Leadership Medal in 1995 and an Exceptional Service Medal in 1997.

April 8, 1993

Marian Anderson, who had gained a reputation as the world's greatest contralto throughout a brilliant and courageous musical career, dies at the age of 91 in Portland, Oregon, of congestive heart failure following a stroke she had suffered earlier that spring.

The recipient of honors and awards throughout the world, Anderson used her $10,000 Bok Award to establish a scholarship fund for young singers. She was the first African American to sing with the New York Metropolitan Opera Company. In 1958, Anderson was named a delegate to the United Nations. She received the Presidential Medal of Freedom in 1963 and the National Medal of Arts in 1986. In 1991, she established the Marian Anderson Center for pediatric sickle cell anemia.

A throng of admirers, including master violinist Isaac Stern, attended her memorial service in June at Carnegie Hall in New York.

April 23, 1993

Cesar Chavez dies in his sleep near Yuma, Arizona, close to his birthplace.

He is said to have had a long, exhausting, but active previous day, embroiled in a legal defense involving the United Farm Workers lettuce boycott. Tired but in good spirits, Chavez exhibited no particular signs of distress or illness when he went to bed. He was found the next morning, lying on his back in bed, a book of Native American drafts in his right hand. He had passed away while reading some time during the night, at the age of 66.

On April 29, 50,000 people from throughout the nation came to the Delano, California, field office of the United Farm Workers, the site where Chavez had conducted his first public fast in 1968. It was the largest funeral ever held for an American labor leader. He was laid to rest at La Paz, California, the site of the United Farm Workers headquarters.

Cardinal Roger Mahoney called Chavez "a special prophet for the world's farm workers." Playwright Luis Valdez said, "We have come to plant your heart like a seed ... the farm workers shall harvest in the seed of your memory."

In 1995, President William J. Clinton posthumously awarded Chavez the Medal of Freedom, the nation's highest civilian honor.

June 1, 1993

Connie Chung joins Dan Rather as co-anchor on the *CBS Evening News*, becoming the first Asian American — and the second woman after Barbara Walters — to anchor a network news program.

She became one of the most recognized personalities in television news.

Born Constance Yu-Hwa Chung in Washington, D.C., on August 20, 1946, Chung graduated from the University of Maryland in 1969 with a degree in journalism. She began her career at WTTG-TV in Washington, D.C., joining the Columbia Broadcasting System in 1971. For CBS, Chung worked as a Washington-based correspondent, covering Watergate, Capitol Hill, and the 1972 presidential campaign.

In 1976, Chung began work at CBS-owned KNXT in Los Angeles, filling in on morning and weekend news programs. She worked for seven years in Los Angeles, while serving as a substitute anchor for the *CBS Morning News*, and *CBS News* evening and weekend broadcasts.

Chung continued on to achieve a successful if sometimes contentious career. At times, she was criticized for using controversial techniques in her interviews and broadcasts.

October 7, 1993

Toni Morrison wins the Nobel Prize for Literature, the first African American woman to win the world's foremost literary award.

Morrison began her first novel — *The Bluest Eye*, released in 1970 — while living and raising a family in Texas. Morrison's most popular book, *Beloved*, was published in 1987. The story, about an escaped slave, captured the coveted Pulitzer Prize for Literature.

Toni Morrison was born Chloe Anthony Wofford on February 18, 1931, in Lorain, Ohio. Her parents — George and Ramah Willis — had brought their four children from the South to Ohio to escape racism. In the small industrial town of Lorain, Chloe Wofford interacted with a mixture of European immigrants, Mexicans, and Southern blacks. Wofford was actually educated in an integrated school long before they were supported by the Supreme Court.

Morrison reportedly did not remember encountering discrimination until she began dating, although she saw it in her father, who had a Marcus Garvey perspective on whites.

Toni Wofford attended Howard University in Washington, D.C., majoring in English. Upon graduation in 1955, she taught English at Texas Southern University. Among her students was Stokely Carmichael, who gained fame as the coordinator of the Student Nonviolent Coordinating Committee. Wofford met and married Jamaican architect Harold Morrison in 1958, whom she would later divorce.

In 1964, Toni Morrison obtained a job as an editor with Random House, where she worked for 20 years. In 1987, Morrison was named the Robert F. Goheen Professor in the Council of Humanities at Princeton University, becoming the first black woman writer to hold a named chair at an Ivy League University.

November 3, 1993

The United States Congress passes a joint measure called the Apology Resolution, signed by President William J. Clinton, acknowledging and apologizing for the United States' overthrowing the Kingdom of Hawaii.

The resolution "apologizes to Native Hawaiians on behalf of the people of the United States for the overthrow of the Kingdom of Hawaii on January 17, 1893, with participation of the agents and citizens of the United States, and the deprivation of the rights of Native Hawaiians to self-determination."

October 16, 1995

The Million Man March, organized by Louis Farrakhan's Nation of Islam, draws some 400,000 (according to the *New York Times*; other estimates ranged as high as 1.5 million).

African American men reportedly traveled by car and by bus from all corners of the country to gather in the Capitol Mall, between the Washington Monument and the Lincoln Memorial. The purpose of the march, in the words of Farrakhan, was to assemble "a million sober, disciplined, committed, dedicated, inspired black men" (Bierbauer) to show the discrepancies in mainstream America's view of African American males.

Despite the turnout, observers inside and outside the African American community expressed distrust of the event organizer, citing Farrakhan as a separatist and a racist, for his comments about European Americans, Jews, and Christians. "If it had originated from our end, we would be there," said Levi Chaplin of Pleasant Lane Baptist Church. "But we can't support somebody that talks against us in one breath, and in one breath hugs us."

Despite controversy surrounding the leader, the march itself proved successful, as participants sought to contest the stereotypical image of black males as criminals, drug dealers, and loiterers.

June 13, 1996

The United States Supreme Court reviews and decides the Rodney King case involving charges of police brutality leveled against four Los Angeles police officers.

District Court judge John G. Davies had sentenced officers Stacey Koon and Laurence Powell to 30 months, which the prosecutors felt was lower than prescribed federal guidelines. The other officers — Timothy E. Wind and Theodore J. Briseno — had already been acquitted.

The Ninth Circuit Court of Appeals had agreed with federal prosecutors, saying that the sentences should have been longer. But by a 9–0 ruling, the United States Supreme Court agreed with Davies, citing the mitigating circumstances — namely Rodney King's resistive behavior — involved in Davies's sentencing. In the decision, the Supreme Court supported the validity of district court sentencing, concluding that the higher courts should generally defer to the lower courts in such matters.

June 23, 1997

Betty Shabazz, widow of famed civil rights leader Malcolm X, dies after suffering for three weeks from burns caused by a fire set by her grandson in her own home.

The 12-year-old grandson, who had been sent to live with Shabazz, apparently set the blaze in reaction to having to move into Shabazz's Yonkers home.

Shabazz, raised in Detroit with adoptive parents, met Malcolm X after attending lectures by the Nation of Islam, while working as a registered nurse in Detroit. After Malcolm X split from Elijah Muhammad in 1964, he and

Betty X took the Muslim surname Shabazz. Betty Shabazz was present with her daughters at the Audubon Ballroom when Malcolm X was gunned down in Harlem on February 21, 1965. Pregnant with twins at the time, Betty Shabazz successfully raised six daughters on her own.

Having attended Tuskegee University in Alabama as an undergraduate, Shabazz returned to school after Malcolm's death, earning her doctorate in education at the University of Massachusetts in 1975. She worked as an administrator at Medgar Evers College in Brooklyn.

In 1994, there was an estrangement between Shabazz and new Nation of Islam leader Louis Farrakhan, growing out a long-held suspicion that Farrakhan had been behind the assassination of Malcolm X. At one point her daughter, Qubilah Shabazz, was accused of trying to hire a hit man to kill Farrakhan. Eventually Betty Shabazz and Farrakhan reconciled at a fundraiser for Qubilah's defense at Harlem's Apollo Theatre. In October of 1995, Shabazz appeared at Farrakhan's Million Man March.

The fire at Betty Shabazz's home was set by the son of Qubilah Shabazz.

June 7, 1998

Jasper, Texas — a town of 7,800 people, ten miles northeast of Houston — is the site of one of the most horrific racial killings of the waning century.

James Byrd — a well known resident of the small town — was beaten and kicked unconscious, then dragged by a logging chain for 2.5 miles along Huff Creek Road, outside Jasper.

While coming home from a party, the intoxicated Byrd was picked up by Lawrence Russell Brewer, John William King, and Shawn Allen Berry, each known as a former convict and a white supremacist. The assaulters drove Byrd up an isolated logging road. There, Berry reportedly beat him, slashed his throat, and sprayed black paint onto his face. Berry then backed his truck over the body, tied the body to the truck bumper with the chain, and dragged it to the edge of a cemetery at an African American church. Along the way, Byrd's body parts — including his decapitated head — were strewn across the pathway.

In response to the outpouring of grief and sympathy from around the world, the Byrd family created the James Byrd Jr. Foundation for Racial Healing. The foundation worked diligently on the passage of hate crime legislation, culminating with the James Byrd Jr. Hate Crimes Act. Passed by the Texas legislature on May 11, 2001, the act strengthened existing hate crime laws.

By November 1999, all three defendants — John William King, Shawn

Allen Berry, and Lawrence Russell Brewer — were convicted of murder in the first degree. Brewer and King were sentenced to death, while Berry faced life in prison for the ghastly murder of James Byrd.

November 3, 1998

David Wu, a Chinese American, is elected to the United States House of Representatives, representing the First Congressional District of Oregon.

A Democrat, Wu became the first Chinese American ever elected to Congress.

Wu was born on the island of Taiwan on April 8, 1955. He earned his bachelor's degree at Stanford University and obtained his law degree from Yale University. With no previous political experience, he captured 52 percent of the vote over public relations consultant Molly Bordonaro.

March 6, 1999

A story of alleged espionage and treason breaks in the *New York Times*.

Wen Ho Lee, a Taiwanese-born American citizen, was accused of providing secrets for the development of nuclear weapons to China. A nuclear scientist working at Los Alamos Laboratory in New Mexico, Lee was accused by Attorney General Janet Reno and the Department of Justice of the crime. Although he spent nine months in solitary confinement, eventually all but one of the 59 charges were dropped.

An 800-page report was completed in May of 1999 by Assistant Attorney General Randy Bellows. The Bellows report indicated not only that the charges had been less than accurate, but that they may not have happened at all. Bellows indicated that racism may have been the motivation.

The report, which allegedly sat on Attorney General Janet Reno's desk for several months, remains largely classified.

In September 1999, United States district judge James Parker of Albuquerque, New Mexico, apologized to Mr. Lee, after criticizing the administration's handling of the case. "The executive branch has enormous power, the abuse of which can be devastating to citizens…. They have embarrassed our entire nation and each of us who is a citizen in it" ("Clinton slams Wen Ho Lee Prosecution").

July 23, 1999

Forty-six people — including 39 African Americans — are arrested as the result of an 18-month undercover drug investigation that would divide the town of Tulia, Texas, as well as highlight the controversies surrounding the War on Drugs.

Forty-one of those people were convicted, based on the word of Tom Coleman, an agent of the Texas Panhandle Regional Narcotics Trafficking Task Force.

However, four years later in 2003, following a lawsuit by the ACLU, most of the convicts were pardoned by Governor Rick Perry in 2003. Agent Coleman was indicted for perjury the same year.

Under the investigation of the American Civil Liberties Union, it was discovered that Coleman usually worked alone, reporting almost exclusively to Swisher County sheriff Larry Stewart and District Attorney Terry D. McEarhern. During Coleman's investigations, drugs buys were never recorded, and no large quantities of drugs, weapons, or cash were ever found. Coleman reportedly had a troubled law enforcement career, often using unorthodox methods resulting in blatant errors. He reportedly had a volatile temper, and was characterized as a racist. Coleman's undercover operation was characterized by the American Civil Liberties Union lawsuit as "an ethnic cleansing of young black males from Tulia." The ACLU asserted that the task force was encouraged — either overtly or covertly — to create a large number of cases by whatever means necessary, to assure its continued federal funding.

The governor's pardons opened avenues for civil law suits on behalf of the defendants. This case is said to illustrate what can go wrong when a drug task force has too much autonomous power. The Texas Panhandle Regional Narcotics Trafficking Task Force numbered among thousands of such task forces created during the 1980s "War on Drugs."

February 4, 2000

The Tulsa Race Riot Commission recommends reparations be made to the aged African American survivors of the Tulsa Race Riot of 1921.

Although no specific amount is recommended for the redress, a preliminary figure of $12 million is among the suggestions by the commission.

The Oklahoma legislature had created the commission in 1998 to investigate the riot, the memory of which had been obscured and repressed by history. The investigation to uncover the uprising included interviews with more than 1,000 persons, 80 of whom were actual survivors of the riot.

The tragedy reportedly had begun on May 20, 1921, when black shoe shiner Dick Rowland rode a downtown Tulsa office building elevator with white elevator operator Sarah Page. Inside the elevator some kind of incident occurred, although there are disagreements about details. Rowland was arrested for assault, although Page never pressed charges. Nevertheless, the match hit the kindling.

A mob of 100 white men, many deputized by the local sheriff, charged the courthouse from which Rowland was scheduled to be released. Seventy-five black men arrived at the jail to protect Rowland. The ensuing altercation resulted in the accidental shooting death of a white man, sending the riot spinning out of control.

The army of white men marched across the railroad tracks to the black district of Greenwood, where more than 1,200 buildings were burnt to the ground. Although the official death toll was 37, the actual number may have been higher than 300, as many survivors remember bodies stacked like firewood.

Today, only one block of the old Greenwood district reportedly stands in the vicinity. The area is occupied by Oklahoma State University at Tulsa.

May 16, 2000

The Oneidas, one of the five members of the Iroquois federation of Indian nations, files a land claim against the State of New York in federal court; the claim encompasses 200,000 acres in western New York, including the city of Syracuse.

The land claim is one of several filed by Iroquois federation nations during the last two decades of the twentieth century. The Cayugas filed a land claim in 1980 at the northern tip of Cayuga Lake. The Senecas laid claim for 18,000 acres on Grand Island, located in the Niagara River outside Buffalo. The Mohawks claimed 15,000 acres in St. Lawrence and Franklin counties. All of these nations cited historic treaties with the white man dating back to George Washington as the bases of claiming title to these lands.

The land claims raised several longstanding issues for the Iroquois nations — and Native American nations in general — concerning their historic dealings with European Americans. It highlighted the innumerable eighteenth and nineteenth century "treaties" through which Americans illegally obtained hundreds of thousands of Indian acreage. It also raised fiscal fears for states and municipalities, which anticipated losing millions in tax dollars once lands came under possession of the sovereign tribal states. Finally, there was anxiety on both sides about the huge bill that would be amassed for the steady stream of litigations surrounding these land claims.

The Indians, however, said the land claims were about redressing ancient wrongs and securing a brighter future for their descendants.

July 11, 2000

The New York Times releases the results of a nationwide poll on race relations in the United States.

Conducted to measure attitudes and opinions about race, the telephone survey involves 2,165 adults, composed of 934 blacks and 1,107 whites. The outcome provides the following insights into the current climate of American race relations:

- Fifty-seven percent of all persons surveyed said they felt race relations to be generally good, an improvement of 16 percent from 1990.

- Seventy-nine percent of blacks and 63 percent of whites approved of interracial marriage. In 1991, only 44 percent of whites and 78 percent of blacks approved.

- Seventy-four percent of those surveyed said there had been real progress in reducing racial discrimination. 78 percent of whites saw real progress made, while 58 percent of blacks saw real progress. Each group had raised their percentage by 25 percent since 1992.

- Forty percent of blacks said that race relations were generally bad, citing no real progress since the 1960s.

- Forty-five percent of blacks and 39 percent of whites said they believed all whites disliked blacks.

- Forty-five percent of whites and 45 percent of blacks said they believed all blacks disliked whites.

- Ninety-four percent of blacks and 93 percent of whites said they would vote for a qualified black candidate for president, if the candidate was nominated by the party to which they belonged. At the same time, 55 percent of whites and 62 percent of blacks said they did not think the country was ready to elect a black president.

- Eighty-five percent of whites said they did not care if their neighborhood was predominately populated with either whites or blacks. Yet, two-thirds of whites said they thought most whites preferred to live in a neighborhood populated mostly with whites. Moreover, 85 percent of whites said they actually lived in a neighborhood composed of few or no blacks.

- Seventy-three percent of all persons surveyed — including 73 percent of whites, and 80 percent of blacks — said their opportunities for success in life were greater than their parents'.

January 22, 2001

Dr. Condoleezza Rice is named national security advisor by President George W. Bush.

Rice was the first African American — and the first woman — to hold such a position among presidential advisors.

A member of Stanford University faculty since 1981, Rice had completed six years as University Provost before Bush appointed her. An expert in international studies — particularly Eastern European and Soviet affairs — Rice served in the George H. W. Bush administration from 1989 through 1991. During this period — which witnessed German reunification and the end of the Soviet Union — Rice served as director of Soviet and Eastern European affairs on the National Security Council.

Born in Birmingham, Alabama, on November 14, 1954, Rice earned her bachelor's degree in political science at the University of Denver. She continued on to earn her master's degree at the University of Notre Dame, then returned to the University of Denver for her Ph.D. Rice received honorary doctorates from Morehouse College (1991), the University of Alabama (1994), the University of Notre Dame (1995), and the Mississippi College of Law (2003).

Dr. Rice served on the board of directors for organizations such as Chevron Corporation, Charles Schwab Corporation, the Hewlett Foundation, the RAND Corporation, the National Council for Soviet and East European Studies, and KQED, a Public Broadcasting Service station in San Francisco.

Three years after her appointment, Rice came under severe pressure by the 9/11 Commission to testify in public concerning the George W. Bush administration's handling of al-Qaeda, its pursuit of the war in Iraq and — particularly — what it did not do to protect the United States from the terrorist attacks on September 11, 2001.

February 19, 2001

Arkansas legislators set aside a state holiday to honor Daisy Bates, the mentor to the nine black students who integrated Central High School in the 1957 desegregation battle.

Set for the third week of every February, it is the only holiday in the nation to honor an African American woman.

In a little-recognized story from the volatile days of September 1957, Daisy Bates and her husband Lucius served as mentors — and her home the safe harbor — for the Central High Nine. These nine African American high school students had endured epithets and abuse to desegregate the high school in Little Rock, Arkansas.

Born in 1912 in Huttig, Arkansas, Bates was elected president of the Arkansas Conference of the National Association for the Advancement of Colored People in 1952. Her husband was the publisher of the weekly *Arkansas State Press.*

Throughout the crisis in Little Rock, the nine students would gather at the Bateses' home at 1207 W. 28th Street, which offered a needed shelter from the pressures outside as well as a place to strategize over the desegregation plans of Little Rock Central High School. The house was also a gathering place for the press and a target for those who bitterly opposed the cause of integration.

The house on W. 28th Street in Little Rock, Arkansas, became a National Historic Landmark.

June 25, 2001

A group called Project USA, known for advocating for reducing immigration, bristles under charges of racism.

As documented in the *Christian Science Monitor,* when its "Truthmobile" entered a parade in Mason City, Iowa, extolling the detrimental effects of immigration on U.S. population, parade officials forced the vehicle off the parade route. Vance Baird, festival coordinator, complained later about the "type of racism and bigotry that this float emphasized."

Craig Nelson, director of the New York based Project USA, responded by saying it was the growing population of the United States, not skin color, that concerns the organization.

The 2000 Census showed that the United States had gained 32.7 million residents, while women born in the U.S. exhibited a reproduction rate of less than two. The gap, said Project USA, was filled by immigration.

June 26, 2001

The 2000 Census reveals that in the 1990s, for the first time in the 20th century, the African American population grew faster in the southeastern United States than in any other region.

This reversed the Great Migration trend that had typified most of the century.

Starting in the early 1990s, African Americans flocked to the deep South, adding 3.5 million blacks to the region. The region that first accepted Africans in bondage, the deep South now displays monuments to the history of African Americans. After the last exodus of blacks from the South ended in the 1960s, the Southern economy boomed, while many of the racial stigmas diminished.

Reportedly, one of the magnets to the South was the affordable housing available in suburban areas to the increasing number of middle class blacks. African Americans began to develop new all-black neighborhoods — a kind of segregation by choice. In these communities, African Americans started to find a new community voice, developing a powerful voting bloc that could influence political policy.

Meanwhile, the great Southern black colleges — such as Alcorn State University in Mississippi, Morehouse College in Georgia, Howard University in Washington, D.C., and Tuskegee University in Alabama — once again had become the centers of higher learning for the black community. But whereas in the past the black colleges had been a way of keeping blacks separate from whites, the black colleges had now become the post-graduate choice of young African American scholars. By 1993, these institutions awarded one-third of the 1.1 million undergraduate degrees earned by African Americans.

June 29, 2001

The National Japanese American Memorial opens in Washington, D.C.

Transportation Secretary Norman Mineta, who remembers gathering at the wait station at the Santa Anita racetrack in 1942 as an 11-year-old boy, cut the ribbon to officially open the monument, which was dedicated to the memory of the 30,000 Japanese American soldiers who fought in World War II while their families and friends waited out the war in internment camps.

Representative Mike Honda (D–San Jose, California), another young World War II internee, said, "Japanese Americans came here with a promise and the promise was broken. But they held true to the promise. Their spirit and patriotism never wavered" (Epstein, p. A3–A4).

July 3, 2001

Charlie Robertson, 67, mayor of York, Pennsylvania, is charged with the 32-year-old murder of Lillie Belle Allen, who had been killed by gunfire while searching for a grocery store.

Robertson, a one-time white power proponent claiming to have reformed, in 1969 was a police officer embroiled in the race riots that purged the city. The situation came to public attention after a local newspaper did a retrospective on the riots in 1999.

Lillie Belle Allen, 27, was the daughter of a black preacher South Carolina. She died in a hail of bullets from the guns of members of a white supremacy gang. One of the gang members, Charlie Robertson, reportedly shouted "White Power" during a rally, as he handed out ammunition to members of the white gang.

Three days later, a police officer named Henry Schaad was killed by gunfire while sitting in the back of an armored vehicle, allegedly by a black gang member. The town was ripped apart by a racial war, which featured the burning of buildings, and armed gangs — black and white — roaming neighborhoods divided by skin color.

Neither murder, however, was investigated for 32 years, as the town tried to bury the incident and to move past the racial flames that burned.

July 6, 2001

An off-duty North Carolina state trooper by the name of Todd Williams is pulled over by local police along Highway 17 in Jacksonville, for no reason other, as Williams saw it, than the color of his skin.

The officers reportedly pulled him over, pointed a gun at him, then searched him. Finally, the officers gave him a ticket for speeding and sent him off — without so much as an apology.

The case became one of many focusing on the issue of racial profiling. Williams sued in federal court for unreasonable search and seizure, but the judge found in favor of the two officers, illustrating the degree of latitude the courts appeared to be willing to give police.

Legal experts said that to win a racial profiling case, it had to be demonstrated incontrovertibly. Since the mid-eighties, with the administration's fervent "War on Drugs," the United States Supreme Court had led the charge in allowing law enforcement to use racial profiling as a tactic.

According to the American Civil Liberties Union, tens of thousands of innocent motorists on highways across the country were the victims of racial profiling. The practice was often presented as a means to justify the end of improved public safety, but it was a practice that quickly eroded the civil liberties provided in the Constitution. In a discussion of the consequences, law professor Jack Glaser asserts, "Affirming the consequent may sound like a tolerable error if one wants to improve public safety: All one has to do is accept that some innocent people will have to be inconvenienced in order to protect others. That makes sense if one is willing to disregard the Fourth Amendment, which prohibits 'unreasonable searches and seizures' without 'probable cause,' and the Fourteenth Amendment, which guarantees 'equal protection'" (Glaser, p. A25).

July 8, 2001

President Kweisi Mfume of the National Association for the Advancement of Colored People speaking to nearly 20,000 NAACP delegates, stresses the importance of equal access to a safe environment.

Mfume's comments came during the association's ninety-first annual national convention, in New Orleans, Louisiana.

Mfume addressed the exposure of African American babies to lead paint in old buildings. He cited that 40 percent of homes still had some lead-based paint in them, while low-income children were eight times more likely to live in homes in which lead paint was a problem. African American children were five times as likely as European American children to suffer from lead poisoning, according to the Centers for Disease Control. While prior NAACP battles concerned economic and social justice, Mfume's comments highlighted how the fight had turned to environmental justice as well.

Earlier in the week, Mfume had pressed the newly elected Bush administration to take a "meaningful and quantifiable approach" (Axtman, p. 2) to issues such as racial profiling, election reform, and racial disparities in the death penalty. He had said the NAACP would also pressure the administration on issues of education, economic development, criminal justice, and foreign policy. President Bush, who was invited to the conference, sent instead a representative with a videotaped greeting to the members.

July 16, 2001

The ninth Circuit Court of Appeals decides twenty Native American tribes have no right to the settlement decided in the 1998 Tobacco Accord.

The tribes had filed suit because they did not benefit from the Tobacco Accord of August 1998 between 46 states and the tobacco industry. The accord had paid $200 billion, used to treat ill smokers, in exchange for promises by states to drop a legal suit against tobacco companies.

The tribes' law suit, filed in San Francisco in 1999, sought 1 billion in compensation and punitive damages and claimed that although Native Americans had been counted for census data used to determine how settlement money would be distributed among the states, they had received no money from the accord. The suit claimed that the omission amounted to racial discrimination and a breach of Native American sovereignty. The suit said that Native American tribes had been left out of the settlement, even though United States territories had been included.

The court of appeals decided the Native Americans had no legal standing to sue the tobacco companies because they had not suffered injury by being excluded. The panel's argument was that the Native Americans had not submitted evidence of paying to treat ill smokers and had not submitted claims to the tobacco companies.

July 17, 2001

Several studies cited in the media suggest American society is moving toward a true multicultural society.

New figures from the United States Census Bureau, for example, revealed a rising number of multiracial individuals, clouding obvious visual distinctions. According to the census, one in 40 Americans identified herself or himself as a product of two or more racial groups. Fourteen of the nation's 100 largest cities boasted a multiracial group composing at least five percent of the population.

In the meantime, *The Washington Post*, the Henry J. Kaiser Family Foundation, and Harvard University released a survey in which biracial couples reported widespread tolerance and even acceptance of their relationships. Fifty-three percent of whites, 77 percent of African Americans, 68 percent of Latinos, and 67 percent of Asians said it made no difference whether one married someone of the same or a different race. Four out of ten Americans reported having had dates with someone of another race. Forty-six percent of black-white couples claimed being married to someone of a different race made marriage harder, compared with 30 percent of Hispanic-white couples and 32 percent of Asian-white couples. Additionally, 65 percent of black-white couples reported that a parent initially had had a problem with the relationship, compared with 24 percent of Latino-white, and 24 percent of Asian-white couples.

At the same time, a Sacramento, California, businessman worked to develop a Racial Privacy Initiative, proposed for the 2002 California Ballot. Sponsored by Ward Connerly, the initiative proposed removing questions of race from applications for jobs, schools, and housing. Connerly — the author of *Creating Equal: My Fight Against Racial Preferences*, and a member of the University of California Board of Regent's anti–affirmative action efforts — argued that in a polyglot society, such questions are not only unethical and intrusive, but irrelevant and misleading. Critics of the measure argued that if the measurement of race were excluded, it would be impossible to observe and guard against the encroachment of racism.

Optimists observing the studies suggested that the rise of multiracial individuals might do much to eliminate the idea of racism in the United States. Multiracials seemed to be appearing in all levels of society, as the melting pot was truly beginning to melt.

July 18, 2001

A study by Harvard's Civil Rights Project announces that United States schools seem to be slipping back toward segregation.

Many schools in the last ten years, the study says, had become less integrated, not more. In particular, Hispanic Americans had amassed in non-white schools.

Responding to the study, some observers said the focus should be on student achievement, no matter what the racial composition. But others warned against the slippery slope toward segregation and against the accompanying idea of "separate but equal" facilities.

Gary Orfield of the Harvard Study said, "Our research consistently shows that schools are becoming increasingly segregated and are offering vastly unequal educational opportunities" (Chaddock, p. 3).

August 14, 2001

With the increased visibility of multicultural society, many scholars — such as those at the Center for the Study of White American Culture — support the view for the need for white studies.

The nonprofit group in Roselle, New Jersey, proposed that white Americans were in need of insight into their culture as much as any other group.

Customarily, when racial studies were offered by academic institutions, the focus remained on Hispanics, African Americans, Asians, and Native Americans. However, with three out of four Americans describing themselves as white, and another 5.5 million assuming an identity of white plus one or more race, it implied a need to further investigate what exactly it meant to be white.

Discussions of white culture were customarily identified with white supremacists, the stigma of a racism firmly attached. However, Ray Winbush, director of the Race Relations Institute at the historically black Fisk University in Nashville, Tennessee, is among a host of scholars supporting the revisiting of the notion. "We have black studies, women's studies, Latino studies ... the fact is that white culture needs to be discussed in depth" (Belsie, "Profile Rises," p. 2).

September 2, 2001

The United States pulls out of the United Nations World Conference Against Racism, Racial Discrimination, Xenophobia, and Related Intolerances.

The conference, held in Durban, South Africa, loses Canada and Israel as participants as well.

The United Nations had organized the conference to address world-wide issues such as the treatment of migrants and refugees, discrimination against Indian untouchables, and apologies and reparations for slavery. However, the George W. Bush administration objected to what Secretary of State Colin Powell cited as the "hateful language," proposed for the final conference statement, expressed against Israel. The statement's language with regard to the Jewish homeland and the treatment of Palestinians was characterized as racist. Representative Tom Lantos, (D–San Mateo, California) commented that the conference had become a "mockery" because of some participants' "pathological preoccupation" with attacking Israel.

However, many African and Arabian representatives asserted that the United States pulled out because of its squeamish reluctance to address the demands of many African countries. These nations had demanded reparations from Western governments for the enslavement of tens of millions of Africans between the eighteenth and twentieth centuries. These nations asserted that President George W. Bush decided not to send high level delegates to the conference specifically because the African nations had been seeking apologies and lawsuits against Western countries on the behalf of families of the 11 million of their people shipped into slavery.

September 11, 2001

The unthinkable occurs, the worst incident of terrorism ever on United States soil.

At 8:45 A.M., American Airlines Flight 11, a Boeing 767 aircraft carrying 92 people, slammed into the north twin tower of the World Trade Center in downtown Manhattan. At 9:03 A.M., a second Boeing 767 airliner, United Airlines Flight 175, hit the second tower, killing 65. Within two hours, both towers crumbled, taking nearly 3,000 lives — from the United States and other countries, including rescuing police and firefighters — with them.

At 9:45 A.M., American Airlines Flight 77 struck the Pentagon in Washington D.C., killing 64 on board. Later, a fourth airplane — United Airlines Flight 93 — crashed in a field outside Pittsburgh. Indications are that the plane had been overtaken by terrorists, who were then overtaken by the passengers, who may have forced the plane to crash. This disaster cost 45 lives.

The tragedy was the work of the terrorist network al-Qaeda, led by millionaire Osama bin Laden. Born in Saudi Arabia and trained by CIA agents during the Russian invasion of Afghanistan in 1979, bin Laden was believed to have orchestrated the attacks with a network of 19 terrorists, all believed to be Muslim.

Predictably, many American citizens turned in anger toward their Islamic neighbors, whether American citizens or visitors. Random acts of violence and terrorism bent on revenge — the very ideals that fueled the deadly hijackings — were unleashed upon the innocent. Shades of "Strange Fruit" reappeared.

At the same time, however, many other Americans came to the support and aid of Muslims targeted by the rash and myopic. These Americans implored their fellow citizens to employ patience and restraint, and to discern their neighbors from their enemies.

It would remain to be seen if America could learn from its more than 100 years of racist and reactionary history.

October 26, 2001

In fevered response to the September 11, 2001, terrorist attacks, President George W. Bush signs the USA Patriot Act, which Congress had passed two days prior.

The Patriot Act gave the administration much broader authority to act in combating terrorism, both real and perceived. It increased the powers of the Justice Department to overtly and covertly track and gather communications, and to conduct surveillance over citizens and noncitizens alike. The Patriot Act increased powers to detain and deport persons suspected of terrorist activities, and allowed the Justice Department greater search and seizure powers. In addition, the act gave the Treasury Department more power to combat money laundering.

While many claimed the act — and even more powerful measures — was necessary to conduct the "War on Terrorism," others warned that the new powers would curtail the very human liberties for which Americans pride themselves.

Between the years 1970 and 2000, the estimated Muslim population in the United States had grown from 30,000 to more than 1 million people. Within months of the passage of the Patriot Act, hundreds of individuals appearing to be of Middle Eastern or Muslim heritage were persecuted by the government, harassed and detained under suspicion of terrorism. Their loyalties were questioned and their library records infiltrated, as they fell under surveillance due to the expanded powers of the Patriot Act. Muslim officials began to speak out against the injustice, fearing such retribution as had befallen Japanese Americans under Executive Order 9066 during World

War II. Critics such as the American Civil Liberties Union claimed the War on Terror seriously violated civil protections guaranteed under the First, Fifth, and Sixth Amendments, for citizens and noncitizens alike.

At the same time, the increased scrutiny of Middle Eastern and Muslim individuals in the American media seemed to increase curiosity toward this segment by other groups of American society. Suddenly, Muslim groups found themselves in contact with other cultures and religions within American communities, providing unique and unexpected opportunities for greater interaction and mutual understanding among the groups.

March 24, 2002

African American actors receive Oscars after a long wait.

Thirty-eight years after Sidney Poitier captured the Best Actor Oscar, African Americans claimed the Best Actor and the Best Actress awards at the Seventy-fourth Academy Awards ceremony at the prestigious new Kodak Theater in Hollywood. Halle Berry won the Oscar for her role in *Monster's Ball*, while Denzel Washington was named Best Actor for his leading role in *Training Day*.

Poitier himself was on hand for the festivities, as he was presented with the Honorary Lifetime Achievement Oscar. Poitier had won the Best Actor award for 1963 for his portrayal of Homer Smith in *Lilies of the Field*.

Washington paid tribute to Poitier, pointing to the veteran star and saying, "I'll always be chasing you." Berry gave a particularly emotional acceptance speech, accepting the honor on behalf of the "nameless, faceless women of color" who followed her.

April 4, 2002

New Mexico becomes the first state of the Union to include questions about federal Indian law on its state bar examination.

The questions focused not on issues pertaining to law within the 450 individually recognized tribes, but on issues of federal law that superseded state and local laws. Such issues might include tribal jurisdiction, as well as the relationship between tribes and federal government.

In December 2001, a Navajo law student named Calvin Lee, a law professor named Kip Bobroff, and an Isleta Pueblo tribal judge named William Johnson appeared before an advisory committee of the New Mexico Supreme Court. They requested the addition to the bar exam, which the Court ordered in February of 2002.

It is thought that Indian law affects about ten percent of New Mexico's citizens, in situations such as child welfare, criminal jurisdiction, zoning, and gambling. There are currently 22 individual tribes dwelling within the state of New Mexico.

Montana is reportedly the second state working on adding Indian law to the state exam.

May 1, 2002

May is declared Asian/Pacific American Heritage Month.

President George W. Bush issued a proclamation, stating that Congress — through Public Law 102–45 — had designated the month of May as Asian/Pacific American Heritage Month, to commemorate the first immigration of Japanese to the United States.

In his proclamation, Bush cited the Asian and Pacific Island cultures as one of the fastest growing segments of American society. He recognized millions of Asian and Pacific Americans "whose love of family, hard work and community has helped unite us as a people and a nation."

The idea of an Asian/Pacific American Heritage Week first emerged in 1977, when congressmen Frank Horton (NY) and Norman Mineta (CA) introduced a house resolution. A month later, senators Daniel Inouye (HI) and Spark Matsunaga (HI) introduced a similar bill. In 1978, President Jimmy Carter signed a joint congressional resolution designating the annual celebration.

Three and one-half months later, the president issued another, similar proclamation, stating that Congress — through Public Law 100–402 — had designated September 15 through October 15 as National Hispanic Heritage month. September 15 is Independence Day for five Latin American countries: Costa Rica, Honduras, El Salvador, Nicaragua, and Guatemala.

Bush's proclamation expanded what had originally been National Hispanic Heritage Week, which began in 1968 under the Lyndon Johnson administration. The week was expanded into a whole month in 1988. Bush says he joined "with all Americans in celebrating this rich and diverse culture and encourage all citizens to recognize the important role of Hispanics in creating and building this great nation."

During the 2000 presidential election, Hispanics voted for Democrats by a 2–1 margin, while Asian Americans voted 54 percent for Al Gore and 41 percent for George W. Bush. Thus, most critics saw the proclamation as a purely political move, a means for Bush to attract support from increasingly powerful Hispanic and Asian-Pacific political blocs in the United States.

May 10, 2002

Questions of racism lead to a Maryland moratorium on executions.

Maryland Governor Parris L. Glendening ordered a moratorium on executions, pending a study to determine if capital punishment in his state was imposed because of race. The governor issued the order simultaneous to granting a stay of execution for Wesley E. Baker, convicted of the 1991 murder of a woman during a purse snatching. Baker was one of nine African Americans among 13 men on death row in the State of Maryland. With the governor's order, Maryland became the second state to suspend all executions. Governor George Ryan of Illinois halted capital punishment in 2000 because of the same fear of injustices.

The National Coalition to Abolish the Death Penalty, the Reverend Jesse Jackson, and others took the opportunity to educate the populace about the injustices found in the imposition of capital punishment. Jackson went so far as to call the death penalty "legal lynching." During subsequent investigations, several alarming statistics came to light, giving substance to the severe reservations about the distribution of death penalty sentences among the races. Not only did great disparities exist among the races of those convicted, but also among the races of the murder victims:

• While only 28 percent of Maryland's population was black, African Americans made up 70 percent of those waiting on death row. Thus, Maryland had the highest concentration of African Americans on death row.

• In Georgia, blacks convicted of killing whites were sentenced to death 22 percent of the time, while whites convicted of killing blacks were sentenced to death 3 percent of the time. While the blacks composed 40 percent of Georgia's population, 77 percent of its capital punishments had been imposed upon African Americans.

• In Alabama, African Americans made up 25 percent of the population, but composed 43 percent of death row inmates; since the resumption of the death penalty, 71 percent of those executed there had been black.

• In Florida, those who killed whites were eight times more likely to receive the death penalty than those who killed blacks.

• Nationwide, 50 percent of murder victims were black, while 85 percent of victims in death penalty cases were white. Since 1976, only four white defendants had been executed for killing a black person, while 75 black defenders had been executed for killing a white person. African Americans who murdered whites were 19 times as likely to be executed as whites who killed blacks.

May 22, 2002

Bobby Frank Cherry is convicted of murder in the 1963 bombing of the 16th Street Baptist Church in Birmingham, Alabama.

The jury of nine — consisting of six whites and three African Americans — found Cherry guilty in the murders of the little African American girls Addie Mae, Denise McNair, Cynthia Wesley, and Carole Robertson.

The conviction brought a close to one of the most horrific incidents in the history of American race relations. The multiple murder convictions meant an automatic life sentence, bringing to justice the last of the former Ku Klux Klansmen connected with the 1963 bombing. Robert Chambliss had finally been convicted of his part in the act in 1977, dying in prison in 1985. Thomas E. Blanton, Jr., was still sitting in solitary confinement, while Herman Frank Cash died untried in 1994.

Although presumably done to intimidate the Birmingham black community, the bombing of the 16th Street Baptist Church perhaps did more to rally a sympathetic white community to the subject of black civil rights than any incident before or since.

June 17, 2002

Federal agencies are partially barred from using racial profiling.

The Department of Justice, under the administration of George W. Bush, issued guidelines barring agents of 70 federal law enforcement agencies from engaging in racial profiling, which is using race or ethnicity as a basis for their investigations. The guidelines were contradictory, however, as they allowed these agencies to single out those appearing to be Middle Easterners, and others, to help "identify terrorist threats and stop potential catastrophic attacks."

On the one hand, the guidelines prohibited these agencies from employing racial profiling techniques such as increasing traffic stops or drug arrests in certain neighborhoods based on racial composition. However, racial components could be considered in the search for an individual suspect. Additionally, these agencies could target Middle Eastern or other ethnic groups that were suspected of terrorist plots.

Only seven of the 70 federal agencies — including the Federal Bureau of Investigations, the United States Customs Office, the Drug Enforcement Agency, the Bureau of Alcohol, Tobacco, and Firearms, and the newly created Department of Homeland Security — had already set up policies concerning racial profiling. These agencies employed more than 120,000 law enforcement officers for the federal government.

The ACLU and other critics contended that the Justice Department's announcement were mere "guidelines." These critics questioned how much the guidelines would actually be enforced. Advocates for Middle Eastern Americans questioned the many exemptions of the policy, which would indeed allow for the racial profiling of Middle Easterners.

March 27, 2003

Arlo Looking Cloud, a 49-year-old homeless man, is arrested in Denver, Colorado, for the 1976 murder of Anna Mae Pictou-Aquash, an activist with the American Indian Movement (AIM).

Anna Mae — of the Canadian Mi'kmaq tribe — had been one of the AIM force who occupied the village of Wounded Knee in 1973 in protest of the deplorable conditions at the Pine Ridge Reservation.

It was Anna Mae who once was quoted as saying, "The whole country changed with only a handful of raggedy-ass pilgrims that came over here in the 1500's. And it can take a handful of raggedy-ass Indians to do the same, and I intend to be one of those raggedy-ass Indians."

Three years after Wounded Knee, Anna Mae's body was found in a deep ravine on February 24, 1976, by a cattle rancher on the reservation near Wanblee, South Dakota. She had been shot execution-style in the back of the head. She had disappeared from her Denver home months earlier.

For 27 years, the murder of Anna Mae was a legend among the Pine Ridge Indians and a mystery that might never have been resolved without the dogged efforts of Bob Ecoffey. An Oglala Sioux, Ecoffey had climbed through the ranks of law enforcement, becoming a United States Marshal and finally a Bureau of Indian Affairs manager for the Pine Ridge Reservation.

With the help of Denver detective Abe Alonzo, Ecoffey finally cracked the case in 2002. Arlo Looking Cloud was a Lakota Indian who had been a security guard for AIM during the occupation of Wounded Knee. Another man, John Graham, was also indicted, and later fought extradition from Vancouver, B.C., for the murder.

There had been belief within the AIM that Pictou-Aquash was an informant for the FBI, which had been keeping the AIM under surveillance for its involvement in the Wounded Knee uprising. However, many Indians believed that the FBI had had her executed, or at least had shown little interest in discovering her murderer. In any case, the wheels of justice — at least for Native Americans — once again had proven to be achingly slow.

Arlo Looking Cloud was convicted of murder in the first degree and was given a life sentence.

June 23, 2003

The Supreme Court gives the nod to narrow uses of affirmative action.

On this date, the United States Supreme Court ruled on two lawsuits challenging the University of Michigan's use of race as a factor of admission in its undergraduate school and in its law school admissions policy. Through its rulings, the Supreme Court continued the volatile discussion of affirmative action in college admissions that had been highlighted in earnest with the case of the *Regents of the University of California v. Bakke* 25 years earlier. The basic question remained: How many African Americans, Asian Americans, Hispanic Americans, and European Americans should be allowed into class?

In *Grutter v. Bollinger*, the University of Michigan Law School denied admission to Barbara Grutter, a white female Michigan resident with a grade point average of 3.8 and a 161 LSAT score. Grutter, the petitioner, claimed the law school's admissions policy gave greater chances to certain students simply because of race.

In the Court's 5 to 4 ruling in favor of the law school, Justice Sandra Day O'Connor wrote that the Equal Protection Clause of the Fourteenth Amendment to the United States Constitution did not prohibit the law school's "narrowly tailored" use of race in admissions decisions, to further a compelling interest in obtaining the educational benefits that flow from a diverse student body. The court cited the importance of diversity in both major business — which anticipated an increasing global market — and the military, which valued the advantage of a highly qualified and diverse officer corps.

In *Gratz v. Bollinger*, the court voted to reverse the specific university undergraduate policy, while still allowing race as a consideration for admission.

Jennifer Gratz and Patrick Hamacher, both Michigan residents and white, applied for the undergraduate LSA (College of Literature, Science, and the Arts). Denied admission, they brought suit against the university for its admissions policy. This policy automatically assigned 20 points — out of the required 100 points needed for admission — to minorities who otherwise qualified for admission. At the same time, the admissions policies admitted virtually all African Americans, Hispanic Americans, Asian Americans, and Native Americans who were minimally qualified. The petitioners claimed the policy violated the Equal Protection Clause of the Fourteenth Amendment.

Chief Justice William Rehnquist declared that existing affirmative action law as established in the *Regents of the University of California v. Bakke* allowed for race to be a factor in admissions. However, Rehnquist declared, it must not be a "deciding factor." The point factor given by the University of Michigan to minorities, Rehnquist wrote, was not "narrowly tailored" to achieve the interest in educational diversity that the respondents claimed justified their program.

Some said if preferences were not given to minorities, 75 percent of African American applicants would be kept out of accredited law schools. The number of African American doctors could drop 71 percent. Ironically, the West Point Military Academy used numeric targets for race at 10–12 percent for blacks, and 25 percent for minorities. This admission policy put West Point at odds with President George W. Bush's push against racial quotas. Experts predicted that without such targets, the country's officer corps would become mostly white, negatively affecting the morale of troops, 40 percent of whom are minority.

The question of affirmative action continued to pit against each other two highly touted American values: colorblindness and integration.

September 17, 2003

The nation's largest Latino radio network fetches a prime price.

In a transaction that showcased the growing importance of Hispanic Americans in the media and the marketplace, Univision Communications purchased the Hispanic Broadcasting Corporation for $3.5 billion. The radio network became Univision Radio, which would reach 80 percent of the Latino population in the United States, nearly 10 million listeners. Univision Radio joined the Univision Network, reaching 98 percent of all Hispanic television households. It also joined Galavision, the nation's leading Spanish language cable network.

By this time, Hispanic Americans composed the fastest-growing segment of United States population. At 37 million — up from 14.6 million in 1980 and 22.4 million in 1990 — Hispanic Americans outnumbered African Americans as the largest minority. In cities like Miami, Florida, Hispanics were actually the majority. The purchasing power of Hispanic Americans stood at $580 billion a year, growing at 12 percent annually.

The merger between Hispanic Radio Corporation and Univision underscored the growing power of the Spanish-language media in the United States. Every major market in the country had at least two Spanish radio and television stations; San Diego had 25.

Radio station KWEX of San Antonio, Texas, became the first Spanish-language UHF station in the United States, the first link in what would become the Spanish International Network (SIN), and eventually Univision.

In 1970, Univision became the first U.S. broadcasting network to televise the World Cup soccer championship. A. Jerrold Perenchio — who had owned and operated Spanish-language broadcasting stations for 25 years — acquired Univision Hallmark in 1992. In September 1996, Univision went public on the New York Stock Exchange. By 2003, Univision remained not only the largest Spanish-language broadcasting network in the United States, but the fifth-most-watched American network overall.

December 3, 2003

Rohit "Ro" Khanna, an attorney from the Twelfth Congressional District in California, announces his candidacy for Congress, opposing the 12-term democrat Tom Lantos. A graduate from Yale Law School in 2001, Khanna voiced strong opposition for the Iraq War and the Patriot Act, two policies under the Bush administration strongly supported by Lantos.

Khanna's candidacy illustrated the emergence of Asian Indian Americans as a political and economic power in the United States. By this time, Asian Indian Americans were a population of 1.8 million, .06 percent of the nation's total population. (In 1965, there had been about 19,000 Asian Indians in the United States.) The median household income for Asian Indian Americans is $61,322, 46 percent higher than the national average. This makes the Indian Americans the wealthiest immigrant group in the nation.

Khanna's campaign was the latest in a series of Asian Indian Americans running for political office. Bobby Jindal had lost a tight race for governor of Louisiana. Kumar Barve had been named majority leader of the Maryland House of Delegates, the lower chamber. If Ro Khanna won, he would become the first Asian Indian American in Congress since Dalip Singh Saund in 1957.

Khanna lost the March 2, 2004, primary election by a resounding 3–1 margin. Throughout the day, his campaign headquarters reportedly received racially-motivated threats by phone against his running for Congress.

December 31, 2003

Several studies conducted in 2003 indicate the fluctuating poverty gap between whites and people of color.

A study from Manchester College in North Manchester, Indiana, showed the difference between the poverty rates of whites and minorities narrowed 19.4 percent in the years between 1995 and 2002. Still, in 2002 7.8 percent of whites lived below the poverty line, while 22.7 percent of blacks, 10.2 percent of Asians and Pacific Islanders, and 21.8 percent of Hispanics lived below the poverty line. At this pace — according to the Manchester study — poverty parity will not be achieved until sometime between 2018 and 2031. Meanwhile, the jobless rate for African Americans rose from 7.6 percent in 2000 to 10.8 percent in 2003. In 2002, nonwhites were 162 percent more likely than whites to be poor.

A study from Harvard University's Joint Center for Housing Studies showed the disparity between whites and people of color in a more creative way. It showed that more than 400,000 homes worth $1 million existed in the United States. The study determined that one out of 72 white homeowners owned a million-dollar house, compared to one out of 762 minority homeowners. Meanwhile, one out of 17 white homeowners owned a house worth $500,000, while only one out of 33 minorities did so. The study also showed that people of color owned 16.5 percent of all homes, but only 1.8 percent of the million-dollar homes.

Nevertheless, people of color seemed to be making gains in homeownership. According to the Harvard study, the number of minority homeowners surged by 58.8 percent between 1993 and 2002.

January 7, 2004

From the East Room of the White House, President George W. Bush introduces his new temporary worker program, which would become known as the Guest Worker Plan. In his address, Bush characterized the United States as a country of immigrants, saying, "America is a stronger, better nation because of the hard work and faith and entrepreneurial spirit if immigrants." This plan would allow undocumented immigrants currently living in United States to apply for a work permit for up to three years, if they can prove their employer could not find a U.S. citizen willing to take the job.

The Guest Worker proposal appeared to be an important step by the Bush Administration, acknowledging the failure of the current immigration system. The proposal is also of vital interest to the millions of laborers who work — as farm laborers, maids, service workers, and other low-paying positions — without permission in the United States. The plan would likely be popular among business leaders, since many businesses prefer to hire illegal immigrants, who fear deportation and therefore will accept substandard labor environments.

Critics, however, said the current overburdened immigration system could not possibly deal with a new wave of applications to the temporary worker program. There was also concern that the guest worker program would drive down wages for domestic workers. Some even compared it to the old "Bracero" program, anticipating similar abuses. Many characterized

the proposal as simply a ploy by the Bush campaign during an election year
to improve his image among Hispanic voters.

Some of the most adamant critics of the Guest Worker Program were
the agents of the United States Border Patrol. These agents regularly worked
ten hours a day, often by themselves in dangerous situations, contributing
to the highest attrition rate among any federal agency. The agents criticized
the president's program for inviting across the border the very illegal immigrants the Border Patrol has been struggling to keep out.

The federal government estimates between eight and fourteen million
illegal immigrants live in the United States, with 60 percent from Central
or South America. Meanwhile, the apprehension rate of illegal immigrants
crossing the United States border dropped 44 percent between the year 2000
(1,676,438 apprehensions) and 2003 (931,438).

May 16, 2004

A study released by University of California, Los Angeles' Institution
for Democracy, Education, and Access (IDEA) revealed that the latest form
of segregation in the schools is created more by divisions in income, rather
than those of race. However, the impact on the minority culture communities may still be significant. The result for many American school districts has
been the emergence of high-end white schools, along with substandard black
and brown schools. This disparity creates another version of the so-called "separate but equal" concept — involving institutions that are always separate but
never equal. This issue, first handed down in *Plessy v. Ferguson*, continues to
plague the American public education, but now with a different twist.

Brown v. Board of Education was handed down by the United States
Supreme Court in 1954, to outlaw racial segregation in the public school.
But UCLA's study revealed that the Linda Brown of the early 21st century
is a child in poverty, who can be of any color, living in any region. She is
being raised by parents who cannot afford to supplement schools with com-
puters, books, art classes, and needed equipment. In California alone, one
million poor, ethnically isolated students are challenging — with the help of
the American Civil Liberties Union — state education officials in class action
lawsuits. The lawsuits claim that the schools for these poor students are worse
than those attended by the rest of California's 6.2 million students.

The study cites all ethic minorities are being segregated — not by standards of race or culture, but by financial status. For example, according to
IDEA, while Hispanic students comprise nearly half of enrollment and
Caucasian one-third, 63 percent of whites go to all-white schools, while 47
percent of Hispanics attend schools with 10 percent or less white students.

The radical solution, the institute suggests, is the financial integration of neighborhoods. "Since the 1950's, Californians have created profoundly segregated neighborhoods...," said John Rogers of IDEA. "The strong relationship between race and income has meant that most low-income neighborhoods are Latino and African American, and most middle and upper-income neighborhoods are white."

The issue of segregated schools may no longer be a question of black, white, red, yellow, or brown, but a question of green.

September 24, 2004

The Smithsonian Institution opens the new National Museum of the American Indian, on a 4.25 acre site east of the National Air and Space Museum, south of the United States Capitol Building. Located at Fourth Street and Independence Avenue, the five-story building boasts 250,000 square feet of floor space. More than 27,000 people visit the museum that day.

Among the Native American museum architects and designers who contributed to the creation of the museum are: Lou Weller, Caddo (tribe); Douglas Cardinal, Blackfeet; Johnpaul Jones, Cherokee/Choctaw; Ramona Sakiestewa, Hopi; Donna House, Navajo/Oneida. The Table Mountain Rancheria Enterprises also assisted in the design.

The museum offers several features emblematic of Native American cultures. The museum exterior featured a sheath of Kasota dolomitic limestone from Minnesota. These pieces of Kasota stone vary in size and surface treatment, giving the building the appearance of a stratified stone mass that has been carved by wind and water. The "Native Landscape" covers 74 percent of the museum, comprised of four main habitats designed to replicate the natural world of the American Indian: forest, wetlands, meadows, and traditional croplands. The landscape is comprised of more than forty boulders, seven hundred trees, along with 33,000 individual plants from more than one hundred fifty species. The Museum also contains more than one million tribal objects, artworks, and artifacts. There is even a fire-pit equipped kitchen in the museum cafeteria which serves Indian-inspired food such as quahog clam chowder, Peruvian mash potato cakes, smoked seafood, and bison chili.

November 4, 2004

Six weeks following the opening of the National Museum of the American Indian, President George W. Bush issues a Presidential Proclamation, declaring November 2004 as Native American Indian Heritage Month.

The Proclamation declares, "As the first people to call our country home, American Indians and Alaska Natives have a noble history in this land, and have long shaped our Nation. During National American Indian Heritage Month, we celebrate our commitment to respect and preserve the rich Native American traditions and cultures. The enduring experiences of tribal communities are a cherished part of our national story....

"Now, therefore, I, George W. Bush, President of the United States of America, by virtue of the authority vested in me by the Constitution and laws of the United States of America, do hereby proclaim November 2004 as National American Indian Heritage Month. I encourage all Americans to commemorate this month with appropriate programs and activities and to learn about the rich heritage of American Indians and Alaska Natives."

Bush used the platform of the proclamation to tout his administration's support of American Indians and Alaskan natives by providing funds for school construction and repairs and educational improvement. However, *U.S. News and World Report* stated the health care of the 2.5 million tribal members is worse than any other U.S. minority or majority group. The life expectancy for Indians is five years lower than any other group, with greater rates of infant mortality, tuberculosis, alcohol abuse, and diabetes. Retiring Senator Ben Nighthorse Campbell of Colorado, the lone Indian member of Congress and one of the few champions for the improvement of Indian health care, described Native Americans as the country's "first endangered species."

Because of the Administration's dismal record on health care, government-to-government relationships with tribes, and environmental protection, many Indian leaders characterized his gestures toward Native Americans as much too little, much too late.

January 20, 2005

George W. Bush is inaugurated to his second term as President of the United States, following an election in which he captured only 51 percent of the popular vote. Although Bush claimed his victory to be a mandate from the American people, the election seemed to polarize the voters of the United States along political and racial lines. Indeed, the resulting election revealed little support for Bush from voters from ethnic and racial minorities.

While, according to CNN, Bush captured 58 percent of the white vote, among non-white men, the re-elected president captured only 30 percent of the votes. Among non-white women he fared even poorer, with only 24 percent of non-white women voted for Bush.

Dr. Ron Walters, director of the African American Institute at the University of Maryland, said only 11 percent of African American voters supported George Bush in 2004, even though voter registration among blacks had nearly equaled that of whites. Despite conflicting claims by the Republican Party, Walters reported 90 percent of African Americans voted Democratic, whether they had actually registered as a Democrat or a Republican. These votes revealed the unresolved issues which concern African Americans most: unemployment (11 percent for blacks, 5.2 percent for whites), education (80 percent blacks go to schools with more than 50 percent black, 60 percent white go to schools more than 50 percent white), and health care.

The Bush campaign seemed to improve his standing with Hispanic voters, however. Utilizing ploys such as introducing the Guest Worker proposal in January 2004, and catering to concerns of conservative Catholic Latino voters around issues such as gay and abortion rights, Bush captured 44 percent of Latino voters in 2004. In the 2000 campaign, he won only about 33 percent of the Hispanic vote.

In the 2004 election, 44 percent of Asian voters, and 40 percent of all others minority groups chose George Bush as president.

April 1, 2005

A civilian border patrol effort based in Tombstone, Arizona, called the "Minuteman Project" is launched, drawing as many as reportedly one thousand volunteers for what is characterized as a "massive neighborhood watch." The volunteers descended upon Arizona's Cochise County to "assist" the United States Border Patrol in keeping watch on the international border between Mexico and the United States. Cochise County reportedly has the busiest illegal-immigrant corridor in the nation, with roughly one fifth of the 1.1 million undocumented immigrants arrested this year coming from the county.

According to *The Arizona Republic*, the volunteers of the Minuteman Project are to be trained to act as "legal observers," instructed to alert the Border Patrol when they spot undocumented immigrants crossing the U.S./ Mexican border. Minutemen volunteers claim to have no ties to racism or xenophobia, and they are supposed to avoid personal confrontations with the border crossers.

One of the biggest Congressional supporters of the project is Representative Tom Tancredo (R–Colo), who has advocated for closing the border between the two nations. State lawmakers backing the efforts include Sen. Jack Harper (R–Surprise), Sen. Thayer Verschoor (R–Gilbert), Sen. Karen Johnson (R–Mesa), Rep. Andy Biggs (R–Mesa), and Rep. Russell Pearce (R–Mesa).

Despite some popular response to the project, not everyone seems to wholeheartedly support the efforts of Minutemen. The Mexican government says they will file criminal complaints against anyone violating the law. Also, the Arizona chapter of the American Civil Liberties Union announced they will be recruiting observers to observe the Minutemen, to make sure they are not trampling on anyone's rights. The Border Patrol itself is trying to discourage participation, fearing unwanted conflict which would make the Patrol's jobs ever harder. Even President George W. Bush says he's against vigilantism in the United States of America.

April 13, 2005

The National Geographic Society and IBM announce an ambitious study to track the spread of cultures throughout the globe. Dubbed the Genographic Project, the goal of the venture is to collect at least 100,000 samples of human DNA from people all over the world. In an effort utilizing genetic analysis and computer technology, the Genographic Project hopes to explain the appearance of various ethnicities and cultures in far-flung sectors of the globe. This includes such sojourns as the possible voyages of peoples from Africa to Arabia, India, southeast Asia and Australia more than 50,000 years ago.

It is hoped the study will create the largest and most comprehensive public database of anthropological genetic information ever assembled. An earlier project — called the Human Genome Diversity Project, conducted in early 1990s — collected 1064 genetic samples from 52 population samples around the world.

Some scientists say the project could re-ignite questions on the use of technology in studying human history, race, and genetics. Critics have raised questions about ethical and cultural issues surrounding the collection of data from specific indigenous groups. For example, many American tribes indicated no interest in providing information they already know, and don't need outsiders telling them their own histories. Many felt they would be exploited again. However, supporters say this is not an exercise in classifying people, but in understanding the histories of ancestors.

The Genographic Project will be spearheaded by scientists from research institutions such as the Laboratory of Human Population Genetics in Moscow, the Center for Excellence in Genomic Science in India, and the Center for Genome Information at the University of Cincinnati. For IBM the project is intended to raise its profile as a provider of technology to research institutions, academic and governmental.

Scientists are allowing anyone to join the project by buying a "Participation Kit." Participants will use a plastic stick to scrape mucous membrane cells from inside the cheek and mail to NGS. The kit costs $99.95 plus shipping and handling. Proceeds will fund future research.

Because of wars, environmental disasters, and increasing globalization, National Geographic says there is a sense of urgency about the project. The world is gradually becoming less culturally and genetically diverse as the melting pot expands.

April 14, 2005

Rep. Bill Thomas, R–Bakersfield, the powerful chair of the House Ways and Means Committee, clashes with the Bush Administration over his legislation, H.R. 1492, to authorize $38 million in federal funds to preserve the camps in Arizona, Utah, and California where Japanese Americans were held during World War II. The Bush Administration opposed the bill due to costs of preserving the camps.

Testifying before the House Resources Subcommittee on National Parks, Thomas proposed his bill in honor of Fred Korematsu, the man who defied FDR's Executive Order 9066 in 1942. Korematsu had died on March 30, 2005, at the age of 86. Thomas also honored his longtime friend, the late Rep. Robert Matsui, D–Sacramento, who had been sent as a boy to Tule Lake in Northern California. Matsui, who died New Year's Eve 2004, was a co-sponsor of the bill. Thomas also advocated the bill in honor of his longtime friendship with Democratic State Assemblyman Fred Mori, the immediate past president of the Japanese American Citizens League, who supported the bill. Other co-sponsors included Rep. Doris Matsui (D–Sacramento) and Rep. Mike Honda (D–San Jose), both of whom had spent part of their childhoods in internment camps.

The bill would require nonprofit groups and local government to provide 25 percent matching funds for the federal grants. It would cover ten internment camps, including Tule Lake in California, Topaz in Utah, Heart Mountain in Wyoming, and Gila River in Arizona. The money would go to buy property now privately owned, to restore historical buildings and create museums and visitor centers.

The National Park Service, which would administer the program, said it has no objection to commemorating the internment episode. Agency officials said it would be difficult to administer the program during the current time of tight budgets and huge maintenance backlogs.

May 1, 2005

This date marked the second anniversary of the day President George W. Bush declared from the deck of the U.S.S. *Lincoln* "major combat operations in Iraq have ended." The war had been waged because of the Bush

Administration's belief that weapons of mass destruction — which would never be found — existed in Iraq. The War in Iraq seemed to culminate on December 14, 2003, with the capture of Saddam Hussein outside the dictator's hometown of Tikrit, Iraq. However, the occupation proved far from over, as the casualty list continued to grow, affecting persons of all colors. By May of 2005, the fatalities figure — according to the United States Department of Defense — would reach more than 1543.

Between March 2003 and April 2004, more than 735 soldiers were killed in Iraq, by both hostile and non-hostile fire. By a year later, the figure more than doubled. Caucasians would account for 1118 or 72.4 percent of the fatalities; Hispanics would make up 177 or 11.4 percent; African American comprise 168 or 10.8 percent; Asian American deaths would be 31–32 percent; and others would make up 31–32 percent of the Iraq War fatalities.

While ethnic minorities make up 31 percent of the overall United States population, and 35 percent participation in all active military personnel, they represent 27.5 percent — or 398 deaths — of all military deaths in Iraq.

An article by Brian Gifford in the journal *Armed Forces & Society* reported a preponderance of deaths among Hispanics in the early days of the war. "If any group of minority service members faces an elevated risk of casualties, it is Hispanics in high-intensity combat conditions. When U.S. tactics dictate a more active, aggressive role in finding and attacking enemy targets, Hispanics incur casualties in excess of their participation in ground combat units. In less intense environments, the Hispanic casualty rate more closely resembles their presence in the military as a whole."

Meanwhile, during the initial war phase of the conflict, Caucasians represented 65 percent of all active duty personnel. However, they were underrepresented in deaths, with 60.9 percent of deaths. This probably reflects that whites served in greater numbers in the relatively protected officer corps, and also heavily populate the more selective "support" functions far from the scene of battle.

However, by May of 2005, the death rate among Caucasians rose to 70.6 percent. This suggests that the increasing guerrilla nature of the tactics undertaken by Iraqi insurgents had placed more than the front combat line at risk. Urban conflicts with Iraqi civilian militias, ambushes of military convoys, and mortar attacks on rear command positions provided little safety for soldiers in elite specialties or rear locations.

By May of 2005 — two years after Bush declared "mission accomplished" aboard the U.S.S. *Lincoln*— the occupation of Iraq would offer no end in sight.

Bibliography

ARTICLES

"ACLU to Monitor Minuteman Project." *World Daily Net*, March 10, 2005.

Adams, Jane. *Independent Magazine*, January 1901.

Asimov, Nanette. "Segregation by Income." *San Francisco Chronicle*, May 16, 2004, p. A1.

Axtman, Kris. "From equal access to environmental justice." *The Christian Science Monitor*, July 13, 2001, p. 2.

Baldus, D.C., and C.L. Pulaski. "Comparative Review of Death Sentences: An Empirical Study of the Georgia Experience." *Journal of Criminal Law and Criminology* 74 (1983): 661–753.

Barone, Michael. "The 51 percent nation." *U.S. News & World Report*, November 15, 2004, p. 33.

Belsie, Laurent. "Blacks leaving cities for suburbs." *Christian Science Monitor*, July 5, 2001, p. 1.

_____. "Profile rises for multiracial people." *Christian Science Monitor*, July 17, 2001, p. 3.

_____. "Scholars unearth new field: white studies." *The Christian Science Monitor*, August 14, 2001.

Bierbauer, Charles. "Million Man messenger, not message, causing division." *CNN: U.S. News*, October 15, 1995.

"Birmingham Bomb Kills; Four Negro Girls Killed; Riots Flair; 2 Boys Slain." *New York Times*, September 16, 1963, p. 1

"Biracial couples report better acceptance of their relationships." *San Francisco Chronicle*, July 6, 2001, p. A 15.

"Black men converge on Washington for rally." *USA Today*, February 16, 1996.

Bragg, Rick. "38 Years After Bombing, Girl's Murderer is Convicted." *New York Times*, May 22, 2002, p. A1.

Brooke, James. "With Sermons and Protest, New York Hails King." *The New York Times*, January 20, 1986, p. B3.

Buchanan, Paul D. "Japanese American Citizens League Remembers Executive Order 9066." *San Mateo Daily Journal*, February 19, 1991.

Buchanan, Paul D. "Muslim Center Finds Welcome in County." *San Mateo Daily Journal*, December 30, 2002, p. 3.

"Bush: Too little, too late for Native Americans." *Indian Country Today*, October 15, 2004.

Carlsen, William. "Rights violations, abuses alleged by detainees." *San Francisco Chronicle*, p. A12.

Carroll, Susan. "Volunteer patrols stir uneasiness on border." *The Arizona Republic*, April 1, 2005.

Chaddock, Gail Russell. "US schools slip back toward segregation." *Christian Science Monitor*, July 17, 2001, p. 3.

Chen, David W. "Battle over Iroquois Land Claims Escalates." *The New York Times*, May 16, 2003, p. A1.

"Chinese Exclusion Measure Passed." *San Francisco Chronicle*, April 29, 1902.

Clines, Francis X. "Death Penalty Is Suspended in Maryland." *New York Times*, May 10, 2002, p. A20.

"Clinton Slams Wen Ho Lee Prosecution." *ABC News,* September 15, 1999.

Coile, Zachary. "Tears of joy and hard memories." *San Francisco Chronicle*, June 30, 2001.

Collier, Robert. "Indian Americans Coming On, Challenging Latinos." *San Francisco Chronicle*, February 29, 2004, p. A9.

Connerly, Ward. "The irrelevance of race." *San Francisco Chronicle*, July 8, 2001, p. C8.

Constable, Pamela. "Africans demand apology for past slavery." *San Francisco Chronicle*, September 2, 2001, p. A12.

_____. "Race talks rocked by walkouts." *San Francisco Chronicle*, September 4, 2001, p. A1.

Cooper-Plaszewski, Kimberly. "Open Forum: In defense of multi-racial identity." *San Francisco Chronicle,* July 25, 2001, p. A19.

Cuba, Prince. "Black Gods of the Inner City." *Gnosis: A Journal of Western Inner Traditions*, fall 1992.

Doyle, Charles. "The USA Patriot Act: A Sketch." Congressional Research Service, Library of Congress, April 18, 2002.

Elder, Janet, and Kevin Sack. "Poll Finds Optimistic Outlook but Enduring Racial Division." *The New York Times*, July 11, 2000, p. A1.

Epstein, Edward. "Emotional call for internment memorials." *San Francisco Chronicle*, April 15, 2005, p. A1.

Epstein, Edward. "Quiet Remembrance for World War II Survivors." *San Francisco Chronicle*, June 29, 2001, pp. A3–A4.

Ford, Peter. "Xenophobia follows US terror." *The Christian Science Monitor*, October 11, 2001.

Francis, David R. "Charges of racism cloud immigration arguments." *Christian Science Monitor*, June 25, 2001, p. 17.

Glaser, Jack. "The Fallacy of Racial Profiling." *San Francisco Chronicle*, December 5, 2001, p. A25.

"Government Lifts Wounded Knee News Blackout." *New York Times*, May 4, 1973, p. 15.

Guthman, Edward and Stein, Ruthe. "Awards to Berry, Washington Eclipse 'Beautiful Mind.'" *San Francisco Chronicle*, March 24, 2002, p. D1.

Hartill, Lane. "A Brief History of Interracial Marriage." *The Christian Science Monitor*, Boston, July 15, 2001, p. 15.

Healy, Bernadine, M.D. "The shame of a nation." *U.S. News & World Report*, October 4, 2004, p. 54.

Hull, Michael D. "The Japanese-American 442nd Regimental Combat Team." *World War II Magazine*, July 1996.

Hutcheson, Ron, and Dave Montgomery. "Bush Guest Worker Proposal: Firestorm engulfs plan to give illegal immigrants legal status." *Detroit Free Press*, January 8, 2004.

Jean, Heller, "Syphilis Victims in the U.S. Went Untreated for Forty Years." *New York Times,* July 6, 1972.

Jonsson, Patrik. "Courts balk at limiting racial profiling." *The Christian Science Monitor*, July 6, 2001, p. 1.

"Justices Back Trial Judge on Sentences in King Case." *San Francisco Chronicle*, June 14, 1996, p. A4.

Konga, Deborah. "Bush urged to address racial issues." Associated Press article. *San Francisco Chronicle*, July 8, 2001, p. A10.

Kozinn, Allen. "Marian Anderson Is Dead at 96; Singer Shatters Racial Barriers." *New York Times*, April 9, 1993, p. 1.

Krebs, Albin. "Louis Armstrong, Jazz Trumpeter and Singer, Dies." *New York Times*, July 7, 1971.

LaSalle, Mick. "Hispanic stars were big during classic studio era." *San Francisco Chronicle*, Sunday, September 16, 2001, p. 38.
Marks, Alexandra. "A Pennsylvania town faces up to old race tensions." *The Christian Science Monitor*, Boston, June 29, 2001, p. 1.
Mathis, Nancy. "On Behalf of a Nation, an Apology." *Houston Chronicle*, May 16, 1997.
Miller, Sarah. "For African-Americans, Trend Is back to the South." *Christian Science Monitor*, Boston, Tuesday, June 26, 2001.
Nakao, Annie. "The Flowering of Lili." *San Francisco Examiner*, January 27, 1997.
_____. "Gala reopens wounds for Japanese Americans." *San Francisco Chronicle*, September 5, 2001, p. A1.
"New Negro Riots Erupt on Coast; Three Reported Shot." *New York Times*, August 13, 1965, p. 1.
"Ole Miss Partly Furls the Confederate Flag." *San Francisco Chronicle*, April 21, 1983, p. 7.
Pimentel, Benjamin. "DNA study of human migration." *San Francisco Chronicle*, April 13, 2005, p. A1.
Pimentel, Benjamin. "Images of Racism." *San Francisco Chronicle*, July 17, 2001, p. A11.
Pressley, Sue Anne. "Racism Suspected in Texas Slaying." *San Francisco Chronicle*, June 9, 1998, p. 1.
Price, Jess. "On the Road." *New Mexico Magazine*, March 1989, p. 28.
"Rice firmly refuses to testify publicly at 9/11 panel." *San Francisco Chronicle*, March 24, 2004, p. A5.
"Roosevelt Stirs Up a Sensation." *San Francisco Chronicle*, October 19, 1901.
Ross, John. *Anderson Valley Advertiser*, June 13, 2001, p. 3.
Rubenstein, Steve. "A Joyous Day of Marching and Speeches." *San Francisco Chronicle*, January 20, 1986, p. 1.
Scheer, Robert. "Wen Ho Lee: Presumed guilty until proven innocent." *San Francisco Chronicle*, August 26, 2001, p. C4.
Shea, Rachel Hartigan. "What's the Place of Race." *U.S. News and World Report*, March 31, 2003, pp. 46–50.
Sink, Mindy. "New Mexico: Bar Exam to Include Indian Law." *New York Times*, April 4, 2002, p. A20.
Streisand, Betsy. "Latino Power: Big media tune into the nation's largest minority." *U.S. News and World Report*, March 17, 2003, pp. 34–26.
"Tehran Students Seize US Embassy." *New York Times*, November 5, 1979.
Turner, Wallace. "Caretaker, 19, Is Freed in 5 Los Angeles Slayings." *The New York Times*, August 13, 1968.
"Violence Mars Boston Busing." *New York Times*, September 12, 1974.
Walsh, Kenneth T. "Well-Timed Reform." *U.S. News & World Report*, January 19, 2004, p. 33.
Wides, Laura. "Muslims call Patriot Act a threat." *San Francisco Chronicle*, December 20, 2002, p. A6.
Yardley, Jim. "Panel Recommends Reparations in Long-ignored Tulsa Race Riot." *The New York Times*, February 5, 2000, p. A1.
Zimmerman, Eilene. "Border agents feel betrayed by Bush guest-worker plan." *The Christian Science Monitor*, Tuesday, February 24, 2004, p. 3.

BOOKS

Aaron, Hank. *I Had a Hammer*. New York: HarperCollins Publishers, 1991.
African American Journey. Chicago: The World Book, 2001.
Aldred, Lisa. *Thurgood Marshall: Supreme Court Justice*. New York: Chelsea House Publishers, 1990.
Alvarez, Luis. *Luis Alvarez: Adventures of a Physicist*. New York: Basic Books, Inc., 1987.

Anderson, Marian. *My Lord, What a Morning.* New York: The Viking Press, 1956.

Bacon, Margaret Hope. *The Quiet Rebels: The Story of the Quakers in America.* Philadelphia: New Society Publishers, 1985.

Ballentine, Betty, and Ian Ballentine. *The Native Americans: An Illustrated History.* Atlanta: Turner Publishing Inc., 1993.

Buchanan, Paul D. *Historic Places of Worship.* Jefferson, N.C., and London: McFarland and Company, Inc., 1999.

Buddhist Church of America Archives. 75th anniversary edition. San Francisco: Buddhist Church of America, 1974.

Bugliosi, Vincent. *Helter Skelter: The True Story of the Manson Murders.* New York: W.W. Norton and Company, Inc., 1974.

Camurat, Diane. *American Indians in the Great War: Real and Imagined.* Paris: Institut Charles V, University of Paris VII, 1993.

Carlson, Lewis H., and John J. Fogarty. *Tales of Gold.* Chicago: Contemporary Books, Inc., 1987.

Cole, Maria. *Nat King Cole: An Intimate Biography.* New York: William Morrow and Co., Inc., 1971.

Collins, Bud. *Bud Collins' Modern Encyclopedia of Tennis.* Garden City, New York: Doubleday and Company, Inc., 1980.

Congress and the Nation, 1945–1964. Washington, D.C.: Congressional Quarterly, Inc., 1965.

Craig, Robert D. *Historical Dictionary of Honolulu and Hawaii.* Lanham, MD: The Scarecrow Press, Inc., 1988.

Davis, Kenneth. *Don't Know Much About History.* New York: Avon Books, 1990.

Daws, Gavan. *Shoal of Time.* New York: The Macmillan Company, 1968.

Du Bois, Shirley Graham. *His Day is Marching On: A Memoir of W.E.B. Du Bois.* Philadelphia: J.R. Lippencott Co., 1971.

Du Bois, W.E.B. *Writings.* New York: The Library of America, 1986.

Duster, Alfreda M. *Crusade for Justice: The Autobiography of Ida B. Wells.* Chicago: University of Chicago Press, 1970.

1872–1942: A Community Story. N.p.: Japanese American Citizens League, San Mateo Chapter, 1991.

Espy, Carlos. *The Politics of the Olympic Games.* Berkeley, Cal.: University of California Press, 1979.

Fitzpatrick, Joseph P. *Puerto Rican American: The Meaning of the Migration to the Mainland.* Englewood Cliffs, New Jersey: Prentice-Hall, 1981.

Freeland, Michael. *Gregory Peck.* New York: William Morrow and Company, Inc., 1980, pp. 173–182.

Garvey, Marcus, and UNIA Papers Project. *Marcus Garvey: Life and Lessons.* Los Angeles: UCLA, 1995.

Gerrold, David. *The World of Star Trek.* New York: Bluejay Books, Inc., 1973.

Gottlieb, Agnes Hooper. *1000 Years, 1000 People: Ranking the Men and Women Who Shaped the Millennium.* New York: Kodansha International, 1998.

Greising, David. *I'd Like the World to Buy a Coke: The Life and Leadership of Roberto Goizuela.* New York: John Wiley and Sons, Inc., 1997.

Griswold, Edward N. *Congressional Guide to the U.S. Supreme Court.* Washington, D.C.: Congressional Quarterly, Inc., 1979.

Hadley-Garcia, George. *Hispanic Hollywood.* New York: Carol Publishing Company, 1990.

Hall, Kermit L. *The Oxford Companion to the Supreme Court of the United States.* New York: Oxford University Press, 1992.

Harlan, Louis R. *Booker T. Washington: The Making of a Black Leader, 1856–1901.* New York: Oxford University Press, 1972.

Haskins, James. *The Life and Death of Martin Luther King, Jr.* New York: Lothrop, Lee, and Shepherd Co., 1977.

Haskins, Jim, and Kathleen Benson. *Carter G. Woodson: The Man Who Put "Black" in American History.* Brookfield, Conn.: The Millbrook Press, 2000.

Hazen-Hammond, Susan. *Timeline of Native American History*. New York: The Berkeley Publishing Group, 1997.

Hornsby, Allan, Jr. *Chronology of African American History*. Detroit: Gale Research, Inc., 1991.

Hughes, Langston, and Milton Meltzer. *A Pictorial History of the Negro in America*. New York: Crown Publishers, Inc., 1968.

Jackson, Jesse. *Legal Lynching: Racism, Injustice, and the Death Penalty*. New York: Marlowe and Company, 1996.

Jennings, Peter, and Todd Brewster. *The Century*. New York: Doubleday, 1998.

Jewell, Derek. *Duke: A Portrait of Duke Ellington*. New York: W.W. Norton and Company, Inc., 1977.

Kanellos, Nicolas. *Hispanic Firsts*. Detroit: Gale, 1997.

Kashima, Tesuden. *Buddhism in America*. Westport, Conn.: Greenwood Press. 1977.

Kent, George E. *A Life of Gwendolyn Brooks*. Lexington, Kentucky: The University Press of Kentucky, 1990.

Kieran, John and Arthur Daly. *The Story of the Olympic Games*. Philadelphia: J.B. Lippencott Company, 1973.

Kohn, George C. *Dictionary of Historic Documents*. New York: Facts on File, Inc., 1991.

Kugelmass, J. Alvin. *Ralph J. Bunche: Fighter for Peace*. New York: Julian Messner, 1970.

Lincoln, C. Eric. *The Black Muslims in America*. Trenton, N.J.: African World Press, Inc., 1994.

Logan, Rayford W. *W.E.B. Du Bois: A Profile*. New York: Hill and Wang, 1971.

MacDonald, J. Fred. *Black and White TV: Afro-Americans in Television since 1948*. Chicago: Nelson-Hall Publishers, 1983.

Mair, George. *Oprah Winfrey: The Real Story*. New York: Carol Publishing Company, 1994.

Malone, Mary. *Connie Chung: Broadcast Journalist*. Hillside, N.J.: Enslow Publishing Company, 1992.

Mankiller, Wilma, and Michael Walls. *Mankiller: A Chief and Her People*. New York: St. Martin's Press, 1993.

Means, Howard. *Colin Powell, Soldier-Statesman, Statesman-Soldier*. New York: Donald I. Fine, Inc., 1992.

McCullough, David. *The Path Between the Seas*. New York: Simon and Schuster, 1971.

McWilliams, Carey. *North from Mexico*. New York: Greenwood Press Publishers, 1968.

Marill, Alvin H. *The Films of Sidney Poitier*. Secaucus, N.J.: Citadel Press, 1978.

Mauro, Tony. *Illustrated Great Decisions of the Supreme Court*. Washington, D.C.: Congressional Quarterly, Inc., 2000.

Meier, Matt S., and Feliciano Rivera. *The Chicanos: A History of Mexican Americans*. New York: Hill and Wang, 1972.

Miller, Kelly. "Booker T. Washington as Ambassador and Spokesman." In Miller, *Roosevelt and the Negro*. Washington: Hayworth Publishing House, 1907.

Moore, Gilbert. *A Special Rage*. New York: Harper and Row Publishers, 1971, p. 58.

Musicant, Ivan. *Empire by Default*. New York: Henry Holt and Company, 1998.

Nenn, Daisy. *A Procession of Friends: Quakers in America*. Garden City, N.Y.: Doubleday and Co., Inc., 1972.

Nichols, Nichelle. *Beyond Uhura*. New York: G.P. Putnam Sons, 1994.

Oates, Stephen B. *Let the Trumpet Sound: The Life of Martin Luther King, Jr.* New York: A Plume Book, 1982.

Osborn, Robert. *50 Golden Years of Oscar*. La Habra, Cal.: ESE California, 1979.

Parks, Rosa. *Rosa Parks: My Story*. New York: Dial Books, 1992.

Perry, Bruce. *Malcolm: The Life of a Man Who Changed Black America*. Barrytown, NY: Station Hill Press, 1991.

Personal Justice Denied. Report of the Commission on Wartime Relocation and Internment of Civilians. Washington, D.C.: Government Printing Office, Library of Congress, 1982.

Potter, Lou. *Liberator: Fighting on Two Fronts in World War II*. New York: Harcourt Brace Jovanovich, 1992.

Powell, Colin L. *My American Journey*. New York: Random House, 1995.

Rampersad, Arnold. *The Life of Langston Hughes*. New York: Oxford University Press, 1986.
Redkey, Edwin S. *Black Exodus: Black Nationalists and the Back to Africa Movement, 1990–1918*. New Haven, Conn.: Yale University Press, 1969.
Riley, James A. *The Negro Leagues*. Philadelphia: Chelsea House Publishers, 1997.
Segal, Ronald. *The Black Diaspora: Five Centuries of the Black Experience Outside Africa*. New York: Farrar, Straus, and Giroux, 1995.
Shole, Richard. *The Academy Award Index: The Complete Categorical and Chronological Index*. Westport, Conn.: Greenwood Press, 1993.
Soloman, Burt. *The Baseball Timeline*. New York: Avon Books, 1997.
Stanton, Bill. *Klanwatch*. New York: Grove Weidenfeld, 1991.
Steiner, Steve. *La Raza: The Mexican Americans*. New York: Harper and Row, Publishers, 1968.
Straub, Deborah Gillan, *Hispanic American Voices*. Detroit: UXL, 1997.
Terrell, John Upton. *American Indian Almanac*. New York: Barnes and Noble Books, 1994.
"Tuskegee Syphilis Study Legacy Committee Report." Tuskegee, Ala.: Tuskegee University, 1996.
Urofsky, Melvin I. *The Supreme Court Justices: A Biographical Dictionary*. New York: Garland Publishing, Inc., 1994.
Utter, Jack. *American Indians: Answers to Today's Questions*. Lake Ann, Mich.: National Woodlands Publishing Company, 1993.
Wagenheim, Kal. *The Puerto Ricans: A Documentary History*. New York: Praeger Publishing, 1973.
Wagenknecht, Edward and Anthony Slide. *The Films of D.W. Griffith*. New York: Crown Publishers, Inc., 1975.
Walker, Samuel. *In Defense of American Liberties: The History of the ACLU*. New York: Oxford University Press, 1990.
Wallechinski, David. *Sports Illustrated Presents the Complete Book of the Summer Olympics*. 1996 edition. Boston: Little Brown and Co., 1996.
Ward, Geoffrey C., and Ken Burns. *Baseball: An Illustrated History*. New York: Alfred A. Knopf, 1994.
Ware, Susan. *Forgotten Heroes*. New York: The Free Press, 1998.
Weinberg, Meyer. *W.E.D. Du Bois: A Reader*. New York: Harper and Row, 1970.
Weisbrot, Robert. *Freedom Bound: A History of American Civil Rights Movement*. New York: W.W. Norton Co., 1990.
Wormser, Richard. *American Islam: Growing Up Muslim in America*. New York: Walker Publishing Company, 1994.

WEB SITES

http://news.nationalgeographic.com. Mayell, Hillary. "Global Gene Project to Trace Humanity's Migrations." *National Geographic News*, April 13, 2005.
http://news.nationalgeographic.com. "Fast Facts: National Museum of the American Indian." *National Geographic News*, September 21, 2004.
http://pubsociology.typepad.pub. Gifford, Brian. "Combat Casualties and Race: What can we learn from the 2003–2004 Iraq Conflict?" September 2004.
http://usinfo.state.gov, March 3, 2004. Crawford, Darlisa. "African Americans and the 2004 U.S. Elections: An Interview with Dr. Ron Walters."
http//www.cnn.com/interactive/world/0401/chart/iraq.fatalities/nav.exclude.html.
www2.worldbook.com. "African American Journey: Marian Anderson." World Book, Inc. 2001.
www.san.beck.org/BTW.html. Beck, Sanderson. "Booker T. Washington and Character Education at Tuskegee Institute, 1881–1915." *Literary Works of Sanderson Beck*. 1996.
www.apri.org/Bio-Rand1.htm. "Biographical Notes on A. Philip Randolph, 1889–1979." A. Philip Randolph Institute. 2001.

www.aclu.org. ACLU Position Paper. The American Civil Liberties Union. Fall 1998.

www.aclu.org. "Arrest the Racism: Racial Profiling in America." ALCU.

www.afro.com. "The Million Man March." The Afro American Newspapers.

www.american.edu. "TED Case Studies: Los Braceros: 1942–1964."

www.AmericanIndian.si.edu. Drapeau, Amy. *Facts and Figures from the Grand Opening of the Smithsonian's National Museum of the American Indian*, October 2004.

www.anc.org.za. Profile of Nelson Rolihlahla Mandela. 2003.

www.arhoolie.com. Pedro J. Gonzalez and Los Madrugadores. 2001.

www.asianweek.com. "Dalip Singh Saund: An Asian Indian American Pioneer." September 16, 1999.

www.asianweek.com. "Fred Korematsu Honored by USF." Asian Week Archives. 2001.

www.asianweek.com. Yip, Althea. "Remembering Vincent Chin." 1998.

www.asu.edu. Cesar Chavez. 2001.

www.bioguide.congress.gov. Saund, Dalip Singh. Biographical Directory of the United States Congress. 2003.

www.bioguide.congress.gov. Wu, David. Biographical Information. 2003.

www.bruceleefoundation.com. "About Bruce Lee." Bruce Lee Foundation.

www.ccr-ny.org. "The State of Civil Liberties: One Year Later." Center for Constitutional Rights. 2004.

www.cgi.chron.com. Breaking the Barriers: A Houston Chronicle Special Section. Overlooked Heroine: Althea Gibson.

www.cis.org/articles. Center for Immigration Studies. 1995.

www.civnet.org. Regents of the University of California v. Bakke. 1978.

www.clements.umich.edu.

www.cnn.com. "Betty Shabazz, Malcolm X's widow, dies at 61." June 23, 1997.

www.cnn.com/ELECTION/2004/President. Election 2004, National Exit Poll, CNN.

www.com-org.utoledo.edu. Wollman, Neil. "Poverty Gaps in the U.S. between the Races, Age Groups, and Genders Decreased Steadily Since 1995 — But Still a Ways to Go." Manchester College. 2004.

www.courses.educ.ksa.edu. Biography Information: Rosa Minoka Hill. 2001.

www.core-online.org. The History of CORE. 2001.

www.cpusa.org. Margolick, David. "Billie Holiday and 'strange fruit.'" 2000.

www.crime.about.com. Bickel, Bill. "Church Bombing … Birmingham, Alabama … 1963." 2004.

www.cviog.uga.edu. University of Georgia. Southern Manifesto.

www.dickshovel.com. "Ethnic Cleansing: We Have It Too." 1993.

www.electriciti.com. "Ballad of an Unsung Hero: The New York Times." 2001.

www.eugenics-watch.com/roots. Laws Against Mixing Races.

www.faa.gov. Famous Flyers: Bessie Coleman. 2001.

www.farmworkers.org. The Bracero Program.

www.fasereports.org. "Jamie Escalante named to Teacher's Hall of Fame." 2000.

www.fedcivilrights.org. Hispanic Heritage Month. 2004.

www.filmsite.org. Dirks, Tim. "The Birth of A Nation (1915)." 1996–2001.

www.freerepublic.com. Clegg, Roger S. "Perfect Profile: The Bush administration's racial-profiling policy surprises." 2003.

www.gale.com. Celebrating Hispanic Heritage — Timeline. 2001.

www.gale.com/free_resources/chh/bio/ochoa_e.htm . "Ellen Ochoa." 2000.

www.geocities.com. "The Tuskegee Airmen: A Tribute to My Father."

www.harlemglobetrotters.com. The Original Harlem Globetrotters. 2001.

www.history.navy.mil/gaqs/gaq61-2.htm. Cryptology: Navajo Code Talkers. Naval Historical Center.

www.house.gov. "Birth of the Congressional Black Caucus Revisited." 2003.

www.ldfla.org. Garcia, Robert. "Riots and Rebellion: Civil Rights, Police Reform, and the Rodney King Beating." 1997.

www.indiancountry.com. "New York Cayuga Land Claim gets measure of justice." 2001.

www.ins.usdoj.gov. Immigration and Naturalization Services. War Brides Act of December 28, 1945.

www.invent.org. George Washington Carver. 2001.

www.isop.ucla.edu/eas/documents/phlpguit.htm. "United States Senator Albert J. Beveridge Speaks about the Philippine Question." UCLA Center for East Asian Studies.

www.jacl.org. "About JACL." Japanese American Citizens League.

www.JACL.org. Tateishi, John. JACL Supports Legislation to preserve internment camps, April 13, 2004.

www.jchs-harvard.edu. "The State of the Nation's Housing." Joint Center for Housing Studies, Harvard University. 2003.

www.jsc.nasa.gov. Biographical Data. 2001.

www.ksks.essortment.com. Oprah Winfrey biography. 2001.

www.law.umkc.edu. "The Charles Manson Trial."

louisianahistory.ourfamily.com/arkansas/littlerock9.html. "They Just Wanted an Education: The Little Rock Nine."

www.mc.maricopa.edu. Mourning Dove: Coyote Stories. 1998.

www.members.aol.com/Nowacumig. "The Chronological History of the AIM."

www.migrationinformation.org. Jachimowicz, Maia. "Bush Proposes New Temporary Worker Program." *Migration Information Source*, February 1, 2004.

www.mockingbird.chebucto.org. Harper Lee Biography. 2003.

www.mockingbird.chebucto.org. "Mockingbird:The Film." November 2001.

www.muddywaters.com. The Official Muddy Waters Biography. 2001.

www.multiracial.com. The Multiracial Advocate.

www.museum.tv. Negra, Diane M. "Connie Chung, U.S. Broadcast Journalist." 2003.

www.naacp.org. NAACP Timeline. 2001.

www.nativeamericans.com/2004PresidentialProclamation.htm. Presidential Proclamation. Office of the Press Secretary, November 4, 2004.

www.ncadp.org. "Executing Minorities: An American Tradition." 2004.

www.news.bbc.co.uk. "Jesse Jackson — man of many missions." BBC News. 2001.

www.no-smoking.org. Kravets, David. "Indians Left Out of Tobacco Deal." Action on Smoking and Health. 2001.

www.oneida-nation.net. Oneida Indian Nation. Land Claims Information. 2000.

www.pazsaz.com. *The Cosby Show*. Pazazz Entertainment Network. 2001.

www.pbs.org/weta/apr/aprbio.html. A. Philip Randolph Biography. PBS.org.

www.pbs.org. The Chicago Defender. 2002.

www2.pfeiffer.edu/-Iridener/DSS/DuBois/DUBOISW4.HTML.

www.poets.org. Poetry Exhibits. Gwendolyn Brooks.

www.poets.org. Theme of English B by Langston Hughes. Academy of American Poets.

www.poppolitics.com. "An American Story." PopPolitics.com.

www.princeton.edu. "George Washington Carver, Jr.: Chemurgist." 2001.

www.public.asu.edu. Ron Takaki. Online Directory of Asian Pacifica American Artists. 2003.

www.romanticmovies.about.com. Murray, Rebecca. "'A Beautiful Mind' Wins Best Picture." 2004.

www.salon.com. Wilma Mankiller. 2001.

www.seattletimes.newsource.com. Martin Luther King, Jr. 2004.

www.senate.gov. Senator Daniel Inouye's Biography. 2001.

www.showme.missouri.edu. "The Tuskegee Syphillis Study." A Historical View of US Immigration Policy. 1995.

www.spartacus.schoolnet.co.uk/USAlynching/htm. Lynching.

www.spot.colorado.edu. Biographical Information for Luis W. and Walter Alvarez. 2001.

www.stanford.edu Hine. Darlene Clark. "Student Nonviolent Coordinating Committee." Black Women in America: An Historical Encyclopedia. 1993.

www.stanford.edu/group/King. Foster, Autherine Juanita Lucy. The Papers of Martin Luther King, Jr. 2002.

www.texasnaacp.org. Texas NAACP. "The Brutal Murder of James Byrd, Jr. of Jasper." November 11, 2002.

www.thesammy.com. "History of Dr. Sammy Lee."

www.umi.com. The John Collier Papers.

www.umich.edu. "U.S. Supreme Court rules on University of Michigan cases." University of Michigan. 2002.

www.uncp.edu. "Indians Rout the Klan." 2001.

www.univision.net. Univision. 2004.

www.usdoj.gov. "The Ten Year Program to Compensate Japanese Americans Interned During World War II Closes Its Doors." February 19, 1999.

www.vahistorical.org. "Learn About Virginia: Lawrence Douglas Wilder." 2003.

www.voices.cla.umn.edu . "Voices from the Gaps: Gwendolyn Brooks." 2001.

www.wakeamerica.com/past/speeches/1980/jjackson_071784.html. Address to the Democratic Convention by Jesse Jackson. Wake America.

www.watson.org. Cozzens, Lisa. "Early Civil Rights Struggles: Brown v. Board of Education." 1995.

www.whitehouse.gov. "Asian/Pacific American Heritage Month: A Proclamation." 2002.

www.whitehouse.gov. Biography of Condoleeza Rice. 2004.

www.window.state.tx.us. "Bordering the Future: Immigration." 2001.

www.worldbook.com/fun/aajourny. African American Journey. World Book Encyclopedia Presents series, 2003.

www.writetools.com/women/stories. McFadden, Edith. "Edith Spurlock Sampson." Women's Stories. 1999–2000.

www.yvwiiusdinvnohii.net. Thomas, N.L. The Peoples Path's Homepage. 2001.

Index

A&T College, Greensboro, North Carolina February 2, 1960
Aaron, Henry "Hank" July 9, 1948; April 8, 1974; October 24, 1972
Abbott, Robert S. May 5, 1905; June 15, 1921
Abernathy, Ralph December 1, 1955; September 3, 1958; March 7, 1965; April 4, 1968
Academy Awards April 9, 1961; April 10, 1968
Acheson, (Secretary of State) Dean March 1, 1950
Addams, Jane July 15, 1904
Advisory Council of the Milbank Fund July 26, 1972
Afghanistan September 11, 2001
Africa July 6, 1971
African Americans June 7, 1943
African Methodist Episcopal Church March 24, 1916
Age Discrimination in Employment Act 1967; March 25, 1972
Agricultural Adjustment Act January 9, 1938
Alabama November 14, 1915
Alabama State December 1, 1955
Alabama State Normal February 4, 1913
Alaska August 1, 1991
Albany, Georgia July 24, 1962; September 15, 1965
Albuquerque, New Mexico September 22, 1950
Alcatraz Island, San Francisco Bay November 20, 1969; July 3, 1987
Alcorn State University, June 12, 1963; June 26, 2001
Aleut (tribe), June 3, 1942
Aleutian Islands, June 3, 1942
Algeria April 25, 1967
Ali, Muhammad February 26, 1934; April 28, 1967
Alien Land Acts, 1913 May 19, 1913; May 26, 1924
"All deliberate speed" March 12, 1956; September 29, 1958
Allen, Charles H. April 12, 1900
Allen, Lillie Belle, July 3, 2001
Allright, S.E. April 3, 1944
Almeida, Rafael, July 4, 1911
"Aloha Oe'" November 11, 1917
Alvarez, Luis Walter October 28, 1968
Alverio, Rosita Dolores April 9, 1961

American Academy of Arts and Letters Award September 1, 1950
American Airlines Flight 11 September 11, 2001
American Airlines Flight 77 September 11, 2001
American Broadcasting Company (ABC) September 9, 1966; January 23, 1977
American Citizens for Justice June 23, 1982
American Civil Liberties Union (ACLU) January 12, 1920; July 23, 1999; July 6, 2001; May 16, 2004
American Farm Bureau Federation August 4, 1942
American Federation of Labor (AFL-CIO) August 25, 1925; December 5, 1955; August 28, 1963
American Flyweight Title June 13, 1923
American Indian Institute September 10, 1915
American Indian Movement (AIM) February 26, 1973
American Institute for Public Service Jefferson Award April 15, 1988
American Lawn Tennis August 28, 1950
American League July 9, 1948
American Muslim Mission February 25, 1975
American Red Cross Blood Bank April 1, 1950
Americans with Disabilities Act, 1990 March 25, 1972
Amherst College April 1, 1950
Amos 'n' Andy June 11, 1953
Amritsar, India January 3, 1957
Anderson, Marian August 26, 1925; April 9, 1939; January 7, 1955; April 8, 1993
Andersonan, Joseph March 21, 1981
Angel Island January 22, 1910
Anglo-Saxism April 24, 1898; May 19, 1913
Annexation of Hawaii July 7, 1897
Annie Allen September 1, 1950
Anniston, Alabama May 4, 1961
Anthony, Susan B. April 24, 1898
Anti-imperialists April 24, 1898
Anti-miscegenation laws October 1, 1948; June 12, 1967
Apache, Chiricahua February 17, 1909
Apology Resolution November 3, 1993
Arab States September 22, 1950
Arai, Clarence August 29, 1930

195

Arizona June 2, 1924; December 7, 1941; October 1, 1948; August 1, 1991
The Arizona Republic April 1, 2005
Arizona Supreme Court June 2, 1924
Arkansas February 19, 2001
Arkansas National Guard September 24, 1957
Arkansas State Press February 19, 2001
Armstrong, Louis August 4, 1901; June 3, 1921; August 8, 1922; April 5, 1923; July 6, 1971
Aryan race August 3, 1936
Ashe, Arthur August 28, 1950
Asia February 24, 1907; January 22, 1910
Asner, Ed January 23, 1977
Assembly Centers February 19, 1942
Astaire, Fred December 9, 1933
Atascadero, California March 31, 1927
Atlanta, Georgia November 24, 1915; January 15, 1929; November 7, 1967; January 2, 1984; April 29, 1992
Atlanta, Texas June 15, 1921
Atlanta Compromise November 14, 1915
Atlanta University February 1, 1903; July 11, 1905
Atlantic Ocean August 15, 1914
Atom bomb March 1, 1950
Attucks, Crispus March 24, 1916
Auburn, New York March 10, 1910
Audubon Ballroom, New York City February 21, 1965; August 11, 1965
"The Aunties" April 24, 1898
The Autobiography of Malcolm X February 21, 1965; January 23, 1977

Back to Africa movement January 12, 1922; June 10, 1940
Badham, Mary March 21, 1963
The Bahamas April 16, 1964
Baird, Vance June 25, 2001
Baker, Ella May 4, 1961
Baker, Josephine August 28, 1963
Bakke, Allan P. June 28, 1978
Baldwin, Mrs. Ruth Standish Baldwin September 29, 1910
Ballad of an Unsung Hero January 7, 1985
Baltimore, Maryland July 2, 1908; January 2, 1984
Baltimore & Ohio Railroad July 2, 1908
Banuelos, Ramona Acosta December 17, 1971
Barnett, (Governor) Ross B. October 2, 1962
Barred Zone Act May 25, 1924
Bataan Death March April 9, 1942
Bates, Daisy September 24, 1957; February 19, 2001
Bates, Ruby March 25, 1931
"Battle Hymn of the Republic" October 2, 1962
The Battlefield August 4, 1901
Bayard, Rustin August 7, 1957
Bazile, (Judge) Leon June 12, 1967
Beals, Melba Pattillo September 24, 1957
The Beatles July 3, 1960
Beckwith, Byron De La June 12, 1963
Belafonte, Harry August 28, 1963
Bellows, (Assistant Attorney General) Randy March 6, 1999
Beloved October 7, 1993

Berkeley County, South Carolina July 15, 1904
Berlin August 3, 1936
Bernstein, Leonard April 9, 1961
Berry, Shawn Allen June 7, 1998
Best Supporting Actress Award February 29, 1940
Beth Israel Medical Center, New York July 6, 1971
Beveridge, Albert (Senator) April 24, 1898
Beverly Hills, California August 10, 1968
Bichet, Sidney December 4, 1927
Biggs, Andy (Representative) April 1, 2005
bin Laden, Osama September 11, 2001
Birmingham, Alabama May 4, 1961; April 16, 1963; September 15, 1963; March 7, 1965
Birmingham Manifesto April 16, 1963
The Birth of a Nation February 8, 1915
Black, Hugo Black October 5, 1953
Black Beauty September 9, 1966
Black Christ April 9, 1942
Black Migration September 29, 1910; March 24, 1916
Black Muslims January 7, 1946; February 21, 1965
The Black Panther April 25, 1967
Black Panther Party (BPP) April 25, 1967; August 22, 1989
Black Panther Party for Self Defense April 25, 1967
Black Power August 11, 1965; October 16, 1968
Black Star Line March 24, 1916; August 1, 1920
Black Swan Records May 15, 1921
Blackfeet (tribe) September 24, 2004
The Blackman December 2, 1927
Blake, James December 1, 1955
Bledsoe, Tempestt September 20, 1984
Blood and Sand December 9, 1933
Blood for Britain April 1, 1950
Bloody Sunday March 7, 1965
The Bluest Eye October 7, 1993
Bodman, James March 21, 1981
Boghetti, Giuseppe August 26, 1925
Bok Award April 9, 1939; April 8, 1993
Bonet, Lisa September 20, 1984
Bookard, Kitt July 15, 1904
Booker T. Washington High January 15, 1929
Boston, Massachusetts May 19, 1925; January 7, 1946
Boston Braves July 4, 1911; July 6, 1912; April 15, 1947
Boutwell, Mayor Albert April 16, 1963
Boynton v. Virginia May 4, 1961
Bracero program August 4, 1942; July 15, 1954
Brandenberg, Clarence June 9, 1969
Brandenberg v. Ohio June 9, 1969
Brennan, William J. October 5, 1953; March 9, 1964; June 29, 1972
Brewer, Lawrence Russell June 7, 1998
Bridges, Lloyd January 23, 1977
Briseno, Theodore J. March 3, 1991
Brooke, General John R. June 12, 1901
Brooklyn, New York April 15, 1947; April 25, 1967
Brooklyn Dodgers July 4, 1911; April 15, 1947; July 9, 1948; October 24, 1972
Brooks, David Anderson September 1, 1950
Brooks, Gwendolyn May 5, 1905; September 1, 1950

Brookside, California August 7, 1948
Brotherhood of Sleeping Car Porters August 25, 1925 July 1, 1941; December 1, 1955
Brothers, David April 25, 1967
Brown, Andy June 11, 1953
Brown, (Justice) Henry May 18, 1896
Brown, John February 12, 1909
Brown, Linda May 17, 1954; May 16, 2004
Brown, Minnijean September 24, 1957
Brown, Oliver (Reverend) May 17, 1954
Brown Bomber June 22, 1938
Brown Chapel March 7, 1965
Brown II May 17, 1954; March 12, 1956; September 29, 1958
Brown v. Board of Education of Topeka, Kansas May 17, 1954; March 12, 1956; September 24, 1957; September 29, 1958; June 28, 1978; January 24, 1993; May 16, 2004
Bryan, William Jennings April 24, 1898
Bryant, Roy September 23, 1955
Buchanan v. Warley November 5, 1917
Buff, Johnny June 13, 1923
Buffalo, New York May 16, 2000
Buffalo Soldiers March 9, 1916
Bunche, Fred September 22, 1950
Bunche, Olive Johnson September 22, 1950
Bunche, Ralph Johnson September 22, 1950
Bureau of Indian Affairs (BIA) March 4, 1933; June 18, 1934; August 1, 1953; July 3, 1987
Burke Act May 8, 1906
Burlington, North Carolina April 1, 1950
Burnham School of Beauty Culture June 15, 1921
Burns, Tommy July 4, 1910
Burton, Harold H. October 5, 1953
Burton, LaVar January 23, 1977
Bush, George April 21, 1992
Bush, George W. July 8, 2001; September 2, 2001; January 7, 2004; November 4, 2004; January 20, 2005; May 1, 2005
Butler, Norman 3X February 21, 1965
Byrd, James June 7, 1998

Cabazon v. State of California October 17, 1988
Cable Act May 25, 1924
Caddo (tribe) September 24, 2004
Cafe Society April 20, 1939
Cairo, Georgia January 31, 1919
California February 24, 1907; October 1, 1948; August 1, 1991
California Gold Rush April 29, 1902
California Supreme Court October 1, 1948; June 28, 1978
Campanella, Roy July 9, 1948
Campanis, Al April 6, 1987
Campbell, Senator Ben Nighthorse November 4, 2004
Canada September 2, 2001
Cantonese Opera Company November 27, 1940
Capitol Mall April 16, 1995
Cardinal, Douglas September 24, 2004
Caribbean Sea August 15, 1914
Carlisle Indian Industrial School, Oklahoma July 6, 1912

Carlos, John October 16, 1968
Carmen, Julie August 21, 1988
Carmichael, Stokely October 2, 1962; August 11, 1965; October 7, 1993
Carnegie Hall July 3, 1960; April 8, 1993
Carranza, Venustiano (Mexican President) March 9, 1916
Carter, J. (Judge) October 1, 1948
Carver, George Washington June 14, 1927
Cayuga (tribe) May 16, 2000
Cayuga County Courthouse, New York March 10, 1913
Cayuga Lake May 16, 2000
Celler, Emanuel (Congressman) October 3, 1965
Center for Disease Control July 26, 1972; July 8, 2001
Center for Excellence in Genomic Science, India April 13, 2005
Center for Genome Information, University of Cincinnati April 13, 2005
Center for the Study of White American Culture August 14, 2001
Central Europe February 1, 1943
Central High School, Little Rock, Arkansas September 24, 1957; February 19, 2001
Central Intelligence Agency (CIA) February 21, 1965; November 4, 1979; September 2, 2001
Cephalization April 30, 1904
Chambliss, Robert Edward September 15, 1963
Chang-Diaz, Franklin January 12, 1986
Chapel Hill, North Carolina April 7, 1947
Chaplin, Levi April 16, 1995
Charleston, Oscar February 20, 1920
Chattanooga, Tennessee March 25, 1931
Chavez, Cesar Estrada March 31, 1927; January 9, 1938; September 16, 1965; August 21, 1988; April 23, 1993
Chavez, Richard September 16, 1965
Check and Double Check June 11, 1953
Cherokee (tribe) July 3, 1987
Cherokee/Choctaw (tribe) September 24, 2004
Chester, Pennsylvania January 15, 1929
Chicago, Illinois July 27, 1919; August 8, 1922; April 5, 1923; January 7, 1927; April 7, 1947; September 1, 1950; September 23, 1955; August 11, 1965; April 25, 1967; December 8, 1979; June 23, 1982; April 12, 1983; January 2, 1984
Chicago American Giants February 20, 1920
Chicago Chronicle January 27, 1900; May 17, 1900
Chicago Coroner July 27, 1919
Chicago Defender May 5, 1905; June 15, 1921; September 1, 1950
Chicago Giants February 20, 1920
Chicago Municipal Court December 8, 1979
Chicago Tribune July 15, 1904
Chihuahua, Mexico March 9, 1916
Childress, Alvin June 11, 1953
Chimes Blues April 5, 1923
Chin, Lily June 23, 1982
Chin, Vincent June 23, 1983
China April 29, 1902; January 22, 1910
Chinatown, San Francisco December 1, 1958

Chinese Exclusion Act of 1902 April 29, 1902; February 24, 1907
Chinese Exclusion Repeal Act December 17, 1943
Chinese immigrants December 17, 1943
Chippewa (tribe) November 20, 1969
Christine Quintasket August 8, 1936
Chuen, Lee Hoi November 27, 1940
Cincinnati, Ohio June 23, 1983
Cincinnati Reds July 4, 1911; July 6, 1912; October 24, 1972
Citizen's Committee to Test the Constitutionality of the Separate Car Law May 18, 1896
City of Los Angeles v. Lyons April 29, 1992
Civil Liberties Act of 1988 August 10, 1988
Civil Rights Act of 1957 September 9, 1957
Civil Rights Act of 1960 September 9, 1957
The Civil Rights Act of 1964 July 2, 1964
Civil Rights Act of 1964 March 25, 1972; June 25, 1976
Civil Rights Act of 1968 April 11, 1968
Civil Rights Commission September 9, 1957
Civil War May 18, 1896; October 16, 1901; March 10, 1913; November 24, 1915
The Clansman February 8, 1915
Clark, (Sheriff) James March 7, 1965
Clark, Tom C. October 5, 1953
Clarke, C. Carroll May 15, 1921
Clarke, Edward Young January 12, 1922
Clay, Cassius April 28, 1967
Clay, Francis July 3, 1960
Cleaver, Leroy Eldridge April 25, 1967
Cleveland, Grover July 7, 1897; February 5, 1917
Cleveland, Ohio August 3, 1936; November 7, 1967
Cleveland Indians July 9, 1948; October 24, 1972
Clinton, William J. July 26, 1972; April 23, 1993; November 3, 1993
Clune Auditorium February 8, 1915
CNN January 20, 2005
Cochise February 17, 1909
Cogewea, the Half-Blood August 8, 1936
Coleman, Bessie June 15, 1921
Coleman, Tom July 23, 1999
Collier, John March 4, 1933
Collier Trophy October 28, 1968
Collins, Addie Mae September 15, 1963
The Color Purple January 2, 1984
Colorado October 1, 1948
Colored Agricultural and Normal University June 15, 1921
Columbia (space shuttle) January 12, 1986
Columbia Broadcasting System (CBS) June 11, 1953
Columbia Pictures April 10, 1968
Columbia Records May 15, 1921
Columbia University September 29, 1910; November 1, 1920; June 3, 1921
Columbus, New Mexico March 9, 1916
Colville Indian Association August 8, 1936
Colville Reservation August 8, 1936
Colville Tribal Council August 8, 1936
Commissioner of Indian Affairs March 4, 1933

Committee for the Improvement of Industrial September 29, 1910
Committee on Jim Crow in Military Service and Training July 26, 1948
Committee on Urban Conditions Among Negroes September 29, 1910
Commodore Records April 20, 1939
Concurrent Resolution 108 August 1, 1953
Congress of Industrial Organizations (CIO) December 5, 1955
Congress of Racial Equality (CORE) April 7, 1947; August 7, 1957; February 2, 1960;
Congressional Gold Medal February 25, 1942
Connelly, John (Governor) November 22, 1963
Connerly, Ward July 17, 2001
Connor, Eugene "Bull" (Police Commissioner) April 16, 1963
Connor, Howard (Major) February 25, 1942
Constitution Hall April 9, 1939
contralto August 26, 1925; April 9, 1939
Cook, Captain James July 7, 1898
Coolidge, Calvin December 2, 1927
Cooper v. Aaron September 29, 1958
Cooperstown, New York October 24, 1972
Corregidor Island, Philippines April 9, 1942
Correll, Charles June 11, 1953
Cosby, Bill September 15, 1965; September 20, 1984
The Cosby Show September 20, 1984
Cotton, James July 3, 1960
The Cotton Club June 3, 1921; December 4, 1927
Cotton States and International Exposition in 1895 November 14, 1915
Court of Appeals November 19, 1973
Covington, Georgia May 15, 1921
Coyote Stories August 8, 1936
Creating Equal: My Fight Against Racial Preferences July 17, 2001
"Creole Rhapsody" December 4, 1927
Crescent City Florida August 25, 1925
The Crisis: The Record of the Dark Races February 12, 1909; June 3, 1921; March 1, 1950
Cropperville January 9, 1938
Crozer Theological Seminary January 15, 1929
Crusade for Citizenship August 7, 1957
Cuba April 24, 1898; June 12, 1901
Cuban Constitution June 12, 1901
Cuban Giants February 20, 1920
Cullen, Countee June 3, 1921
Culp, Robert September 15, 1965; September 20, 1984

Dallas, Texas November 22, 1963
Dandi, India January 15, 1929
Dartmouth College December 4, 1975
Daughters of American Revolution (DAR) April 9, 1939
Davis, Ossie August 28, 1963
Davis, Sammy, Jr. August 28, 1963
Davis, Sylvester October 1, 1948
Dawes Act August 1, 1953
Dawes Severalty Act of 1887 May 8, 1906
Day, Justice William R. November 5, 1917
Dayton Marcos February 20, 1920

Daytona Beach, Florida September 15, 1965
Deardorff, Roseanne April 14, 1983
Death Valley, California August 10, 1968
Decatur, Mississippi June 12, 1963
Declaration of Rights of Negro Peoples of the World August 1, 1920
Dees, Morris March 21, 1981
Delano, California March 31, 1927; September 16, 1965; April 23, 1993
Delano grape strike September 16, 1965
Del Rio, Dolores December 9, 1933
Democratic National Convention July 17, 1984
Denny, Reginald April 29, 1992
Denver, Colorado April 25, 1967
Department of Agriculture August 4, 1942
de Soto, Rosanna April 15, 1988
Detroit, Michigan September 22, 1950; August 11, 1965; November 7, 1967
Detroit Stars February 20, 1920
Dexter Avenue Baptist Church December 1, 1955
Diamond Grove, Missouri June 14, 1927
Diaz, Porfirio May 25, 1911
Distinguished Service Cross August 21, 1959
District Court, Texas November 19, 1973
Doby, Larry July 9, 1948; April 6, 1987
Donahue, Phil January 2, 1984
Donald, Beulah Mae March 21, 1981
Donald, Michael March 21, 1981
Doohan, James September 8, 1966
Dorchester, Boston September 12, 1974
Douglas, Frederick January 13, 1990
Douglas, William O. October 5, 1953; June 29, 1972; November 19, 1973
Douglass, Frederick February 1, 1903
Dowell, Denzil April 25, 1967
Downing, Al April 8, 1974
Drew, Charles April 1, 1950
Du Bois, W. E. B. (William Edward Burghardt) April 24, 1898; February 1, 1903; July 11, 1905; February 12, 1909; March 24, 1916; July 28, 1917; February 18, 1919; June 3, 1921; January 12, 1922; August 25, 1925; March 1, 1950; August 27, 1963
Dunbar, Paul Laurence January 13, 1990
Duncan, Sandy January 23, 1977
Durban, South Africa September 2, 2001
Durham, North Carolina January 8, 1977
Dutch Harbor, Attu Island June 3, 1942
Dutch Reform Church February 17, 1909
Duvall, Robert March 21, 1963
Dylan, Bob July 3, 1960

Eastern Colored League February 20, 1920;
Ebbets Field April 15, 1947
Ebenezer Baptist Church, Atlanta January 15, 1929; April 4, 1968
Ebens, Ronald June 23, 1982
Eckford, Elizabeth September 24, 1957
Ecole d'Aviation des Freres Caudron at Le Crotoy June 15, 1921
1867 Treaty of Medicine Lodge January 5, 1903
Eighth Amendment June 29, 1972
Einstein Medal October 28, 1968

Eisenhower, Dwight D. September 24, 1957
El Salvador November 6, 1986
El Santuario del Chimayo April 9, 1942
The Electric Company April 9, 1961
Elementary and Secondary Education Act January 2, 1968
Elks Hall, Harlem August 25, 1925
Ellington, Daisy December 4, 1927
Ellington, Edward "Duke" June 3, 1921; December 4, 1927; July 6, 1971
Elliot, (Judge) J. Robert July 24, 1962
Ellis Island of the West January 22, 1910
Emmy Awards April 9, 1961; September 15, 1965; January 23, 1977
The Emperor Jones November 1, 1920
Endo, Misuye June 21, 1943
Enola Gay October 28, 1968
Enter the Dragon September 9, 1966
Epton, Bernard June 23, 1982
Equal Employment Opportunity Commission July 2, 1964; March 25, 1972; November 19, 1973
Equal Protection Clause June 28, 1978; July 6, 2001
Escalante, Jaime April 15, 1988
Espinoza, Joe January 11, 1954
Espinoza, Mrs. November 19, 1973
Espinoza v. Farah Manufacturing Company November 19, 1973
Estevez, Emilio August 21, 1988
Europe January 22, 1910
Europe, James Reese January 1, 1918
Evers, Medgar June 12, 1963
Ex Parte Endo June 21, 1943
The Exclusion Act of 1882 April 29, 1902
Exclusion Act of 1902 January 22, 1910
Executive Order 8802 July 1, 1941; December 7, 1941
Executive Order 9066 December 8, 1941; February 19, 1942; June 21, 1943; August 10, 1988; April 14, 2005

Fabela March 31, 1927
Fahardo, Puerto Rico April 21, 1992
Fairfield, Alabama February 3, 1956
Fan, Lee Jun November 27, 1940
Farah Manufacturing Company November 19, 1973
Farmer, James April 7, 1947
Farrad, W.D. February 26, 1934
Farrad, Wallie February 26, 1934
Farrakhan, Louis Haleem Abdul February 25, 1975; April 16, 1995
Fat Boy October 28, 1968
Faubus, Orville (Governor) September 24, 1957
Federal Bureau of Investigation (FBI) February 21, 1965; April 4, 1968; March 21, 1981
Federal League July 4, 1911
Fédération Aéronautique International (FIA) June 15, 1921
Fellowship of Reconciliation (FOR) April 7, 1947; August 7, 1957
Fields, Joseph December 1, 1958
Fifteenth Amendment June 21, 1915; April 3, 1944

15th Infantry Regimental Band of New York January 1, 1918
Fifth Amendment June 21, 1943
Fifth Circuit Court of Appeals July 24, 1962
Figures, Thomas March 21, 1981
Filipino Americans June 7, 1943
First Amendment March 9, 1964
First Baptist Church, Montgomery, Alabama December 1, 1955; September 3, 1958
Fisk University September 29, 1910; August 14, 2001
Fists of Fury September 9, 1966
Five Civilized Tribes July 3, 1987
Flatheads (tribe) August 1, 1953
Florida April 12, 1900
Flower Drum Song December 1, 1958
Flying Down to Rio December 9, 1933
Folger, Abigail August 10, 1968
Fools Crow, Frank February 26, 1973
Foraker, Joseph B. April 12, 1900
Foraker Act April 12, 1900
"Forbidden Book" January 27, 1900; May 17, 1900
Foreman, George April 28, 1967
Forest Hill Tennis Club, New York August 28, 1950
Forest Lawn Cemetery January 3, 1957
Forrest, Nathan Bedford November 24, 1915
Fort Hill Cemetery, Auburn, New York March 10, 1913
Fort Sill, Oklahoma February 17, 1909
Fortune, Porter April 19, 1983
Foster, Andrew "Rube" February 20, 1920
Foster, Reverend Hugh February 3, 1956
Four Horsemen of the Apocalypse December 9, 1933
The 442nd Regimental Combat Team (RCT) February 1, 1943
447 Bombadiers March 22, 1941
Fourteenth Amendment May 18, 1896; December 12, 1938; June 21, 1943; January 11, 1954; May 17, 1954; December 11, 1961; March 9, 1964; July 6, 2001
Francisco Guilledo (Pancho Villa) June 13, 1923
Frankfurter, Felix October 5, 1953
Franklin County, New York May 16, 2000
Frazier, Joe April 28, 1967
Freedman's Hospital April 1, 1950
Freedom Rides April 7, 1947; May 4, 1961
French Open Tournament August 28, 1950
Fresno, California August 29, 1930; August 7, 1948
Frost Award September 1, 1950
Frykowski, Voytek August 10, 1968
Fullilove v. Klutznick July 2, 1980
Funter Bay, Alaska June 3, 1942
Furman v. Georgia October 2, 1967; June 29, 1972
FUTURES April 15, 1988

G.I. Bill May 3, 1948
Gaines, Lloyd December 12, 1938
Gandhi, Mohandas March 31, 1927; January 15, 1929; April 7, 1947
Garfield High School, East Los Angeles April 15, 1988

Garner v. Louisiana December 11, 1961
Garrity, (Judge) Arthur September 12, 1974
Garvey, Marcus March 24, 1916; February 13, 1920; August 1, 1920; January 12, 1922; June 10, 1940; October 7, 1993
Gennet Records April 5, 1923
Genographic Project April 13, 2005
Gentleman's Agreement of 1907 February 24, 1907; May 19, 1913
George Washington University Law School August 21, 1959
Georgia, Atlanta July 26, 1972
Geronimo February 17, 1909
Ghana, Africa August 27, 1963
Ghost Dance February 26, 1973
Gibson, Althea August 28, 1950
Gibson, Josh June 17, 1939
Gibson Island Club July 2, 1908
Gifford, Brian May 1, 2005
Gila River, Arizona April 14, 2005
Gilliam, Jim "Junior" July 9, 1948
Glover, Danny January 2, 1984; August 21, 1988
Gogh, Vincent Van April 9, 1961
Goldberg, Whoopi January 2, 1984; August 21, 1988
Gone with the Wind February 29, 1940
Gonzales, California March 31, 1927
Gonzales, Colin June 25, 1976
Gonzales, Pedro J. January 7, 1985
Gordon, George William March 24, 1916
Gosden, Freeman June 11, 1953
"Got My Mojo Workin'" July 3, 1960
The Grammy Awards April 9, 1961
Grand Island May 16, 2000
Great Artiste October 28, 1968
Great Britain September 20, 1958
Great Depression August 4, 1942
The Great Emancipator February 12, 1909
The Great (Black) Migration January 9, 1938
Great Migration June 26, 2001
Great Salt March January 15, 1929
The Great Satan November 4, 1979
Great Society January 20, 1965
The Great War June 2, 1924
Great White Hope July 4, 1910
Green, Ernie September 24, 1957
Green Hornet September 9, 1966
Greenberg, Hank October 24, 1972
Greenfield, Elizabeth Taylor May 15, 1921
Greenville, South Carolina July 17, 1984
Greenwich Village, New York April 20, 1939
Greenwood, Mississippi September 23, 1955
Greenwood District February 4, 2000
Griffith, D. W. February 8, 1915
Grove Press February 21, 1965
Grovey v. Townsend April 3, 1944
Guam April 24, 1898
Guess Who's Coming to Dinner? April 10, 1968
Guest Worker Plan January 7, 2004
Guinn and Beal v. United States June 21, 1915
The Gulf War November 4, 1979

Haley, Alex February 21, 1965; January 23, 1977
Hamilton, Charles August 11, 1965

Hammerstein, Oscar, II December 1, 1958
Hampton Institute May 5, 1905
haoles July 7, 1898
Hare, Pat July 3, 1960
Harlan, John M. October 5, 1953; June 30, 1958; December 11, 1961
Harlan, Marshall (Justice) May 18, 1896
Harlem, New York March 24, 1916; June 3, 1921; August 25, 1925; January 7, 1927; December 4, 1927; February 21, 1965; August 11, 1965; April 25, 1967
Harlem Globetrotters January 7, 1927
Harlem Hospital, New York September 20, 1958
Harlem Renaissance March 24, 1916; June 13, 1921; March 1, 1950
Harlem's Poet June 3, 1921
Harper, Jack (Senator) April 1, 2005
Harper & Row September 20, 1958
Harpers Ferry, W.Va. February 12, 1909
Hart-Celler Act October 3, 1965
Hartford, Connecticut August 11, 1965
Harvard University February 1, 1903; September 22, 1950; January 8, 1977; July 17, 2001
Harvard University's Civil Rights Project July 18, 2001
Hastie, William H. April 3, 1944
Havana, Cuba August 1, 1920
Hawaii April 29, 1902; November 11, 1917; August 21, 1959
Hawaii Territorial Senate of Hawaii August 21, 1959
Hawaii Treaty of 1898 July 7, 1898
Hawaii Territorial House of Representatives August 21, 1959
Hay, John (Secretary of State) April 24, 1898
Hayer, Talmadge February 21, 1965
Haynes, George Edmund (Doctor) September 29, 1910
Haynes, Marques Haynes January 7, 1927
Hays, Henry March 21, 1981
Hayworth, Rita December 9, 1933
Hearst newspapers April 24, 1898
Heart Mountain, Wyoming April 14, 2005
Heebie Jeebies April 5, 1923
Heller, J.R. (Doctor) July 26, 1972
Hello Dolly! July 6, 1971
Henderson, Fletcher May 15, 1921
Heney-Webb Alien Land Act May 19, 1913.
Heney-Webb Alien Land Law February 24, 1907
Henry J. Kaiser Family Foundation July 17, 2001
Hepburn, Katharine April 10, 1968
Hernandez, Peter January 11, 1954
Hernandez v. Texas January 11, 1954
Hill, Charles March 18, 1952
Hinckley, Illinois January 7, 1927
Hirabayashi, Gordon June 21, 1943; August 10, 1988
Hirabayashi v United States June 21, 1943
Hiroshima, Japan October 28, 1968
Hitler, Adolf August 3, 1936
Hokkaido, Japan June 3, 1942
Holiday, Billie April 20, 1939
Holliday, George William March 3, 1991; April 29, 1992

Holly Springs, Mississippi July 15, 1904
Hollywood, California January 3, 1957
Home for Colored Waifs August 4, 1901
Homer Smith April 16, 1964
Honda, Mike (Congressman) June 29, 2001
Honda, Mike (Representative) April 14, 2005
Hong Kong November 27, 1940
Honolulu, Hawaii August 21, 1959
Hoopa (tribe) August 1, 1953
Hoover, J. Edgar April 4, 1968
Hopi (tribe) September 24, 2004
Horne, Lena August 28, 1963
House, Donna September 24, 2004
Houser, George April 7, 1947
Houston, Texas April 14, 1983
Howard, Edgar June 18, 1934
Howard University, Washington, D.C. July 2, 1908; April 1, 1950; August 11, 1965; January 8, 1977; January 13, 1990; October 7, 1993; June 26, 2001
Huerta, Dolores September 16, 1965
Hughes, Charles Evans (Chief Justice) December 12, 1938
Hughes, James June 3, 1921
Hughes, Langston May 5, 1905, June 3, 1921
Humacao, Puerto Rico April 9, 1961
Human Genome Diversity Project April 13, 2005
Humphrey, Hubert (Senator) April 1, 1950
Hunter College January 8, 1977
Hunter's Point district, San Francisco, California July 3, 1987
Hussein, Saddam May 1, 2005
Huttig, Arkansas February 19, 2001

I Can't Be Satisfied July 3, 1960
I Feel Like Going Home July 3, 1960
I Spy September 15, 1965; September 20, 1984
Ialoni Palace November 11, 1917
IBM April 13, 2005
Idaho October 1, 1948
Immigrant Act of 1965 October 3, 1965
Immigrant Quota Act of 1921 October 3, 1965
Immigrant Quota Act of 1924 May 26, 1924; June 30, 1952; October 3, 1965
Immigrant Restriction Act November 15, 1935
Immigration Act of 1917 February 5, 1917
Immigration and Naturalization Service (INS) November 6, 1988
The Immigration Reform and Control Act of 1986 November 6, 1986
Imperial Valley, California January 3, 1957
"In a Sentimental Mood" December 4, 1927
In the Heat of the Night April 10, 1968
Independent Magazine July 15, 1904
India September 20, 1958
Indian Citizenship Acts June 2, 1924
Indian Gaming Regulatory Act October 17, 1988
Indiana October 1, 1948
Indianapolis ABC's February 20, 1920
Indians of All Tribes November 20, 1969
Ingalik (tribe) June 3, 1942
Inouye, Daniel (Senator) August 21, 1959
International League April 15, 1947

International Olympic Committee (IOC) July 5, 1912
Inupiaq (tribe) June 3, 1942
Iowa Agricultural College June 14, 1927.
Iran, Tehran November 4, 1979
Iran Hostage Crisis November 4, 1979
Iroquois (tribe) May 16, 2000
Ishi August 29, 1911
Island of Rhodes, Greece September 22, 1950
Israel September 22, 1950; September 2, 2001
Issei generation August 29; 1930 June 30, 1952
Isthmus of Panama August 15, 1914
Italy February 1, 1943
Iwo Jima February 25, 1942

J.B. Lippincott Company March 21, 1963
Jackson, Inman January 7, 1927
Jackson, Jesse April 4, 1968; October 24, 1972; July 17, 1984; March 21, 1981; August 21, 1988
Jackson, Mississippi October 2, 1962
Jackson County, Texas January 11, 1954
Jackson Street Hospital November 27, 1940
Jacksonville, North Carolina July 6, 2001
Jamaica December 2, 1927; June 10, 1940
Jamal-Warner, Malcolm September 20, 1984
James Byrd Jr. Hate Crimes Act June 7, 1998
James Byrd Jr. Hate Foundation for Racial Healing June 7, 1998
Jane Crow January 8, 1977
Japan April 30, 1904; February 24, 1907; November 15, 1935; December 8, 1941; September 20, 1958
Japanese American Citizens League (JACL) August 29, 1930; April 14, 2005
Jasper, Texas June 7, 1998
Jefferson Davis Highway March 7, 1965
Jefferson High School, Los Angeles September 22, 1950
Jeffries, James July 4, 1910
Jim Crow May 18, 1896; July 28, 1917; May 4, 1961
"Joe Camel" April 21, 1992
John Bull April 24, 1898
John Marshall Law School, Chicago December 8, 1979
John the Baptist February 1, 1903
Johns Hopkins University April 21, 1992
Johnson, Andrew September 24, 1907
Johnson, Hiram W. (Governor) May 19, 1913; May 26, 1924
Johnson, James Weldon June 3, 1921
Johnson, John Arthur "Jack" July 4, 1910
Johnson, Karen (Senator) April 1, 2005
Johnson, Lester January 7, 1927
Johnson, Lyndon Baines June 14, 1927; March 21, 1963; November 22, 1963; January 20, 1965; March 7, 1965; October 3, 1965; February 29, 1968; January 24, 1993
Johnson, Thomas 15X February 21, 1965
Johnson-Reed Act May 26, 1924
Johnson Space Center April 3, 1983
Johnston, Philip February 25, 1942
Joint Center for Political and Economic Studies January 20, 2005

Jones, Amos June 11, 1953
Jones, Johnpaul September 24, 2004
Jones, William H. (Congressman) March 2, 1917
The Jones Act March 2, 1917
Joplin, Mississippi June 3, 1921
Journey of Reconciliation April 7, 1947; May 4, 1961
Judge April 24, 1898
Judge Priest February 29, 1940
Jung Fan Kung-Fu Institute November 27, 1940
"Jungle Music" December 4, 1927

Kansas City Monarchs February 20, 1920; April 15, 1947
kapu July 7, 1897
Karnofsky family August 4, 1901
Kasabian, Linda August 10, 1968
Kaufman, (Judge) Charles June 23, 1982
Kazenbach v. Morgan. March 7, 1965
Kennedy, John F. October 2, 1962 June 12, 1963; December 1, 1963; November 22, 1963
Kennedy, Robert May 4, 1961; August 21, 1988
Kenney, Kerry August 21, 1988
Kent College of Law May 5, 1905
Kentucky Club, New York December 4, 1927
Kerner, (Governor) Otto February 29, 1968
The Kerner Commission Report February 29, 1968
Khomeini, Ayttolah Ruhollah November 4, 1979
Kido, Saburo August 29, 1930
King, Alberta Williams January 15, 1929
King, Coretta Scott April 4, 1968
King, John William June 7, 1998
King, Martin Luther, Jr. January 15, 1929; December 1, 1955; August 7, 1957; September 3, 1958; September 20, 1958; May 4, 1961; July 24, 1962; October 2, 1962; April 16, 1963; August 28, 1963; December 1, 1963; March 7, 1965; April 4, 1968; April 11, 1968; October 24, 1972; January 2, 1984; July 17, 1984; January 13, 1990
King, Martin Luther, Sr. January 15, 1929
King, Rodney March 3, 1991; April 29, 1992; February 20, 1996
King City, California March 31, 1927
King Gustav V of Sweden July 6, 1912
King Joe Oliver's Creole Jazz Band August 4, 1901; August 8, 1922; April 5, 1923
Kingdom of Hawaii November 3, 1993
Kingsburg, California March 31, 1927
Kiowa January 5, 1903
Kiska Islands June 3, 1942
Klamath (tribe) August 1, 1953
Knapp, Barbara August 28, 1950
Knight-Pulliam, Keshia September 20, 1984
Knowles, James March 21, 1981
Koenig, Walter September 8, 1966
Koon, Sgt. Stacey C. March 3, 1991
Koop, C. Everett April 21, 1992
Koppel, Ted April 6, 1987
Korean ancestry August 7, 1948
Korean War August 4, 1942
Korematsu, Fred June 21, 1943; August 10, 1988; April 14, 2005
Korematsu v. United States June 21, 1943

Kosciusko, Mississippi January 2, 1984
Krenwinkel, Patricia August 10, 1968
Kroeber, Alfred August 29, 1911
Ku Klux Klan (KKK) February 8, 1915; November 24, 1915; January 12, 1922; September 23, 1955; January 18, 1958; May 4, 1961; September 15, 1963; March 21, 1981
kuklos November 24, 1915
Kwan, Nancy December 1, 1958

Laboratory of Human Population Genetics, Moscow April 13, 2005
La Paz, California April 23, 1993
La Salle College November 27, 1940
LaBianca, Leno August 10, 1968
LaBianca, Rosemary August 10, 1968
The Labor Importation Program August 4, 1942
Ladies Professional Gold Association (LPGA) August 28, 1950
Lake Michigan July 27, 1919
Lake View Cemetery, Seattle September 9, 1966
Langston, Oklahoma June 15, 1921
Lantos, Tom (Congressman) September 2, 2001
Latin America July 6, 1971
Lawrence Livermore Laboratory October 28, 1968
League of Nations February 18, 1919
LeBeauf, Sabrina September 20, 1984
Lee, Amasa March 21, 1963
Lee, Bruce September 9, 1966
Lee, C.Y. December 1, 1958
Lee, Frances March 21, 1963
Lee, Harper March 21, 1963
Lee, Dr. Sammy August 7, 1948
Lee, Vernita January 2, 1984
Lee, Wen Ho March 6, 1999
Lemon, Meadowlark January 7, 1927
"Letter from Jail" April 16, 1963
Levin, Joseph J. March 21, 1981
Lewis, John March 7, 1965
Lewisohn Stadium Concert Award August 26, 1925
Liberia, Africa March 24, 1916
Life January 18, 1958
Lili'oukalani, Queen July 7, 1897
Lillies of the Field April 16, 1964
Lincoln, Abraham February 12, 1909
Lincoln, U.S.S. May 1, 2005
Lincoln Memorial April 9, 1939; August 28, 1963; April 16, 1995
Lincoln University July 2, 1908; December 12, 1938
Liston, Sonny April 28, 1967
Little, Earl May 19, 1925
Little, Louis Norton May 19, 1925
Little, Malcolm May 19, 1925; January 7, 1946
Little Boy October 28, 1968
Little Louie August 4, 1901
Little Rock, Arkansas September 24, 1957; February 19, 2001
Little Rock Nine September 24, 1957
Locke, Alain June 3, 1921
Lodge, Henry Cabot April 24, 1898; February 5, 1917
Lodi, California January 7, 1985

London, England June 10, 1940
Lone Wolf v. Hitchcock January 5, 1903
Loong, Lee Siu September 9, 1966
Lorain, Ohio
Lorraine Motel, Memphis April 4, 1968
Los Alamos Laboratory, New Mexico March 6, 1999
Los Alamos, New Mexico October 28, 1968
Los Angeles, California February 8, 1915; June 7, 1943; August 7, 1948; October 1, 1948; September 22, 1950; August 11, 1965; April 25, 1967; November 7, 1967; April 14, 1983; January 7, 1985; April 29, 1992
Los Angeles County District Attorney March 3, 1991
Los Angeles County Superior Court April 29, 1992
Los Angeles Dodgers, Los Angeles Dodgers April 8, 1974; April 6, 1987
Los Angeles Police March 3, 1991 April 29, 1992
Los Angeles Rams April 15, 1947
Los Madrugadores January 7, 1985
The Lost/Found Nation of Islam in the Wilderness of North America February 26, 1934
Louganis, Greg August 7, 1948
Louis, Joe June 22, 1938; October 24, 1972
Louisiana Supreme Court May 18, 1896
Louisville, Kentucky November 5, 1917
L'Ouverture, Toussaint March 24, 1916
Loving, Mildred June 12, 1967
Loving, Richard June 12, 1967
Loving v. Virginia June 12, 1967 April 10, 1968
Lowerey, J. August 21, 1988
Loyola University Law School, Chicago December 8, 1979
Lucy, Autherine Juanita February 3, 1956
Lucy, Milton February 3, 1956
Lucy, Minnie February 3, 1956
Lumbee Indian (tribe) January 18, 1958
Luque, Dolf July 4, 1911
Lust for Life April 9, 1961
Luzon Island, Philippines April 9, 1942
Lynching July 15, 1904; April 20, 1939

MacArthur, Douglas (General) November 15, 1935
Macbeth August 22, 1989
Madamoiselle January 8, 1977
Madero, Francisco, Jr. May 25, 1911
Mahoney, Cardinal Roger April 23, 1993
Maine June 2, 1924
Major League Baseball June 17, 1939; April 15, 1947 July 9, 1948
Malcolm X May 19, 1925; January 7, 1946; December 1, 1963; February 21, 1965; August 11, 1965; February 25, 1975
"Mammy" February 29, 1940
Man, Sifu Yip Man November 27, 1940
Manhattan, New York City, New York September 11, 2001
Manhattan Project October 28, 1968
Manifest Destiny May 18, 1896 April 30, 1904; June 2, 1924
Manila Bay April 9, 1942
Mankatao State December 4, 1975

Mankiller, Wilma Pearl July 3, 1987
Manson, Charles August 10, 1968
Marble, Alice August 28, 1950
March Against Fear October 2, 1962
March on Washington July 1, 1941; August 28, 1963
March on Washington for Jobs and Equal Protection in Nation Defense July 1, 1941
Marian Anderson Center April 8, 1993
Marlowe September 9, 1966
Marquette University December 4, 1975
Marsans, Armando July 4, 1911
Marshall, Norma Ariza July 2, 1908
Marshall, Justice Thurgood July 2, 1908; April 3, 1944; May 17, 1954; October 2, 1967; January 24, 1993
Marutani, William June 12, 1967
Maryland, Baltimore January 8, 1977
Maryland March 10, 1913; October 1, 1948
Mason City, Iowa June 25, 2001
Mason Street Temple, Memphis April 4, 1968
Massachusetts February 1, 1903
Massachusetts Institute of Technology (MIT) January 12, 1986
Matsui, Doris (Representative) April 14, 2005
Matsui, Robert (Representative) April 14, 2004
Maxton, South Carolina January 18, 1958
Mays, Willie July 9, 1948
Mazzoli, Romano (Congressman) November 6, 1986
McCarran, Patrick A. (Senator) June 30, 1952
McCarran-Walter Act June 30, 1952
McCarthy Era June 30, 1952
McCrary, Michael June 25, 1976
McCullough, David August 15, 1914
McDaniel, Hattie February 29, 1940
McDuffie, John November 15, 1935
McEarhern, Terry (District Attorney) July 23, 1999
McFarland, California March 31, 1927
McGee, W. J. April 30, 1904
McGill Medical College April 1, 1950
McKinley, William April 24, 1898; January 27, 1900; May 17, 1900; July 15, 1904
McKissick, Floyd August 11, 1965
McLairen v. Oklahoma State Regents for Higher Education June 5, 1950
McLarrin, Guilledo June 13, 1923
McNair, Denise September 15, 1963
Medal of Freedom October 24, 1972; April 8, 1993; April 23, 1993
Medical Degree at the University of Puerto Rico April 21, 1992
Meeropol, Abel April 20, 1939
Memphis, Tennesee July 15, 1904; October 2, 1962; April 4, 1968
Mendez, Jose July 4, 1911
Mendota, California March 31, 1927
Menendez, Ramon April 15, 1988
Menominee August 1, 1953
Meredith, James October 2, 1962
Messenger of Allah February 26, 1934
Metropolitan Opera of New York City January 7, 1955

Mexican foreign ministry August 4, 1942
Mexican Revolution May 25, 1911
Mexico November 6, 1988
Mexico City, Mexico October 16, 1968
Mfume, Kweisi July 8, 2001
Miami, Arizona December 17, 1971
Miami, Florida April 16, 1964
Middle East July 6, 1971
Midwestern Writer's Conference Award September 1, 1950
Milan, J.W. September 23, 1955
Miles, Nelson A. (Brigadier General) February 17, 1909
Miles College February 3, 1956
Mill Creek, Deer Creek August 29, 1911
The Million Man March October 16, 1995
Millwood, New York September 17, 1983
Milwaukee Braves April 8, 1974
Milwaukee, Wisconsin January 2, 1984
Mindanaou, Philippines April 24, 1898
Mineta, Norman (Transportation Secretary) June 29, 2001
Minoka-Hill, Rosa March 18, 1952
Minoso, Orestes July 9, 1948
Minuteman Project April 1, 2005
Mississippi, Jackson June 12, 1963
Mississippi River June 3, 1921
Missouri October 1, 1948
Missouri ex rel. Gaines v Canada December 12, 1938
Mobile, Alabama March 21, 1981
Mohammad, Elijah February 26, 1934; January 7, 1946; December 1, 1963; February 21, 1965; February 25, 1975
Mohammad, Farrad February 26, 1934
Mohammed, Wallace Fard February 26, 1934
Mohammad, Warith Deen February 25, 1975
Mohawk (tribe) November 20, 1969; May 16, 2000
Monroeville, Alabama March 21, 1963
Montana October 1, 1948
Montgomery, Alabama February 4, 1913; September 23, 1955; December 1, 1955; November 13, 1956; August 7, 1957; September 3, 1958; May 4, 1961; March 9, 1964; March 7, 1965
Montgomery, Olin March 25, 1931
Montgomery Bus Boycott December 1, 1955
Montgomery County Courthouse September 3, 1958
Montgomery Improvement Association (MIA) December 1, 1955; November 13, 1956
Montgomery Industrial School February 4, 1913
Montgomery Way August 7, 1957
Montreal Royals April 15, 1947; April 6, 1987
"Mood Indigo" December 4, 1927
Morehouse College January 15, 1929; June 26, 2001; January 2, 1984
Moreno, Antonio December 9, 1933
Moreno, Rita April 9, 1961
Morgan, McKinley July 3, 1960
Mori, Fred (Assemblyman) April 14, 2005
Morrison, Harold October 7, 1993
Morrison, Toni October 7, 1993
Mourning Dove August 8, 1936

Municipal Stadium, Cleveland, Ohio July 9, 1948
The Muppet Show April 9, 1961
Murakami, Masanori September 1, 1964
Murphy, Justice Frank June 21, 1943
Murray, Pauli January 8, 1977
My Lord, What a Morning April 9, 1939

NAACP v. Alabama June 30, 1958
Nagasaki, Japan October 28, 1968
Nashville, Tennessee January 2, 1984
Nation of Islam (NOI) May 19, 1925; February 26, 1934; January 7, 1946; February 21, 1965; April 28, 1967
The National Advisory Commission on Civil Disorders February 29, 1968
National Aeronautics and Space Administration (NASA) January 12, 1986
National Air and Space Museum September 24, 2004
National American Indian Heritage Month November 4, 2004
National Association for the Advancement of Colored People (NAACP) July 11, 1905; February 12, 1909; February 4, 1913; February 8, 1915; June 21, 1915; July 28, 1917; June 3, 1921; December 12, 1938; April 20, 1939; February 29, 1940; April 3, 1944; March 1, 1950; June 11, 1953; May 17, 1954; September 23, 1955; December 1, 1955; February 3, 1956; June 30, 1958; June 12, 1963; September 17, 1983; January 24, 1993; February 19, 2001
National Association of Colored Professional Baseball Clubs February 13, 1920;
National Broadcasting Company (NBC) September 20, 1958; September 15, 1965; September 20, 1984; April 6, 1987
National Endowments of the Arts September 1, 1950
National Farm Workers Association September 16, 1965
National Football League April 15, 1947
National Geographic Society April 13, 2005
National Guard July 24, 1962; April 29, 1992
National Historic Landmark February 19, 2001
National Indian Gaming Commission October 17, 1988
National Institute of Health (NIH) April 21, 1992
National Japanese American Memorial June 29, 2001
National League April 15, 1947
National League for the Protection of Colored Women September 29, 1910
National League on Urban Conditions among Negroes September 29, 1910
National Medal of Arts April 8, 1993
National Medal of Science October 28, 1968
National Organization of Women (NOW) January 8, 1977
National Urban League September 29, 1910
National Women's Hall of Fame July 3, 1987
Native Hawaiians November 3, 1993
Native Museum of the American Indian September 24, 2004; November 4, 2004
Navajo Code Talkers Program February 25, 1942

Navajo/Oneida (tribe) September 24, 2004
Nazi Germany April 1, 1950
Negro Leagues July 4, 1911; February 20, 1920; April 15, 1947; July 9, 1948
The Negro Metropolis June 3, 1921
The Negro Speaks of Rivers June 3, 1921
The Negro World March 24, 1916; January 12, 1922
Nelson, Craig June 25, 2001
Nevada October 1, 1948
New Deal March 4, 1933 January 9, 1938
New Deal for the Indians March 4, 1933
New Haven, Connecticut April 25, 1967
New Mexico June 2, 1924
The New Mexico National Guard April 9, 1942
New Orleans, Louisiana August 4, 1901; May 4, 1961; November 7, 1967; July 8, 2001
New Orleans organization May 18, 1896
New York City College August 25, 1925
New York City, New York September 29, 1910; February 8, 1915; March 24, 1916; July 28, 1917; February 13, 1920; July 12, 1920; August 1, 1920; November 1, 1920; August 8, 1922; March 1, 1950; December 1, 1958; February 25, 1975; April 8, 1993
New York Giants July 6, 1912
New York Metropolitan Opera Company April 8, 1993
New York Philharmonic Orchestra August 26, 1925
New York Police Athletic League August 28, 1950
New York Times March 1, 1950; July 26, 1972; March 6, 1999; July 11, 2000
New York Times Company v. Sullivan March 9, 1964
New York Yankees July 4, 1911
Newark, New Jersey August 11, 1965; April 25, 1967
Newcombe, Don July 9, 1948
Newport Jazz Festival July 3, 1960
Newport, Rhode Island July 3, 1960
Newton, Huey April 25, 1967; August 22, 1989
Niagara Falls, Ontario, Canada July 11, 1905
Niagara movement July 11, 1905
Niagara Platform July 11, 1905
Niagara River May 16, 2000
Nichols, Nichelle September 8, 1966
Nieslen ratings September 20, 1984
Nightline April 6, 1987
Nimoy, Leonard September 8, 1966
1912 Olympics July 6, 1912
1920 Alien Land Law February 24, 1907
1924 Immigrant Quota Act December 28, 1945
1960 Olympic Games April 28, 1967
1968 Summer Olympics October 16, 1968
1998 Tobacco Accord July 16, 2001
The 9th Circuit Court of Appeals July 16, 2001
92nd Infantry Division March 22, 1941
Nisei generation February 1, 1943; June 12, 1967
Nitz, Michael June 23, 1982
Nixon, E.D. December 1, 1955
Nixon, Richard M. July 6, 1971; December 17, 1971; March 25, 1972
Nobel Prize for Literature October 7, 1993

Nobel Prize for Peace September 22, 1950
Nobel Prize for Physics October 28, 1968
Norrise, Clarence March 25, 1931
North Atlantic Treaty Organization (NATO) December 8, 1979
North Carolina July 6, 2001
North Dakota October 1, 1948
Northwestern University Law School April 12, 1983
Novarro, Ramon December 9, 1933
Novello, Antonio C. April 21, 1992

Oakland Athletics October 24, 1972; June 13, 1923; April 25, 1967; August 10, 1988; August 22, 1989; April 29, 1992
Oakville, Alabama August 3, 1936
Occidental College August 7, 1948
Ochoa, Ellen April 14, 1983
Ochoa, Joseph April 14, 1983
Oglala (tribe) February 26, 1973
Ohio House of Representatives November 7, 1967
Ohio State University August 3, 1936
Okanagon (tribe) August 8, 1936
Okeh Race Records May 15, 1921; April 5, 1923
Oklahoma June 21, 1915; December 7, 1941; August 1, 1991
Oklahoma Legislature February 4, 2000
Oklahoma State University, Tulsa February 4, 2000
"Ol' Man River" November 1, 1920
Ole' Miss' October 2, 1962
Oliver, "King" Joe August 4, 1901; August 8, 1922
Olmos, Edward James April 15, 1988; August 21, 1988
Olympic Stadium, Berlin January 7, 1927
Olympics August 3, 1936; August 7, 1948
Omaha, Nebraska May 19, 1925; April 25, 1967
101st Airborne Division September 24, 1957
The 100th Infantry Battalion February 1, 1943
Oneida (tribe) May 16, 2000
Oneida, Wisconsin March 18, 1952
Operation Wetbacks July 15, 1954
Oppenheimer, Dr. J. Robert October 28, 1968
The Oprah Winfrey Show January 2, 1984
Oregon October 1, 1948
Orfield, Gary July 18, 2001
Oriental Exclusion Act May 26, 1924
Oroville, California August 28, 1911.
Ortez, Ricardo December 9, 1933
Osage August 1, 1953
Othello November 11, 1920
Our Lord of Esquipulas April 9, 1942
Outstanding Business Woman December 17, 1971
Owens, James Cleveland "Jessie" August 3, 1936
Oxford University March 21, 1963
Oxnard, California March 31, 1927

Pace, Harry Herbert May 15, 1921
Pacific Ocean August 15, 1914
Page, Sarah February 4, 2000
Paige, Leroy "Satchel" January 17, 1939; July 9, 1948
Palestine Conflict September 22, 1950

Pan-African Congress Resolutions February 18, 1919
Panama Canal April 24, 1898; August 15, 1914
Paramount Records May 15, 1921
Parents, Steve August 10, 1968
Paris, France May 25, 1911
Parkland Memorial Hospital, Washington D.C. November 22, 1963
Parks, Raymond February 4, 1913
Parks, Rosa Louise McCauley February 4, 1913; December 1, 1955
Pasadena, California January 31, 1919
Pasadena Junior College January 31, 1919
Patagonia April 30, 1904
The Path Between the Seas August 15, 1914
Patterson, Haywood March 25, 1931
Peace and Freedom Party April 25, 1967
Peace Information Center March 1, 1950
Pearce, Russell (Representative) April 1, 2005
Pearl Harbor, Hawaii December 7, 1941; February 19, 1942; June 3, 1942
Peck, Gregory March 21, 1963
Pediatric sickle cell anemia April 8, 1993
Pennsylvania July 2, 1908
The Pentagon, Washington, D.C. September 11, 2001
Penthouse magazine September 17, 1983
People Are Talking January 2, 1984
Perez, Andrea October 1, 1948
Perez v. Sharp October 1, 1948
Permanent National Origins Act May 26, 1924
Perry, Bruce February 21, 1965
Perry, Rick (Governor) July 23, 1999
Pershing, John "Black Jack" (General) March 9, 1916
Philadelphia Choir August 26, 1925
Philadelphia, Pennsylvania August 26, 1925; April 9, 1939; August 11, 1965; April 25, 1967; December 8, 1979; September 20, 1984
Philippine-American War April 24, 1898
Philippines April 24, 1898; April 29, 1902; April 30, 1904; November 15, 1935; July 4, 1946
Phillips, Lou Diamond April 15, 1988
Pine Level, Alabama February 4, 1913
Pine Ridge Indian Reservation, South Dakota February 26, 1973
Pittsburgh, Pennsylvania September 11, 2001
Platt Amendment June 12, 1901
Pleasant Lane Baptist Church April 16, 1995
Plessy, Homer May 18, 1896
Plessy v. Fergusen May 18, 1896; November 5, 1917; May 17, 1954; May 16, 2004
Poitier, Sidney April 16, 1964; April 10, 1968
Polanski, Roman August 10, 1968
Polo Grounds June 13, 1923
Poole, Paul Robert February 26, 1934
Poplar Bluff, Missouri January 9, 1938
Portland, Oregon April 8, 1993
Potawatomi August 1, 1953
Powell, Colin September 2, 2001
Powell, Laurence March 3, 1991
Powell, Ozzie March 25, 1931
Prague, Czechoslovakia March 1, 1950
Prague, Oklahoma July 6, 1912

Presidential Medal of Freedom July 3, 1987; April 8, 1993
Price, Jess April 9, 1942
Price, Victoria March 25, 1931
Price, Vincent August 22, 1989
Princeton University October 7, 1993
Prohibition August 1, 1920; August 8, 1922
Pro-imperialists April 24, 1898
Project USA June 25, 2001
The Prophet February 26, 1934
Proud Shoes: Profile of An American Family January 8, 1977
Provincetown Playhouse November 1, 1920
Public Broadcasting System (PBS) April 15, 1988
Public Law 280 August 1, 1953
Public Work Employment Act
Puck January 27, 1900
Puerto Rican Supreme Court March 2, 1917
Puerto Rico April 24, 1898; April 12, 1900
Puerto Rico House of Delegates April 12, 1900
Pulitzer newspapers April 24, 1898
Pulitzer Prize September 1, 1950; March 21, 1963; October 7, 1993
Pullman Company August 25, 1925
Purple Heart August 21, 1959

Quarry, Jerry April 28, 1967
Queen Elizabeth Hospital, Hong Kong September 9, 1966
Queen Lili'uokalani November 11, 1917
Quezon, Manual November 15, 1935
Quinn, Anthony December 9, 1933; April 9, 1961

Race records May 15, 1921
Race Relations Institute August 14, 2001
Racial Privacy Initiative July 17, 2001
Radio Station KMPC January 7, 1985
Rainbow/Push Coalition July 17, 1984
Randolph, Asa Philip January 12, 1922; April 25, 1925; July 1, 1941; July 26, 1948; December 5, 1955; August 28, 1963; October 24, 1972
Random House October 7, 1993
Raper, Dr. Arthur July 15, 1904; April 20, 1939
Rashad, Phylicia September 20, 1984
Ray, James Earl April 4, 1968
Reagan, Ronald October 24, 1972; August 10, 1988
Reconstruction May 18, 1896; September 24, 1957
Red Summer July 27, 1919
Reed, James A. May 26, 1924
Reeves, Jeremiah September 23, 1955
Rehabilitation Act, 1973 March 25, 1972
Related Intolerances September 2, 2001
Relocation centers February 19, 1942
Reno, Janet (Attorney General) March 6, 1999
Reno, Nevada July 4, 1910
Republic of Philippines November 15, 1935
Rhodes, Harry January 23, 1977
Richmond, California April 25, 1967
Richmond, Indiana April 5, 1923
Richmond, Virginia January 13, 1990
The Richmond Times October 16, 1901
Rickard, Chief Clinton June 2, 1924

Rickey, Branch April 15, 1947
The Ritz April 9, 1961
Riverside Church, Harlem October 24, 1972
Roberson, Willie March 25, 1931
Robert F. Goheen Professor October 7, 1993
Robertson, Carol September 15, 1963
Robertson, Charlie July 3, 2001
Robeson, Paul November 1, 1920
Robeson County, North Carolina January 18, 1958
Robinson, Bill "Bojangles" June 3, 1921
Robinson, David October 24, 1972
Robinson, Frank October 24, 1972; April 6, 1987
Robinson, Jack "Jackie" Roosevelt January 31, 1919 April 15, 1947; July 9, 1948; October 24, 1972; April 6, 1987
Robinson, Jackie, Jr. October 24, 1972
Robinson, Mallie McGriff January 31, 1919
Robinson, Rachel October 24, 1972
Robinson, Sharon October 24, 1972
The Rock November 20, 1969
Rockefeller, Nelson (Governor) October 24, 1972
The Rockford Files April 9, 1961
Rocky Mountain, Oklahoma July 3, 1987
Rodgers, Richard December 1, 1958
Roe Cloud September 10, 1915
Rogan, Joe February 20, 1920
Rogers, Ginger December 9, 1933
Rogers, Jimmy July 3, 1960
"Rollin' Stone" July 3, 1960
Rolling Fork, Mississippi July 3, 1960
The Rolling Stones July 3, 1960
Roosevelt, Eleanor April 9, 1939
Roosevelt, Franklin D. June 14, 1927; March 4, 1933; July 1, 1941; December 7, 1941; December 8, 1941; February 19, 1942; May 3, 1948
Roosevelt, Theodore April 24, 1898; October 16, 1901; February 24, 1907; February 17, 1909; May 19, 1913
Roosevelt College April 12, 1983
Roosevelt's War Message to Congress December 7, 1941; December 8, 1941
Roots February 21, 1965; January 23, 1977
Rose, William April 10, 1968
Roseland Ball Room May 15, 1921; June 3, 1921; August 8, 1922
Roselle, New Jersey August 14, 2001
Rosenwald Foundation Fellowship August 26, 1925
Ross, John August 4, 1942
Rowlands, Dick February 4, 2000
Roxbury, Boston September 12, 1974
Runyan, Kathryne June 25, 1976
Runyan, Russell June 25, 1976
Runyan v. McCrary et al June 25, 1976
Russell, Bill October 24, 1972
Russia March 1, 1950
Russians April 29, 1902
Russo-Japanese War February 24, 1907
Rustin, Bayard July 1, 1941; April 7, 1947
Rutgers University November 1, 1920
Ruth, George H. "Babe" April 8, 1974

Sabarmati Ashram, India January 15, 1929
Sac and Fox (tribe) July 6, 1912
Sachmo July 6, 1971
Sacramento, California September 16, 1965;
  July 17, 2001
St. Francis of Assisi March 31, 1927
St. James Theatre December 1, 1958
Saint John's University December 4, 1975
St. Joseph's Hospital, Memphis April 4, 1968
St. Louis, Missouri April 30, 1904; May 3,
  1948
St. Louis Browns July 4, 1911
St. Louis Giants February 20, 1920
St. Louis Terriers July 4, 1911
Saint Mary's College, Minnesota December 4,
  1975
St. Regis Mohawk (tribe) March 18, 1952
Sakiestewa, Ramona September 24, 2004
Salinas, California March 31, 1927
Salish (tribe) August 8, 1936
Salt Tax January 15, 1929
Sampson, Edith Spurlock December 8, 1979
San Antonio, Texas November 19, 1973
San Carlos, New Mexico February 17, 1909
San Diego, California August 11, 1965; April 25,
  1967
San Diego State University April 14, 1983
San Francisco, California February 24, 1907;
  January 22, 1910; August 29, 1930; November
  27, 1940; March 1, 1950; October 28, 1968;
  July 17, 1984; July 16, 2001
San Francisco Bay January 22, 1910
San Francisco Chronicle October 16, 1901
San Francisco Giants September 1, 1964
San Francisco Museum of Anthropology
  August 29, 1911
San Francisco State College July 3, 1987
San Jose, Costa Rica January 12, 1986
San Quentin Prison, California January 7, 1985
San Terenzo, Italy August 21, 1959
Sandwich Islands July 7, 1898
Santa Anita Racetrack June 29, 2001
Santa Monica Civic Auditorium April 16, 1964
Santa Monica Civic Center April 10, 1968
Santee River July 15, 1904
Saperstein, Abe January 7, 1927
Saperstein Globetrotters January 7, 1927
satyagraha January 15, 1929
Saund, Dalip Singh January 3, 1957
Savannah, Georgia September 15, 1965
Savoy Ballroom January 7, 1927
The Savoy Big Five January 7, 1927
Scat singing April 5, 1923
Schaad, Henry July 3, 2001
Schmeling, Max June 22, 1938
Schomberg, Arthur June 3, 1921
Scott Medal October 28, 1968
Scottsboro, Alabama March 25, 1931
The Scottsboro Nine March 25, 1931
Seale, Bobby April 25, 1967
Seattle, Washington August 29, 1930; Novem-
  ber 27, 1940; September 9, 1966
Sebring, Jay August 10, 1968
Second Pan-African Congress February 18, 1919

Second World War January 9, 1938; June 22,
  1938
Secretary of Interior February 26, 1973
Sellers, (Police Commissioner) Clyde Septem-
  ber 3, 1958
Selma, Alabama March 7, 1965
Selma, California March 31, 1927
Senate Armed Services Committee July 26, 1948
Seneca (tribe) May 16, 2000
Sengstacke, John May 5, 1905
Separate but Equal clause June 5, 1950; May 17,
  1954
Servicemen's Readjustment Act May 3, 1948
Shah Mohammed Riza Pahlevi November 4, 1979
Shakur, Lumumba April 25, 1967
Sharp, W.G. October 1, 1948
Sheen, Martin August 21, 1988
Shelley v. Kraemer November 5, 1917; May 3, 1948
Shoshone-Bannock (tribe) November 20, 1969
Show Boat November 1, 1920
Siena College December 4, 1975
Simi Valley, Ventura County, California April 29,
  1992
Simmons, William J. November 24, 1915
Simon, Carly August 21, 1988
Simpson, Alan (Senator) November 6, 1986
Simpson-Mazzoli Bill November 6, 1986
Sioux (tribe) January 8, 1939; November 20,
  1969; February 26, 1973
Sixteenth Street Baptist Church September 15,
  1963
Smith, Bessie May 15, 1921
Smith, Lonnie E. April 3, 1944
Smith, Tommy October 16, 1968
Smith v. Allwright April 3, 1944
Smithsonian Institution September 24, 2004
Snyder Act June 2, 1924
Society of American Indians (SAI) January 8, 1939
Somme, France June 15, 1921
Soo, Jack December 1, 1958
Soul on Ice April 25, 1967
The Souls of Black Folk February 1, 1903; June 3,
  1921
South Boston September 12, 1974
South Boston High School September 12, 1974
South Carolina July 15, 1904; August 28, 1950;
  July 3, 2001
South Carolina v. Kazenbach March 7, 1965
South Dakota October 1, 1948
Southern Christian Leadership Conference (SCLC)
  August 7, 1957; May 4, 1961; August 21, 1988
Southern France February 1, 1943
Southern Manifesto on Integration March 12, 1956
Southern Paiute (tribe) February 26, 1973
Southern Poverty Law Center March 21, 1981
Southern Tenant Farmers Union (STFU) Janu-
  ary 9, 1938
Southie September 12, 1974
Soviet Union November 1, 1920; March 1, 1950
Spain April 24, 1898; April 12, 1900
Spanish-American War July 7, 1897; April 24,
  1898; April 12, 1900; May 19, 1913; Novem-
  ber 24, 1915; March 9, 1916
Spann, Otis July 3, 1960

Spielberg, Steven January 2, 1984
"Splendid little war" April 24, 1898
Sporting News Rookie of the Year Award April 15, 1947
Springfield Race Riot of 1908 February 12, 1909
Springfield, Massachusetts August 11, 1965
Springfield, Ohio February 12, 1909
Stand and Deliver April 15, 1988
Stanford University December 4, 1975; November 3, 1998
Star Trek September 8, 1966
State of Alabama June 30, 1958
State of Louisiana December 11, 1961
Statue of Liberty October 3, 1965
Steiger, Rod April 10, 1968
Steiner, Steven August 4, 1942
Stern, Isaac April 8, 1993
Stewart, Larry (Sheriff) July 23, 1999
Stockholm Appeal March 1, 1950
Stockholm, Sweden July 6, 1912; March 1, 1950
Stokes, Carl November 7, 1967
Stone Mountain, Georgia November 24, 1915
"Strange Fruit" April 20, 1939; September 11, 2001
Stride Toward Freedom September 20, 1958
Student Nonviolent Coordinating Committee (SNCC) May 4, 1961; March 7, 1965; October 7, 1993
Subversive Activities Control Act June 30, 1952
Sullivan, L.B March 9, 1964
Summer Elementary School May 17, 1954
Sunni Islam February 25, 1975
Sutherland, George (Justice) February 19, 1923
Sweatt, Herman June 5, 1950
Sweatt v. Painter June 5, 1950
Sweden September 20, 1958
"Sweet Georgia Brown" January 7, 1927
Swimmer, (Chief) Ross July 3, 1987
Swing, Joseph July 15, 1954
Sydney, Australia July 4, 1910
Syracuse, New York May 16, 2000
Syracuse University September 17, 1983

Table Mountain Rancheria Enterprises September 24, 2004
Taft, William Howard February 5, 1917
Tahlequah, Oklahoma July 3, 1987
Takei, George September 8, 1966
Talented Tenth February 1, 1903; August 25, 1925
Tallahatchie River September 23, 1955
Tancredo, Tom (Representative) April 1, 2004
Tate, Sharon August 10, 1968
Tatem, Reese "Goose" January 7, 1927
Temple of Islam, #1 February 26, 1934
Temple of Islam, #2 February 26, 1934
Tennessee November 24, 1915
Tennessee State University January 2, 1984
Tenth Cavalry March 9, 1916
Termination and Relocation Phase, Indian Reorganization Act (IRA) of 1934 August 1, 1953
Teton (tribe) February 26, 1973
Texas Court of Criminal Appeals January 11, 1954
Texas Democratic Policy April 3, 1944
Texas Panhandle Regional Narcotics Trafficking Task Force July 23, 1999

Texas School Book Depository November 22, 1963
Texas Southern University October 7, 1993
"Theme for English B" June 3, 1921
Thind, Bhagat Singh February 19, 1923
Thineland February 1, 1943
13th United States Cavalry March 9, 1916
Thompson, Bill (Senator) April 14, 2005
Thoreau, Henry David January 15, 1929
Thorpe, Jim July 6, 1912
Thousand Year Reich June 22, 1938
Three Years in Mississippi October 2, 1962
The "Thrilla' in Manila" April 28, 1967
Tikrit, Iraq May 1, 2005
Till, Emmitt September 23, 1955
Time magazine April 20, 1939
Tlingit (tribe) June 3, 1942
Tombs Prison, New York December 2, 1927
Tombstone, Arizona April 1, 2005
The Tony Award April 9, 1961
Topaz, Utah April 14, 2005
Topeka, Kansas September 1, 1950
Topeka, Kansas, school board May 17, 1954
Toscanini, Arturo January 7, 1955
Tracy, Spencer April 10, 1968
Traynor, (Judge) J. October 1, 1948
Treasurer of the United States December 17, 1971
Treaty of Laramie of 1868 November 20, 1969
Treaty of Paris April 24, 1898
Trinidad August 11, 1965
True History of the War in the Philippines January 27, 1900
Truman, Harry S February 1, 1943; July 26, 1948; June 30, 1952
Truth, Sojourner March 24, 1916
Truthmobile June 25, 2001
Tubman, Harriet Ross March 10, 1913
Tubman, Nelson March 10, 1913
Tule Lake, California April 14, 2005
Tulia, Texas July 23, 1999
Tulsa Race Riot Commission February 4, 2000
Tulsa Race Riots February 4, 2000
Turner, Henry MacNeal March 24, 1916
Tuscaloosa, Alabama March 21, 1981
Tuscarora (tribe) June 2, 1924
Tuskegee, Alabama February 4, 1913
Tuskegee Airmen March 22, 1941
Tuskegee Army Air Field March 22, 1941
Tuskegee Experiment, Tuskegee Syphilis Study July 26, 1972
Tuskegee Institute, Alabama February 4, 1913; November 14, 1915; March 22, 1941
Tuskegee University October 16, 1901; June 14, 1927; June 26, 2001
Twain, Mark April 24, 1898
24th Colored Infantry April 24, 1898
29th Street Beach July 27, 1919
Tydings, Millard November 15, 1935
Tydings-McDuffie Act of 1935 November 15, 1935; July 4, 1946

Uncle Sam January 27, 1900; April 24, 1898; May 17, 1900
Underground Railroad March 10, 1910
Union Baptist Church August 26, 1925

United Airlines Flight 93 September 11, 2001
United Airlines Flight 175 September 11, 2001
United Artists April 10, 1968
United Farm Workers Union (UFW) January 9,
    1938; September 16, 1965; April 23, 1993
United Klans of America March 21, 1981
United Nations March 1, 1950; January 7, 1955;
    December 8, 1979; April 8, 1993; September 2,
    2001
United Nations' World Conference Against
    Racism, Racial Discrimination, Xenophobia,
    and Related Intolerances September 2, 2001
United States Army April 24, 1898; February 19,
    1942
United States Army 442nd Regimental Combat
    Team August 21, 1959
United States Border Patrol July 15, 1954; Janu-
    ary 7, 2005; April 1, 2005
United States Census Bureau August 1, 1991;
    July 17, 2001
United States Congress April 12, 1900; April 29,
    1902; January 5, 1903; July 15, 1904; May 8,
    1906; February 5, 1917; May 26, 1924; June 2,
    1924; December 8, 1941; December 17, 1943;
    June 30, 1952; August 1, 1953; September 9,
    1957; July 2, 1964; March 7, 1965; January 2,
    1968; April 11, 1968; March 25, 1972; August
    10, 1988; October 17, 1988; November 6, 1988;
    November 3, 1993
United States Constitution July 2, 1908; March
    12, 1956; September 29, 1958
United States Court of Appeals January 24, 1993
United States Department of Defense May 1,
    2005
United States Department of Justice September 9,
    1957; March 6, 1999
United States Department of the Interior June 3,
    1942
United States District Court for the District of
    Kansas May 17, 1954
United States House of Representatives July 15,
    1904; March 12, 1956; August 21, 1959;
    November 3, 1998
United States Immigration and Naturalization
    Service (INS) July 15, 1954
United States Indian Reorganization Act June 18,
    1934
United States Lawn Tennis Association (USLTA)
    August 28, 1950
United States Marine Corps February 25, 1942
United States Marshals October 2, 1962
United States Olympic Committee (USOC)
    October 16, 1968
United States Open Tennis Tournament August
    28, 1950
United States Public Health July 26, 1972
United States Senate March 12, 1956; August 21,
    1959
United States Supreme Court May 18, 1896; Jan-
    uary 5, 1903; June 21, 1915; November 5, 1917;
    February 19, 1923; December 12, 1938; June
    21, 1943; April 3, 1944; April 7, 1947; May 3,
    1948; June 5, 1950; October 5, 1953; January
    11, 1954; May 17, 1954; December 1, 1955;

March 12, 1956; November 13, 1956; Septem-
    ber 24, 1957; June 30, 1958; September 29,
    1958; April 28, 1967; October 7, 1993
United States v. Balsara February 19, 1923
United States v. Bhagat Singh Thind February 19,
    1923
Universal-International December 1, 1958
Universal Negro Improvement Association (UNIA);
    March 24, 1916; August 1, 1920
University of Alabama February 3, 1956
University of California, Berkeley August 29,
    1911; January 3, 1957; October 28, 1968; Janu-
    ary 8, 1977
University of California Board of Regents July 17,
    2001
University of California, Los Angeles January 31,
    1919; September 22, 1950; May 16, 2004
University of California Medical School at Davis,
    June 28, 1978
University of California Regents v. Allan P. Bakke
    June 28, 1978
University of Chicago April 7, 1947; October 28,
    1968
University of Connecticut January 12, 1986
University of Michigan Medical Center, Ann
    Arbor April 21, 1992
University of Mississippi, Oxford October 2, 1962;
    April 19, 1983
University of Missouri December 12, 1938
University of North Carolina January 8, 1977
University of Oklahoma June 5, 1950; Decem-
    ber 4, 1975
University of Punjab January 3, 1957
University of Southern California (USC) Au-
    gust 7, 1948
University of Texas June 5, 1950
Urban League June 11, 1953
Utah October 1, 1948

Valdez, Luis April 23, 1993
Valentino, Rudolph December 9, 1933
Van Houten, Leslie August 10, 1968
Velez, Lupe December 9, 1933
Vendome Movie Theatre April 5, 1923
Vereen, Ben January 23, 1977
Verschoor, Thayer (Senator) April 1, 2005
Villa, Francisco "Pancho" Guilledo March 9, 1916;
    June 13, 1923; January 7, 1985
Vinson, Fred (Chief Justice) M. May 3, 1948;
    June 5, 1950
Virginia, Arlington June 25, 1976
Virginia Union University January 13, 1990
Viva Zapata! April 9, 1961
Vocalion Records May 15, 1921
Vogel, Major General Clayton P. February 25,
    1942

Wagenheim, Kal April 12, 1900
Wake Island April 24, 1898
Walcott, Louis Eugene February 25, 1975
Waldorf-Astoria Hotel, New York July 6, 1971
Walker, Buddy August 28, 1950
Wallace, George (Governor) March 7, 1965
Walters, Dr. Ron January 20, 2005

War Bride Act December 28, 1945
War on Drugs July 6, 2001
War Powers June 21, 1943
Warner Brothers Pictures April 15, 1988
Warren, Earl (Chief Justice) October 5, 1953; January 11, 1954; May 17, 1954
The Warren Court October 5, 1953; September 29, 1958
Wasco, California March 31, 1927
Washington, Booker Taliaferro October 16, 1901; February 1, 1903; February 4, 1913; November 14, 1915; June 14, 1927; March 22, 1941
Washington, D.C. July 2, 1908; August 26, 1925; December 4, 1927; April 9, 1939; April 1, 1950
Washington, George May 16, 2000
Washington, Harold April 12, 1983
Washington, Kenny April 15, 1947
Washington Monument April 9, 1939; April 16, 1995
The Washington Post July 17, 2001
Waterman, T. T. August 29, 1911
Waters, Ethel May 15, 1921; June 3, 1921
Waters, Muddy July 3, 1960
Wa-Tho-Huk July 6, 1912
Watson, Charles "Tex" August 10, 1968
Watts District, Los Angeles August 11, 1965; April 29, 1992
Waxahachie, Texas June 15, 1921
Way of the Dragon September 9, 1966
The Weary Blues June 3, 1921
Webber, J.B. (Sheriff) August 29, 1911
Webster, Bob August 7, 1948
Weems, Charles March 25, 1931
Weisberg, Stanley (Judge) April 29, 1992
Weller, Lou September 24, 2004
Wells-Barnett, Ida Bell July 15, 1904; May 5, 1905; February 12, 1909
Wesley, Cynthia September 15, 1963
West Baltimore, Maryland July 2, 1908
West Side Story April 9, 1961
Westmoreland, California January 3, 1957
Wheeler, Burton K. June 18, 1934
Wheeler-Howard Act June 18, 1934
White, Edward D. (Justice) January 5, 1903
White, George Henry (Congressman) July 15, 1904
White House October 16, 1901; July 26, 1972
White House's Hispanic Heritage Award April 15, 1988
White Man's Burden April 24, 1898
White power July 3, 2001
Whitfield, Owen (Reverend) January 9, 1938
Wichita, Kansas September 10, 1915
Wickard, Claude August 4, 1942
Wilde, Jimmy June 13, 1923
Wilder, Lawrence Douglas January 13, 1990
Williams, Eugene July 27, 1919; March 25, 1931
Williams, Hosea April 4, 1968
Williams, "Smokey" Joe February 20, 1920
Williams, Spencer, Jr. June 11, 1953

Williams, Todd July 6, 2001
Williams, Van September 9, 1966
Williams, Vanessa September 17, 1983
Wills, Maury April 6, 1987
Wilson, Woodrow March 9, 1916; February 5, 1917; July 28, 1917
Wimbledon Championship of Tennis August 28, 1950
Wims, Keziah Corine Wims September 1, 1950
Winbush, Ray August 14, 2001
Wind, Timothy E. March 3, 1991
Winfrey, Oprah January 2, 1984
Winfrey, Vernon January 2, 1984
Wing Chun Kung Fu November 27, 1940
Winnebago (tribe) September 10, 1915
WNET January 7, 1985
Wofford, Chloe Anthony October 7, 1993
Wofford, George October 7, 1993
Wofford, Ramah October 7, 1993
Women's Medical College, Pennsylvania March 18, 1952
Woolworth's February 2, 1960
World Community of Al-Islam in the West February 25, 1975
World Flyweight Champion June 13, 1923
World Series October 24, 1972
World Trade Center November 4, 1979; September 11, 2001
World War I January 1, 1918; June 15, 1921; June 2, 1924; August 25, 1925; August 4, 1942
World War II April 29, 1902; November 1, 1920; August 29, 1930; March 22, 1941; June 3, 1942; August 4, 1942; December 17, 1943; December 28, 1945; May 3, 1948; April 1, 1950; October 4, 1968; August 10, 1988; June 29, 2001; April 14, 2005
World's Fair, 1904 April 30, 1904
Wounded Knee February 26, 1973
Wovoka (tribe) February 26, 1973
Wright, Andy March 25, 1931
Wright, Roy March 25, 1931
Wright, Walter January 7, 1927
Wu, David November 3, 1998
Wyoming October 1, 1948

Yaha August 29, 1911
Yahi August 29, 1911
Yale University September 29, 1910; September 10, 1915
Yankee Stadium June 22, 1938
Yankton Sioux (tribe) February 26, 1973
Yarmouth, S.S. August 1, 1920
Yatabe, Thomas August 29, 1930
York, Pennsylvania July 3, 2001
Yuma, Arizona March 31, 1927; April 23, 1993
Yup'ik (tribe) June 3, 1942

Zapata, Emil April 9, 1961
Zoot Suit Riots June 7, 1943
Zoot Suits June 7, 1943